THE COMPLETE IDIOT LETTERS

THE COMPLETE IDIOT LETTERS

*One Man's
Hilarious Assault
on
Corporate America*

PAUL ROSA

REGNERY PUBLISHING, INC.
WASHINGTON, D.C.

Library of Congress Cataloging-in-Publication Data

Rosa, Paul.
     The complete idiot letters : one man's hilarious assault on corporate America / Paul Rosa.
         p.   cm.
    ISBN 0-89526-395-5 (pbk. : alk. paper)
    1. Letters—Humor. 2. Complaint letters—Humor. 3. Consumer complaints—Humor. I. Title.
PN6131.R66 1997
816' .54—dc21
                                       97-29932
                                          CIP

Published in the United States by
Regnery Publishing, Inc.
An Eagle Publishing Company
422 First Street, SE, Suite 300
Washington, DC 20003

Distributed to the trade by
National Book Network
4720-A Boston Way
Lanham, MD 20706

Printed on acid-free paper.
Manufactured in the United States of America
Design by Marja Walker

10 9 8 7 6 5 4 3 2 1

Books are available in quantity for promotional or premium use. Write to Director of Special Sales, Regnery Publishing, Inc., 422 First Street, SE, Suite 300, Washington, DC 20003, for information on discounts and terms or call (202) 546-5005.

THE COMPLETE IDIOT LETTERS

Coppertone Suntan Lotion	1
60 Minutes	3
General Electric Light Bulbs	7
Bradford Exchange Collector Plates	9
American Veterinary Medical Association	12
Postmaster General	14
Fruit of the Loom	16
Ford Modeling Agency	19
Campbell Soup Company	22
Ragu Spaghetti Sauce	25
Charles J. Givens Organization	27
United States Marine Corps	30
Trojan-Enz Condoms	33
Oscar Mayer Foods	35
Tyson Foods	39
Student Loan Servicing Center	41
Exxon Gas	43
American Medical Association	46
Advil Pain Reliever	48
Timex Corporation	50
General Motors	52
Hooters Restaurants	54
Harley-Davidson Motorcycles	56
Toshiba Televisions	58
Eveready Batteries	61
Chemical Bank	63
Cheyenne Mountain Zoo	65
Ken-L Ration Dog Hero of the Year	67
L&F Products—Lysol Toilet Bowl Cleaner and d-Con Rat Traps	70
TV Guide	76
The Pillsbury Company	78
Roget's Thesaurus	81
American Airlines	83
Smucker's Jelly	85
Denver Nuggets Professional Basketball Organization	89
Heinz Ketchup	91
Ford Motor Company	93
KFC Corporation	95
The Wardley [Aquarium] Corporation	97
NBC Meteorologist Mike Daniels	102

3M Video-Tapes	104
American Birding Association	107
Amway Corporation	109
LensCrafters	112
Frito-Lay, Inc.	114
Duraflame	116
Robitussin Cough Medicine	118
St. Ives Swiss Formula Hair Conditioner	120
Royal Velvet Towels	122
Cliffs Notes	124
I Can't Believe It's Not Butter	126
Amtrak	128
Oil of Olay	130
Coors Brewing Company	132
Creamette Spaghetti	134
Pearle Vision Center	136
Kraft Cheese	138
Armitron Wristwatches	140
Hugo Boss Eau de Toilette	142
U.S. Olympic Committee	144
Sinton Dairy Foods Company	146
First Alert Smoke Detectors	149
Trident Sugarless Gum	151
Iditarod Trail Committee	153
El Paso County Marriage License Bureau	157
Colorado Springs Gazette Telegraph	163
Earl Scheib Automobile Painters	165
International House of Pancakes	167
Kinko's Service Corporation	169
Safeway Inc.	171
Russell Stover Candies	173
Delta Airlines	175
Colorado Department of Transportation	179
The U.S. Playing Card Company	181
Kleenex Tissues	186
Scrabble Board Game	188
Miller Brewing Company	190
Crouch Fire & Safety Products, Inc.	192
Autozone	194
Johnson Wax	196
American Society of Plastic Surgeons	198
Columbia House Record Club	200
Dial Soap	202

117 E. Espanola St.
Colo. Springs, CO 80907
October 10, 1993

Coppertone Suntan Lotion
SolarCare, Inc.
1745 Eaton Ave.
Bethlehem, PA 18015

Dear False Advertisers,

Damn it, I'm **mad**! Nothing gets my dander up higher than a claim that is unsubstantiated! Apparently it has gotten to the point in this country where corporations can make any sort of assertion they want, feeling no obligation whatsoever to back it up! Well I, for one, am fed up! As a man who has been teased since boyhood (in Utah, pop. 1,704,200) about his pale skin, I thought it was high time I did something about. I had two options. I could ignore the shallow comments of those who cared little for my feelings, or I could fold under the enormous societal pressure to look more "acceptable." As a coward, I chose the latter.

After purchasing the first bottle of <u>suntan</u> lotion of my life last Wednesday, I excitedly sped home ("To hell with the posted speed limits!" I bellowed). Repairing to the bathroom, I covered myself from face to toe with Coppertone <u>Suntan</u> Lotion and joined my sedentary family in the living room. I applied another layer of your <u>suntan</u> lotion to my person before retiring for the evening. The next morning I rushed to the bathroom to see if your product did as advertised, but alas, I saw absolutely no sign of a tan! My wife (Juji) suggested that I "try it for a couple more days before giving up." Well, I love my wife, and this seemed like a reasonable suggestion, so I enthusiastically "lathered up" again with <u>suntan</u> lotion. I repeated the process several times that day, but the following morning my skin was still as white as the bleached bones of a woolly mammoth. My son (Kurt) teased me by saying, "Can you turn down your skin a bit Dad, I lost my sunglasses?" After smacking him, I returned to the bathroom to give your <u>suntan</u> lotion one final, skeptical try. The following morning I was still as pale as Casper (the ghost, not Wyoming), and angry as a cornered wolverine! Juji then wisely recommended I contact you with my concerns.

So I'm writing this letter to tell you that your product simply doesn't work! I used half a bottle of the stuff this week, and my skin is completely unchanged, except for being quite slimy. Have some people actually reported darker skin when using your product, or is this just another scam (like Rogaine with Minoxidil)? Maybe I was vain to think that Coppertone <u>Suntan</u> Lotion could change my dull, middle-aged life, but I can dream, can't I? I would appreciate a response to these allegations and some proof that your product helps *some* folks in their quest for "nicer" skin! An (XL) T-shirt for Kurt would be welcome too.

Fit to be tied,

Paul Rosa

(Pale) Paul C. Rosa

SolarCare Technologies
Corporation

DIAGNOSTICS

MEDICAL

PERSONAL CARE

March 4, 1994

Paul C. Rosa
119 East Espanola Street
Colorado Springs, CO 80907

Dear Mr. Rosa:

I agree, a written reply to your letter *is* a fair request.

As I understand it, you purchased a product from Coppertone that advertised your skin would become darker if you applied a coating of the suntan lotion. I hope I got it right.

The only "sun" product that STC offered, in conjunction with Coppertone, was a product called SunSense® Towelette. It was designed in a towellete form for easy application and storage. The purpose of this product was to provide protection from the sun; it shields against UVA-UVB rays. The product was not intended to be a tan accelerator.

It is possible that you purchased a product from Coppertone that was meant to be a tan accelerator and in that case you may want to contact Coppertone directly.

I have enclosed several packets of the SunSense Towelettes for you and your family. If we can be of further assistance, please feel free to contact us toll free at 1-800-869-3538, ext 3009.

Thank you.

Sincerely,

Jacqui Grandizio

Jacqui Grandizio
Technical Assistance/Customer Service

1745 Eaton Avenue • Bethlehem, Pennsylvania 18018-1799
610-882-1820 • FAX 610-882-1830

119 E. Espanola St.
Colo. Springs, CO 80907
October 11, 1993

Fan Mail
60 Minutes
524 West 57th St.
New York, NY 10019

Ahoy, News Trackers!

Your show is tops in my book, my friends, and also in the books of many fine folks nationwide (the Nielsens don't lie)! Every Sunday night I settle in front of the Sony Trinatron with my lovely wife (Mai Lin) and a bowl of peanuts, to learn about the earth through the knowing words of Mike Wallace, Morley Safer, Ed Bradley, Steve Kroft, Lesley Stahl, and Andy Rooney. News-show pretenders come and go like Oprah's sensible diet, but 60 Minutes remains the undisputed heavyweight informer ("UHI" we call it).

I shared a chairlift in Aspen with Ed Bradley several years ago, and he seemed like a fine gentleman! We talked about the terrific snow conditions and other interesting topics, but I failed to tell him that he's been one of my news heroes since I was a teenager in Deschutes, OR (pop. 62,142). I guess I was just too nervous, so please tell him for me now! I also think I saw Lesley Stahl last year in New York, but I'm not sure. I saw a woman about a block away on 5th Avenue, and it certainly *looked* like her. She was wearing a black skirt with a fashionable blazer, and appeared quite natty. She's a splendid news lady as well and proves that your show could use a few more. Perhaps Brenda Vaccaro would join the staff!

I'm sure I've never seen Mike, Morley, Steve, or Andy (he's probably shy), but I always keep my eyes peeled for my idols. Do any of you ever visit southern Colorado? I'd be happy to take one or more of the team to a delicious dinner (Dutch treat) at Jose Muldoon's. Just look me up when you get to town!

Yes, I'm a huge fan of the show, but I feel the following topics need more coverage:

⇨ Eggs - They're delicious and important to millions!
⇨ Rust - It's *everywhere* and it's troublesome!
⇨ Unusual vegetables - Yams, rutabagas, etc. are sweeping America!
⇨ Dog Groomers - A misunderstood breed (no pun intended).
⇨ Mice - Those pesky critters won't be denied!

So, keep up the fine work, but try to include the above topics. I'd also appreciate a *letter* addressing my advice. Andy's autograph and an (XL) T-shirt would be cherished as well.

Actually "44 Minutes!"

Paul Rosa

Paul C. Rosa

117 E. Espanola St.
Colo. Springs, CO 80907
November 15, 1993

Morley Safer
60 Minutes
524 West 57th St.
New York, NY 10019

Dear Mr. Safer,

Just a word to let you know how much your quality reporting has meant to me! Every Sunday night, I settle in front of the television with the family (my wife, Mya, and my kids Jay Hawk, Renee, Leon, Becki, and Whipper). The entire 60 Minutes gang is terrific, but (this is a secret) you have a considerable edge over Ed, Steve, Lesley, and Andy, and a slight advantage over Mike. No one else in the vast news world presents fascinating, well-researched pieces like you do, my friend. With the terrific values you exude, I would venture to guess that you were raised in an eastern state, possibly Massachusetts or Virginia. Am I correct? As you are my favorite 60 Minutes dude (a family nickname), I have chosen to contact you directly with a problem.

On October 11 of this year, I sent a letter to you folks, explaining my devotion to the program and offering some suggestions for future shows. I have now waited five weeks and still haven't received a response, so I am somewhat incensed. I realize that the staff is busy circling the globe, excavating fascinating news pieces, but what good is that if you have an angry audience? I think it is very important to respond to public input, as they are the bread and butter (so to speak) of your success. My father (Rupert) used to say to me, "Son, if you're not treated with respect, *demand* it!" So that's what I'm (politely) doing!

Mr. Safer, I am enclosing a copy of my original letter and urge you to respond as quickly as possible to my suggestions. It is difficult to watch your program when something is gnawing at my conscience. Since you seem like a thorough, well-meaning man, I ask you to make my letter a personal priority. Your time is appreciated, and I look forward to a swift response in the enclosed SASE. Lastly, does 60 Minutes offer (XL) T-shirts? You are gracious!

I have a crush on Lesley,

Paul Rosa

Paul C. Rosa

Dear Paul Rosa:

Well, I guess it's fallen to me to give you a response.
Thank you for the non-work conversation on the chairlift. It
was greatly appreciated.

None of us live in southern Colorado but I have a home in
Woody Creek. It is my second home and I would like to spend
more time there than I do. However, all of this work that
you see every Sunday keeps us all on the road far too much.

Thank you for taking the time to write(so many times). For
now, I think we'll accept your wonderful compliments and
pass on the story ideas.

By the way, Andy refuses to sign autographs.

Sincerely,

Ed Bradley
7 September 1994

Paul C. Rosa
119 E. Espanola St.
Colorado Springs, CO. 80907

CBS/BROADCAST GROUP

CBS Inc., 524 West 57 Street
New York, New York 10019
(212) 975-3166

Ray Faiola, Director
Audience Services

·Dear Mr. Rosa: September 13, 1994

Andy Rooney has asked me to extend his thanks for your praise and
support; it is always encouraging to receive such pleasant and
thoughtful comments from the members of our audience. We regret to say,
however, that requests for autographs and photographs are so numerous
that Mr. Rooney is unable to comply with them.

We appreciate your taking the time to write and hope that you will
continue to find CBS News broadcasts informative and interesting.

Cordially,

Ray Faiola

Ray Faiola
Director, Audience Services

Mr. Paul C. Rosa
117 E. Espanola Street
Colorado Springs, CO 80907

119 E. Espanola St.
Colo. Springs, CO 80907
October 17, 1993

G. E. Light Bulbs
General Electric Company, Nela Park
Cleveland, OH 44112

Dear Illuminators,

What can I say that hasn't already been said a thousand times? Since I was a small rascal growing up in busy Fauquier, VA (pop. 35,889) and sleepy Hunter, AL (pop. 550), I've marveled at the consistent, powerful impact of General Electric Light Bulbs. Without them (and their inferior counterparts) our nighttime lives would be comprised of a series of unpleasant, stumbling episodes. The summer population of Alaska would increase thirty-fold as bruised citizens flocked to the "land of twenty-hour sunshine." This glorious, last bastion of wildlife would soon be reduced to a vast sea of Taco Bell wrappers and discarded tennis shoes. Don't be humble; the G.E. Light Bulb has actually helped preserve many species that would otherwise be critically exposed to "Murray and Irene, the Winnebago nightmares." I now want you to pause for a moment and shake the hand of the worker to your immediate left. You've *earned* the sentimental gesture, my friends!

I am faithful to the dependable 60 watt G.E. Light Bulb (Avg. lumens 870, Avg. life 1000 hours). Wow, what a super product we have here! You *say* Avg. life 1000 hours, but that's an estimate that simply doesn't do this bulb justice! I once had a 60 watt bulb in my winery that lasted an astonishing 2800 hours (I keep detailed records). It might have shone forever had not my clumsy 6'9" worker (Ned Wompley) shattered it with his misplaced forehead. My research indicates that your 60 watt bulbs have an average life of 1274 hours and 18 minutes, given that they are not prematurely broken. Rare is the corporation that does not make false, overblown claims to take advantage of the (often gullible) consumer. Your forthrightness is to be admired.

And now a few questions. In the cartoons which are so popular among my seven children (George, Fay, Bobo, Renee, Nipsy, Cray, and Sylvia Anne), the animated characters sometimes "get" light bulbs over their heads, indicating the formation of a good idea. How did this originate? I went to the local public library (Penrose), but no such information existed. None of my friends could educate me either, so I decided to go straight to the source. What's the answer? Also, I am somewhat troubled by the light bulb in my refrigerator. This 40 watt (120 volt) bulb supposedly switches on only when the door is opened. But (here's my question), how can we be **sure**?! If the bulb shines *constantly*, no one would be the wiser, and refrigerator light bulb profits would be about 288 times higher than they should be! This is based on a (generous) estimate of five minutes of daily "open refrigerator door time." The genesis of this potential atrocity would lie in the mechanics of the door, but refrigerator makers really have no incentive to cheat...**unless** they receive kickbacks from light bulb producers! Now I'm sure G.E. is above such evil, but the other companies? I'm not so sure!

Please get back to me with your ideas on the above topics, and, if possible, please send several (XL) T-shirts. Other thoughts from you are welcome as well! And keep up the super work!

Brightly,

Paul Rosa

Paul C. Rosa

GE Lighting

General Electric Company
Nela Park, Cleveland, OH 44112

March 8, 1994
File Reference: I-94-004020

Mr. Paul C. Rosa
119 E. Espanola St.
Colorado Spgs, CO 80907

Dear Mr. Rosa:

This is in response to your recent letter detailing the
life of our 60 watt standard light bulb. According to your
letter, you had one 60 watt GE light bulb last 2800 hours
and another only lasted 1274 hours and 18 minutes and was
prematurely broken.

Quality and customer satisfaction are very important to all
of us here at GE Lighting. We want to assure you that we
are dedicated to the design and manufacture of the best
lighting products of their type anywhere in the world and
for that reason, enclosed are some coupons for 60 watt soft
white light bulbs.

As to your question regarding the cartoon characters that
get the light bulb over their heads indicating a formation
of a good idea, we really don't know where that originated.
The only thing I can suggest is a letter to Disney who was
a pioneer in animation and cartoons.

As to the question regarding your refrigerator 40 watt
light bulb. There is a button along the edge of the
refrigerator door where the door hinges that may be
depressed to allow you to be sure that the light is going
out. If the light is staying on, you may run into some
problems with the refrigerator continuing to run to
compensate for the heat that is being generated by the
light bulb.

Thank you again for your thoughtful letter. If I can be of
any further service, please do not hesitate to write.

Sincerely,

Paul L. Cwiok, Manager
Incandescent Product Service

PLC/ms

117 E. Espanola St.
Colo. Springs, CO 80907
October 20, 1993

Customer Service
The Bradford Exchange
9345 Milwaukee Ave.
Niles, IL 60714-1393

Dear Giving Ones,

Every Sunday, at roughly 6:15 a.m., I anxiously seize the newspaper from the hands of my faithful paper boy (Chris) and dash back to the warmth of my living room. Once there, I eagerly extract the "Parade Magazine" portion and flip -with a rehearsed efficiency- to the page that features the *glorious* Collector Plates. I am *never* disappointed with the spectacular artwork, and quickly pick up the phone to talk with my mother (Marge) in California. Her enthusiasm invariably matches (or surpasses) mine, and within the hour her (double) order has been "entered" for the latest, greatest masterpiece. As her credit card features a nifty "cash back" feature, it is prudent to have her pay for both of our orders *initially*. Let me assure you, friends, I conscientiously reimburse her without fail (I am a strict Scientologist)! This month's Collector Plate, Best Friends, was so breathtaking that I thought it was time I finally wrote to you fine folks and thanked you for the years of pleasure you've given me. In fact it was 7:00 a.m. last Sunday (October 17), and my mother had just placed the order, when I exclaimed (out loud), "I must no longer be derelict! Those folks *deserve* a letter!"

Some of my favorite plates this year have been Before the Hunt (a winter moon reveals the buffalo spirit), The Rock and Roll Legend (the spectacular Elvis stamp), Running with the Wind (the spirit of America's wild creatures), and Joe DiMaggio (joltin' Joe's 56-game hitting streak). But with Best Friends (girls pretending to have tea) you have outdone yourselves! Kudos! Your offerings have been superb, but I *would* still like to see some plates featuring flightless birds, windsocks, and large cars from the 70's!

And now, some plate questions. Occasionally all of my dinner plates are dirty and I am forced to eat (unhappily) out of a bowl or basin. Is it okay to eat from a Collector Plate or will this ruin it? Are the plates dishwasher safe? Remember, this eventuality comes up perhaps twice yearly, but it *is* a trying one, to be sure! Have any artists considered painting Collector Saucers? Cups? Urns? Next, I have noticed that the plates are always "individually numbered by hand." Of what *relevance* is this, and why is it done by hand? Lastly, the order forms consistently read, "Please **enter** my order for (plate title)." What is my order being entered *into*? I'm puzzled!

Your diligence regarding the above questions is appreciated! And remember, your efforts bring much joy into a world that has (arguably) gone awry. God bless The Bradford Exchange!

Do you have (XL) T-shirts?

Paul Rosa

Paul C. Rosa

The World's Largest Trading Center in Collector's Plates
Regularly Serving More than Four Million Collectors

Worldwide Quotations for All Issues by Mail & Telephone
Mail Order & to the Trade   Charter Member NALED

THE BRADFORD EXCHANGE

9333 MILWAUKEE AVENUE, NILES, ILLINOIS 60714   708-966-2770
TELEX: BGE-NILES   TELEFAX: 708-966-3121   CABLES: BRADEX-CHICAGO

November 30, 1993

Mr. Paul C. Rosa
117 E. Espanola St.
Colorado Springs, CO   80907

Dear Mr. Rosa:

We are always pleased to hear from our clients and appreciate
your giving us the opportunity to be of assistance.

Limited edition collector's plates traded on the Bradford
Exchange are for display purposes only. They should never be
used for serving food because of the rare metallic pigments
fired into the plates for color fidelity.

We suggest you clean your collector's plates with a mild soap
solution and thoroughly rinse and dry. Or, you may wish to use
a feather duster or soft, damp cloth for periodic cleaning.
Please do not place your plates in a dishwasher.

Please contact us if we can provide additional information.
Our toll free number is 1-800-323-5577.

Sincerely,

June Owens

June Owens
Account Executive

JO/ln/cs

117 E. Espanola St .
Colo. Springs, CO 80907
October 22, 1993

Consumer Concerns
American Veterinary Medical Association
1931 North Meacham Road, Suite 100
Schaumburg, IL 60173-4360

Dear Beast Masters,

Lord, where do I begin? American vets are certainly the best in North America! I have
owned three cats:

① Mitzi (1952-1968)
② Agnes (1969-1981)
③ Jesse (1982-Present)

As you can plainly see, my pets have all lived to a ripe old age (Jesse is still going strong)
and I have several compassionate vets (and of course, luck) to thank for this! My cats'
three vets have been:

① Dr. Leonid Krivzcher (Mitzi; Pittsburgh, PA)
② Dr. Jackie White-Zwillenbergerski (Agnes; Jasper, AR)
③ Dr. Cal Pierce (Jesse; Colorado Springs, CO)

These three devoted doctors represent(ed)* the American Veterinary Medical Association
with pride and devotion. I take my hat off to each of them, and if Jesse wore a hat I bet I
could convince *her* to take it off too! If these doctors are typical of the vets practicing in
this country, our cats, dogs, horses, pigs, llamas, emus, hamsters, etc. are in good hands!

As I feel quite "close" to the AVMA, it is with confidence that I pose a question. In my
travels as an espresso coffee-maker salesman, I have noticed (in *every* state!) the following
bumper sticker: **"If you have your freedom, thank a vet!"** Now I realize many vets
have proudly served our country, but you don't hear carpenters or lawyers bragging about
their military accomplishments! Why do veterinarians feel the need to gloat? Our nation's
highways would be a miserable, distracting place to be if we saw endless stickers like, "If
you have your freedom, thank a dentist," or, "If you have your freedom, thank a welder."

Please get back to me with an explanation, good people. I have absolutely no other
complaints, and await your swift reply. Finally, do you offer (XL) T-shirts? God bless!

Pets are fun,

Paul Rosa

Paul C. Rosa

*Dr. Krivzcher, who was quite old in 1968, is presumably deceased...or a centenarian!

AMERICAN VETERINARY MEDICAL ASSOCIATION
1931 N. MEACHAM ROAD, SUITE 100 • SCHAUMBURG, ILLINOIS 60173-4360
PHONE 708-925-8070   FAX 708-925-1329

October 28, 1993

Paul C. Rosa
117 E. Espanola Street
Colorado Springs, CO 80907

Dear Mr. Rosa:

Thank you for your kind words regarding your experience with veterinarians. The American Veterinary Medical Association has over 54,000 member veterinarians and we like think all of them are compassionate, caring, and concerned about your pets. We are always pleased to receive complimentary statements about veterinarians.

Incidentally, I suspect a local chapter of the Veterans of Foreign Wars or American Legion is supplying the bumper stickers that you see. That is the reason the AVMA prefers the word veterinarian rather than the term "vet". We reserve that shortened version for former servicemen and women, or the shiny little chevrolet corvette.

Most sincerely,

Bruce W. Little, DVM
Assistant Executive Vice
President

BWL/ kmg

117 E. Espanola St.
Colo. Springs, CO 80907
October 24, 1993

Mr. Marvin Runyon, Postmaster General
475 Lenfant Plaza, SW
Washington, DC 20260-2100

Dear important, high-ranking, public servant,

First of all, I'd like to thank you for the unbelievably fine work carried out by the proud employees of the United States Postal System (USPS). Many times, when I send a letter to my mother, Henrietta, in my home town of Sibley, IA (elev. 1,670 ft.), the parcel often arrives three days later! Your swiftness and efficiency have impressed me since I was a wayward little girl in Sibley, IA (I already mentioned the town, didn't I?). I don't know if you regularly send congratulatory notes (and such) to the scores of postal workers, but the next time you do, please include this poem:

Through rain and snow and sleet and slush
you bring the letters that mean so much!
Sometimes you smile and sometimes you frown
but you're real important in this nice town!
                                        © 1993, P. Rosa

I'd be proud if you signed my name (I won't accuse you of forgery, I swear!). But I'm not 100% pleased with the post office. I've learned more and more about feminism lately, so glaring societal problems have surfaced to my conscience. The issue relevant to *you* is the name, "U.S. **Mail**." This sounds suspiciously like "male," and probably makes little girls feel somewhat inferior to their penis-toting counterparts! Why not switch it to "U.S. **Femail**" for awhile? Then you would be representing both sexes! You could change the name every few months to insure fairness! This goes for **mail** boxes as well. **Femail** boxes should appear at every *other* designated location. And folks who deliver the mail/femail should be called simply, "transporters," eliminating all sexism.

I would appreciate a swift response to my above ideas, and your (possible) schedule for implementing my suggestions. In today's world we must make sure that each baby born in America (from North Carolina to Idaho and beyond) receives a fair shot at the American dream. I can still remember my mother waking me up for grade school in Sibley (pop. 3,051) with the following inspirational words: "Honey, having a vagina is no crime! Now put on your trousers or skirt (my choice) and make me proud!" I would fairly leap from my sleeping surface, determined to "do" better than the day before! Please write soon! And an (XL) T-shirt would be treasured!

                                        Not a lesbian,

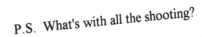

                                        Paula C. Rosa

P.S. What's with all the shooting?

**UNITED STATES
POSTAL SERVICE**

May 17, 1994

Ms. Paula C. Rosa
117 E. Espanola St.
Colorado Springs, CO 80907-7428

Dear Ms. Rosa:

Thank you for writing to the Postmaster General of the United States Postal Service concerning the term " U.S. Mail".

THe term "U.S. Mail" has no relationship to the word "male". Nor, is there any sexual connotation associated with the term "mail". The English definition of the word "mail" is to " .use a bag".

Thanks again, for writing.

Sincerely,

Mauro M. Licciardello

Mauro M. Licciardello
Senior Consumer Affairs Associate

Reference:41070201:lmw

475 L'ENFANT PLAZA SW
WASHINGTON DC 20260-2200
202-268-2284
202-268-2304

117 E. Espanola St.
Colo. Springs, CO 80903
October 26, 1993

Customer Concerns and Services
Fruit of the Loom Corporation
233 South Wacker Drive
Chicago, IL 60606

Dear Supporters,

Underwear. Perhaps more than anything else in this world (besides oxygen), underwear is completely taken for granted. I have stepped into Fruit of the Looms at least 10,000 times in my life, and never once stopped to *truly* appreciate the terrific comfort and support they offered. Again, I always took them for granted, and perhaps therein lies your genius! Well, my hard-working heroes, I am taking the time here to let you know that your efficient, understated efforts are appreciated by one Paul Rosa in Colorado Springs! Right now, I'd like you to say to yourselves, "My dedication has been rewarded. The consumer has spoken and he is pleased!" I know this may seem a bit silly, but regular self-affirmations are healthy for one's soul. Just ask my Great Uncle Leo, age 102, who is *still* bagging his own leaves!

As a cherubic youngster growing up in attractive Milford, NH (pop. 6,000), my father, Paul Sr., showed me how to step into Fruit of the Looms ("One leg at a time," he'd say). I've never forgotten his gentle lesson and remain faithful to your brand to this day! Oh sure, I've been tempted by overzealous salesmen to try Jockeys or Calvin Kleins, but I always manage to wave them away with a flip of my wrist. I will wear Fruit of the Looms until the day I die, unless of course I am forced to wear adult diapers.

And now, my friends, a few questions if you don't mind. I'm never sure how long I should wear underwear before discarding them. Sometimes I think I should keep them for only eight months, while other times I feel they should be worn until the first "extra" hole appears. Do you have any guidelines or (better still) pamphlets you can share with me? I'd be grateful! Secondly, is it permissible to put a pair of underwear on a *cat*? My cat (Jesse) is almost eighteen, and her bowels are looser than, well, Madonna! A small pair of Fruit of the Looms (filled with cotton) is just the trick for keeping my carpets spotless. I assure you that she is placed into her litter box twice daily to relieve herself with dignity, so the SPCA can put away their fountain pens, thank you very much! Do adult diapers for cats even *exist* (the adult diaper theme unpleasantly returns), or should I just keep using your product? Thirdly, why is it called a "*pair* of underwear," when there is clearly only one article of clothing involved? This has agitated me for some time now! Finally, I love your mischievous commercials, featuring the gentlemen dressed as fruit. I think I would look dashing in the *grape* suit and was wondering if you were currently interviewing prospective employees. I work out several times weekly on the Thighmaster, so my body has lost little definition!

I look forward to a rapid reply to my queries, and politely request an (XL) T-shirt if you have one to spare. And any other literature you can send my way would be cherished. Keep up the splendid work!

Here comes the comma,

Paul Rosa

Paul C. Rosa

Fruit of the Loom, Inc.

May 25, 1994

Mr. Paul C. Rosa
117 E. Espanola St.
Colorado Springs, CO 80903

Dear Mr. Rosa,

Thank you for your letter of October 26, 1994. It only arrived on my desk within the last week. With regard to your questions, let me address them in the order you raised them.

1. We have no pamphlet on the wearing of our underwear products. You are the best judge as to when you think the product needs to be replaced. So much will depend on your personal life style.

2. Of course you may use our underwear products for your cat if you so desire. I'm glad they are getting the job done.

3. I'm not aware of an adult diaper for cats being commercially available. Likely you will have to make do with your current arrangement.

4. Perhaps underwear is referred to by the pair due to often being worn as a top and bottom. That's about the best I can do.

5. The Fruit "guys" have been retired and are no longer actively used in our commercials.

Again thank you for your interest in Fruit of the Loom and your loyal, customer status. We appreciate your support.

Regards,

Mark A. Steinkrauss
Vice President - Corporate Relations

NB: Please enjoy the enclosed Fruit of the Loom tee shirt as requested.

5000 Sears Tower
Chicago, Illinois 60606 ▪ 312/876-1724

Fruit of the Loom, Inc.

June 6, 1994

Mr. Paul C. Rosa
117 East Espanola Street
Colorado Springs, CO 80903

Dear Mr. Rosa:

Thank you for your recent letter regarding our men's underwear.

We were glad to hear that you like our products so well because of
the comfort and support they provide.

In response to your questions, how long you wear your underwear is
a personal matter. Assuming they are otherwise serviceable, why
not wear them until they get holes in them?

Secondly, if putting underwear on your cat solves the problem with
her loose bowels and your carpeting, again, why not? Other pet
owners do so for the very same reasons.

Thirdly, I can only speculate that it is from habit...a pair can
be defined as a single thing compared to two like parts such as
scissors and pants.

Finally, we are not using the "Fruit of the Loom Guys" in commercials at the present time.

Thank you again for sharing your comments with us; enclosed is an
article on the history of men's underwear which we hope you will
find interesting.

Sincerely,

Lois Meyerson
Consumer Services

LM:lc

Enclosure

/gc

One Fruit of the Loom Drive
P.O. Box 90015
Bowling Green, KY 42102-9015   502-781-6400

117 E. Espanola St.
Colo. Springs, CO 80907
October 27, 1993

Men's Division (Model Review)
Ford Modeling Agency
344 E. 59th Street
New York, NY 10022

Dear Glamour Reviewers,

Hell, I've *always* been good looking. In 1941, when I was only six years old, my father said, "Damn, if he was any better looking I'd think he was a *girl*!" I took that as a compliment, and the remainder of my youth in tranquil Cotuit, MA (pop. 1300) was spent playing stickball, doing chores, and growing into a dashingly handsome young man. During World War II, my father's plane was heavily damaged in southwest Germany, but he managed to parachute to safety. Three years in detention camps did little to dampen the enthusiasm and verve which had become his signature traits (so to speak) in Cotuit.

In 1954, I matriculated at Princeton University and began my arduous (geological) studies. Four years later, as valedictorian of my graduating class, I began my lifelong service to the stimulating world of rocks and minerals. In 1978, I was awarded the prestigious Kettenheimler Award, given bi-annually to the geologist who "contributes the most to the advancement of sedimentary studies." In the past, this award has been won by the likes of Richard Nigro, Mikhail Katz, and Agnes Wilkes Barnlowiz, so I was honored, indeed! At this point (1978), I was, as my wife, Cileen put it, "a remarkably distinguished-looking fellow." Indeed, my ruggedly-casual good looks have remained intact to this day, and, as a 58 year old retiree, I felt it was time I wrote to you. Allow me to explain, my friends.

I read recently that Cindy Crawford, Cheryl Tiegs, and a handful of *male* models make upwards of $10,000 a day for simply striding down a "runway" in an insolent fashion. Now, I never dreamed of taking advantage of my "lucky roll of the genetic dice" (except for a few times in college) but I certainly wouldn't mind jumping on the sturdy back of this cash cow! I haven't the slightest idea how to go about pursuing a modeling "career," but my best friend (Shamtar Kikavastamalsen) suggested I contact you, as his daughter (Birla Kikavastamalsen) is convinced you are a terrific organization. I am enclosing a xeroxed copy of a recent photo, taken near the mineral baths in Glenwood Springs, CO. I would appreciate it if you would review my face and consider me for inclusion in your "stable of stars." My physique has been described (again, by my wife) as, "sinewy and supple," and I recently took third place in the Denver Invitational Arm-wrestling Tournament (55-60 age group). I look forward to your response in the convenient self-addressed, stamped envelope (SASE) I have enclosed. Thank you and God bless! Lastly, do you have (XL) T-shirts? I'm a collector!

With all of my *original* teeth,

Paul Rosa

Paul C. Rosa

FORD MODELS, INC.

344 East 59th St., New York, New York 10022-1592

Tel (212) 753-6500

Fax (212) 644-6731

Telex 234443 - F M A U R

Dear Mr. *Rosa*

   After careful evaluation of your photograph(s), we unfortunately feel that you are not qualified for a successful career in modeling here at the Ford Model Agency.

   It is always difficult to discourage someone from an endeavor which he is sincerely interested in, but we feel we cannot falsely encourage someone to make a costly mistake.

   We are sorry that this must be a form letter. However, we do receive many letters everyday and it would take a full staff to answer each one individually.

                    Sincerely,

                    Ford Models, Inc.

Ford Brazil
Rua Dr. Renato
Paes de Barros 784
Sao Paulo, Brazil 04035
Tel 55 11 820-6277
Fax 55 11 829-9344

Ford Florida
800 Ocean Drive
Miami Beach, Florida 33139
Tel (305) 534-7200
Fax (305) 534-8220

Ford France
242 rue de Rivoli
75001 Paris, France
Tel 33 (1) 40-20-98-40
Fax 33 (1) 40-20-98-44

117 E. Espanola St.
Colo. Springs, CO 80907
October 28, 1993

Consumer Complaints, Questions, and Concerns
Campbell Soup Company (V8 Vegetable Juice)
Camden, NJ 08103-1701

Dear Health Nuts,

What can I say about the Campbell Soup products that hasn't been said a *million* times before? Your terrific soups, beverages and sauces are the envy of the soup, beverage and sauce world! Since I was a vibrant little guy growing up in dusty Claremore, OK (pop. 12,085), I have enjoyed a plethora of your life-sustaining offerings. I can still vividly remember the way my mother, Claire, would call me in for lunch: "Paul, lunch is ready!" she would lyrically chirp, and I would drop everything to rush to the kitchen and discover what delicacy she had prepared for me. Admittedly, my favorite lunch was Campbell's Chicken Noodle Soup with hot dogs cut into it and an ice cold glass of chocolate milk. After wolfing down this splendid delight and kissing my mother affectionately on the cheek, I would hurry back (energy renewed) to the playground to join my best pals, Billy Ray, Earl and Quan Chai Ling. Oh, what a carefree life that was, my friends! But perhaps my letter is straying a bit.

Since I was always such a huge fan of your soups, I decided (in 1992) to try some of your *other* fine products. My favorite was soon V8 Vegetable Juice, with its tart bouquet and nutritious benefits. Some of the popular sodas of the day (Coca-Cola, Pepsi-Cola, Dr. Pepper, Jolt, etc.) are so loaded with sugar and caffeine that one would be a *fool* to drink more than 1248 ounces a year (two cans a week). So I was soon drinking V8 Juice *and* Campbell Soups, and I never felt more fit and enterprising in all my years (31). I didn't have a care in the world until last week, when my second-best friend (Tye) convinced me of something.

I had never considered the meaning of **"V8"** until Tye brought up the subject last week while we played squash at the YMCA. He insisted that this title has satanic implications based on the following (admittedly sound) logic: The letter "V" is the twenty-second letter of the alphabet. If one takes the two digits in twenty-two (two and two) and adds them, we arrive at the sum of four. If one takes the average of four and eight (from V8), we "reach" the number *six*. If we now turn our attention to the back label, we can clearly see that the first entry reveals that a serving size is *six* fluid ounces while the last entry states that V8 contains *six* percent of the U.S. recommended daily allowance of iron. As Tye patiently explained, the number six, taken three times, is *666!*

"Good lord, **666** is the number of Beelzebub, the dark lord!" I shouted, as this fact was pointed out to me. I immediately ceased drinking V8, but would like to give you the opportunity to explain this (too much of a) coincidence. I certainly am upset by my possible lifelong support of the antichrist...and your trickery! Please respond *at once*, and, if possible, send an (XL) T-shirt.

A God-fearing Christian,

Paul Rosa

Paul C. Rosa

Campbell Soup Company

November 8, 1993

Mr Paul Rosa
117 E Espanola St
Colorado Springs, CO   80907

Dear Mr Rosa:

 Thank you for contacting us about the Campbell's "V8" 100%
Vegetable Juice. We appreciate your taking the time to share
your concern with us.

We trust that you will continue to use and enjoy Campbell's
high quality products.

Sincerely,
Patti Cranmer
Consumer Representative
0006772980

CHRONOLOGY

Campbell Soup Company

1869   Joseph Campbell, a fruit merchant, and Abram Anderson, an ice box manufacturer, form first partnership to can tomatoes, vegetables, jellies, condiments, and mince meat. First plant in Camden, N.J.

1876   Anderson leaves partnership. Arthur Dorrance and Joseph Campbell form new firm.

1891   Company name changed to Jos. Campbell Preserve Co.; incorporated in New Jersey ten years later.

1894   Arthur Dorrance succeeds Joseph Campbell as President. Campbell retires and dies in 1900, ending association of Campbell family with the Company.

1897   Dr. J. T. Dorrance, nephew of Arthur, joins the Company after studying in Europe, and originates the concept of Canned Condensed Soup.

1898   Campbell's Soups red-and-white label first introduced. Colors suggested by Cornell University football uniforms.

1899   First advertising on New York City streetcars.

1900   Campbell's Soups win Gold Medallion for excellence at Paris Exposition; Medallion featured on labels ever since.

1902   Profitable every year since 1889, Company pays first in unbroken series of cash dividends.

1904   Campbell's Pork & Beans are introduced. Philadelphia artist Grace Gebbie Drayton creates the Campbell Kid characters.

1942   Sales top $100 million mark.

1946   Arthur C. Dorrance dies and is succeeded as President by James McGowan, Jr.

1947   Campbell opens third soup plant in Sacramento, Calif., and begins to grow its own mushrooms at Prince Crossing, Ill.

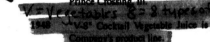

1948   "V-8" Cocktail Vegetable Juice is added to the Company's product line.

1950   First Campbell television advertising.

1953   James McGowan, Jr., retires and W. B. Murphy is elected President. Campbell Soup Fund is organized.

1954   Company goes public with one class of common stock and is admitted to trading on the New York Stock Exchange.

1955   Company makes major entry into frozen foods with acquisition of C. A. Swanson & Sons, originator of the "TV Dinner."

1957   New corporate headquarters opens in Camden. Napoleon, Ohio, plant begins production. Company establishes International Division.

1958   Sales exceed $500 million. Campbell enters continental Europe with Campbell's Soups, S.p.A., and plant at Felegara, Italy.

1959   New plant at King's Lynn, England, opens. Campbell's de Mexico, S.A. de C.V., and Campbell's Soups (Aust.) Pty. Limited are formed.

1960   Plants open in Chestertown, Md.; Listowel, Ontario; and Portage la Prairie, Manitoba.

1961   Company acquires Pepperidge Farm, bakery products manufacturer, and Biscuits Delacre, Belgian cookie and confection maker.

1962   New plants open in Shepparton, Australia; Nieppe, France; and Villagran, Mexico.

117 E. Espanola St.
Colo. Springs, CO 80907
October 29, 1993

Consumer Affairs
Ragu Foods Company
Rochester, NY 14606

Dear Spaghetti Coverers,

My favorite meal of all time would have to be spaghetti (with Ragu Sauce), a crisp garden salad (with ranch dressing), a loaf of French bread (with butter), and a bottle of red wine (with my girlfriend). Perhaps after this terrific feast, I will indulge in a sinful slice of cheesecake (with strawberries). I tell you, folks, that's living (with gusto)! I think what my father, Earl, said many years ago, still holds true today: "When you've got a good woman by your side and a plateful of spaghetti in front of you, there's *nothing* a man can't do!" Actually, I always thought it would be difficult to play tennis with a plateful of spaghetti in front of you (the woman admittedly could be your mixed doubles partner), but I never challenged my father. You see, he had a combustible temper and didn't hesitate to use his meaty fists when angered. But he died in a freak lawnmower accident in 1978, so my days of fearing him are past, my friends! It's time to re-focus this letter...

As I implied earlier, my favorite spaghetti sauce is Ragu (Old World Style), and I have a remarkable (related) discovery to share with you! One night last April, I spilled a substantial quantity (four ounces?) of your rich sauce on my bare left (lower) leg. I quickly washed it off, but was surprised to discover that this area of skin was noticeably smoother and more supple the following day. So I "tried" some Ragu on my hands and, sure enough, the results were similar: luxurious, creamy skin. "I believe I may be onto something here!" I roared, as I decided to push the experiment to its next (logical) level. One day I submerged my entire head in a huge cauldron of warm (70° F) Ragu Spaghetti Sauce, and remained motionless for approximately 15 seconds. After withdrawing my (messy) noggin, I allowed the sauce to "sink in" for another full 20 minutes. Then I bathed and retired for the evening, praying that my efforts would be rewarded.

WERE THEY EVER!!! The following morning, my face, scalp, and hair felt more healthy and pliant than they had since my adolescent days in quaint Alma, NE (pop. 1,369)! Since this triumphant day, I have consistently dipped various body parts in tubs of Ragu, and my skin is the envy of all who behold it! When I was younger (and more naive) I considered immersing myself completely in Nivea Creme to stay "younger," but that stuff costs a fortune! Ragu is reasonably priced- although I would appreciate a quantity discount- and probably achieves better results than a plywood box full of Nivea *ever* could! Besides, I don't care for stuffy cosmetic companies (ha!).

Well, my startled chums, have you ever heard of such a thing? Have you considered incorporating a Ragu <u>skin</u> <u>care</u> <u>line</u>? Please send all available details on Ragu (I'm an information nut), especially concerning benefits to the skin! An (XL) T-shirt would be grand as well. Write soon! God bless!

Saucily,

Paul Rosa

Paul C. Rosa (skin like velvet)

VAN DEN BERGH
FOODS COMPANY

Consumer Information Center
55 Merritt Boulevard
Trumbull, CT 06611

November 18, 1993

Mr. Paul Rosa
117 E. Espanola St.
Colorado Springs, CO   80907

Dear Mr. Rosa:

We have received your request for information about our
company and the products we manufacture. We are pleased to
learn of your interest.

In response to your request, we are enclosing the literature
we presently have available about our products. We hope you
will find this information helpful and informative.

We appreciate your contacting us. If we can be of any
further help, please give us a call using our toll-free
number, 1-800-328-7248, Monday through Friday between 8:30
am and 8:30 pm Eastern Time. One of our Representatives
will be happy to assist you.

Sincerely,

Pat Anderson

Pat Anderson
Representative, Consumer Information

117 E. Espanola St.
Colo. Springs, CO 80907
October 31, 1993

Charles J. Givens
c/o The Charles J. Givens Organization
P.O. Box 161148
Altamonte Springs, FL 32716-1148

Dear Mr. Givens,

I just finished reading a portion of your terrific book, "More Wealth Without Risk," and thought I should write you a spirited congratulatory letter. The chapters I found most impressive -again, I didn't read the *entire* book- were: chapter one (Developing Your Financial Blueprint), chapter two (Becoming Your Own Financial Expert) , and chapter four (Avoiding Rental Car Insurance Rip-offs). I skimmed some of chapters five through thirty-seven, and they looked very informative as well. Chapter twenty-one (Give Yourself A Tax-Free Raise) and chapter thirty (The Money Movement Strategy) seemed like they might be particularly interesting. I've made it a point to finish the book eventually.

Based on the first four chapters, which I read almost *completely*, it is apparent that you are truly a "money expert," my friend! You are also (I don't need to tell you this!) a lecturer, entrepreneur, investor, television and radio personality, self-made multimillionaire, best-selling author, and nationally syndicated newspaper columnist! Many folks can't even claim *two* of these "titles!" It's pretty clear that you are in the correct line of work, something few Americans can boast. Don't even *think* of switching careers...just add to the existing ones!

One thing that (I think) your books truly teach is that a person can become financially independent if they are willing to take the time to educate themselves and develop a handful of effective financial strategies. You probably believe that everyone is responsible for their own financial well-being and should work *very* hard. When I was a teenager in sunny Corona, NM (pop. 236), my Uncle Shoboda would always say to me, "Paul, there's no substitute for hard work, fierce determination, and cold beer!" My uncle meant well, but he was a blithering alcoholic. He also enjoyed dressing like a woman, but that's another story.

Anyway, Mr. Givens, as I am getting very sleepy, I think I should wind this letter down. I *did* want to tell you that I am extremely bored with my current job as a book store custodian, and was thinking of quitting. I'm sure that another job will come along (they always do), but I'm very low on money. Since you seem to have more than you know what to do with, I would like to <u>borrow</u> some, say $30,000. If you agree to this, I can finally get the rest I need. I can also finish reading your book, as my free time will be well utilized. Please let me know if you can accommodate me, and send an (XL) T-shirt with your (speedy) reply.

Needing a vacation,

Paul Rosa

Paul C. Rosa

July 12, 1994

Paul C. Rosa
117 E. Espanola St.
Colorado Springs, CO 80907

Dear Mr. Rosa:

Thank you for your note attached to a copy of your letter addressed to Mr. Givens. We understand your desire to reach him personally. Mr. Givens has helped millions of people like you. Due to the volume of mail that comes to his office, as well as his heavy travel schedule and personal media appearances, Mr. Givens has asked me to reply to your letter. We have no record of your October letter. However, I apologize for the delay in our reply.

Although we sympathize with your situation, we do not have the resources to assist non-members with their questions. Furthermore, Mr. Givens does not make loans. He does not have more money than he knows what to do with. He is very focused on each of his projects. He does own a bank which conducts business with residents in several Central Florida counties. However, I can advise you to first get better acquainted with the loan officer at the bank where you do most of your business. Find out what lending services they offer. Discuss your situation and ask for suggestions.

In addition, I suggest that you investigate other local banks and financial institutions to determine if they are interested in you and doing business with you as a lender. As a rule, loans are best arranged with local lenders who know you and your reputation. If any of the lending institutions you talk to are not interested in financing your needs, ask them to refer you to reputable lenders.

Mr. Givens says it is essential to: **"Get to know a bank loan officer for more financial clout"**! Also, it is important to follow his Strategy #3-1: **When borrowing money, never take "no" for an answer.** Of course, you must have a clearly defined purpose and a business plan.

Explore other private lending sources. Unfortunately, bankers can be very inflexible with people in your situation. Work continuously on building your credit. Borrow what you can and pay back your loans. Do this in increasing amounts. Over time you will build your credit limits.

                        continues

                                        921 Douglas Avenue
                                   Altamonte Springs, FL 32714
                                        407-774-3400

Paul C. Rosa
July 12, 1994
Page 2.

I believe you would benefit from being a member of the Charles J. Givens Organization which was formed to provide a support team to help people like you understand and implement Mr. Givens' strate- gies. We invite you to join America's largest and most exciting financial help organization. Membership brings you many benefits which include the Financial Library, access to our talented Hotline Consultants, and our monthly membership publication **Success InSight**.

If membership is beyond your means at this time, you can learn many of Mr. Givens' strategies by getting his latest books **More WEALTH WITHOUT RISK** and <u>**SuperSelf**</u> Doubling Your Personal Effectiveness. They can be found at your local bookstore or public library.

For more information about joining the Givens Organization, please call 1-800-365-4101 and ask how to become a member. In the mean- time, we wish you every success in reaching your financial goals.

Sincerely,

Roger Easton
Research Consultant
Charles J. Givens Organization, Inc.

117 E. Espanola St.
Colo. Springs, CO 80907
November 1, 1993

General Carl Mundy, Jr.
United States Marine Corps Headquarters
Washington, DC 22222

Dear General Mundy,

Ah, the ***United States Marine Corps.*** I just have to *say* those four words and I feel a palpable shiver running up the length of my spinal column! The proud history and tradition of "The Corps" are as undeniable and majestic as a glorious Lippizaner Stallion! Since I was an inconsequential runt growing up in dreary Currituck, NC (pop. 11,089), I've decorated my bedroom(s) with Marine Corps posters and other paraphernalia (buttons, ribbons, banners, statuettes, etc.). I have zealously looked forward to the day when I would turn eighteen and could enlist, just like my father (Carmen) and my Uncle (Manny Lee)!

I am now a seventeen year old high school senior, and am quite eager to get the ball rolling (so to speak). I was taught by my mother to "go straight to the top" when seeking information, so I decided to write to you, sir. Please take a few moments to address the questions of a well-scrubbed eager beaver (me):

1. Do we get to shoot guns fairly soon after enlisting? I really like guns.
2. Are the Marine Corps barracks well ventilated? I have frightful asthma.
3. How good is the food ("chow" in military speak)? Describe a typical meal.
4. Do the shower facilities afford privacy? I'm a bit of an introvert, I guess.
5. Is gum chewing permitted? I am fairly addicted to the stuff!
6. Are "extra-firm" mattresses available for those Privates with "problem backs?"
7. What about blankets/comforters; may we bring our own? Pillows? House plants?
8. Are there strict physical requirements for getting into The Corps? I carry 230 pounds on my 5'6" frame, but am quite sturdy. Are pimples frowned upon?

I know how busy you are, sir, so I won't bore you with any more of the questions you must hear a million times a year from naive, bright-eyed kids like me! But if you could draft a letter to me, I would not only be honored, but content that my information was...precise! Please don't forward my letter to a "lesser" officer, as I would be most comfortable with *your* learned reply. I'm sure you understand, as one day you yourself were standing on the daunting precipice which is young adulthood! I restlessly await your reply, General Mundy! Lastly, if you have any spare (XL) T-shirts you can send my way, I'd be speechless!

Semper Fi,

Paul Rosa

Paul C. Rosa

117 E. Espanola St.
Colo. Springs, CO 80907
December 20, 1993

General Carl Mundy, Jr.
United States Marine Corps Headquarters
Washington, DC 22222

Dear General Mundy,

Well. sir, it has now been forty-nine days since my first missive was dispatched to you. I fully grasp the busy schedule you must have, what with administrating and scheduling and such, but I feel seven weeks is *plenty* of time to respond to a mercurial lad such as myself. Now I wouldn't dream of treating you with disrespect (lord knows, you've earned *that*!), but I feel you've been somewhat derelict in your responsibilities.

As you recall, I explained that I have dreamed of joining "The Corps" since I was knee-high to a donkey (or thereabouts). As a high school senior, I am eager to get the ball rolling (if you will) and find out all I can about your operation and its many virtues. Again, it made sense to me to go to the top man, which I have been assured, sir, is you. With my final semester quickly approaching (January 14), it is imperative that I pounce on all available information and get my future into second gear. With this urgent "shift" in mind, I can't stress enough how important it is that you reply in an expeditious fashion. Good gravy, my very future depends on it, General!

I would appreciate it if you could answer the eight questions in my first letter (re-submitted for your convenience), as well as the following four additional queries that recently floated to my conscience:

9. Are balding recruits permitted to keep their existing hair long?
10. How often do recruits get to cavort with the ladies?
11. If I change my mind (unlikely), is it "easy" to leave The Corps?
12. Walkmans. Yes or no?

There. I won't take up any more of your valuable time, but I would truly be thankful if you made yourself comfortable behind your large, oak (am I right?) desk and drafted me a note. A self-addressed, stamped envelope is inserted for your convenience. Thank you much!

With my future on the line,

Paul Rosa

Paul C. Rosa

DEPARTMENT OF THE NAVY
HEADQUARTERS UNITED STATES MARINE CORPS
2 NAVY ANNEX
WASHINGTON, DC 20380-1775

IN REPLY REFER TO:

1100
MRA
JAN 1 2 1994

Mr. Paul C. Rosa
117 E. Espanola Street
Colorado Springs, CO 80907

Dear Mr. Rosa:

This is in response to your letters of November 1, 1993, and
December 20, 1993, addressed to the Commandant of the Marine
Corps. I am responding on behalf of General Mundy.

Surely you did not expect a personal reply from the Commandant
since the questions you posed were neither serious nor sincere.

If you are truly interested in becoming a Marine, your local
Marine recruiter can provide basic information about enlistment
criteria. To be of assistance, I have forwarded your name and
address to our recruiter in Colorado Springs.

Sincerely,

LYNETTE M. MARTIN
Major, U.S. Marine Corps
Head, Administration Branch
Marine Corps Recruiting Command
By direction of the
Commanding General

117 E. Espanola St.
Colo. Springs, CO 80907
November 1, 1993

Consumer Affairs
Trojan-Enz Condoms
Division of Carter-Wallace, Inc.
New York, NY 10105

Dear Sperm Stoppers,

After happily using your terrific product for thirteen years, I felt it was *high* time I contacted you and said, "God bless the dedicated men and women who manufacture Trojan-Enz Condoms!" My affiliation with your company began on my prom night in 1980, when my girlfriend (Becky Lee Manholtz) and I shared a blissful evening on the Mt. Carmel Golf Course in north-central North Dakota. We enjoyed many more wonderful trysts that summer before the relationship disintegrated into a petty, mean-spirited nightmare of accusations and insults. Admittedly we were both young and quite stupid, so one must forgive our transgressions. Something we were *both* happy with though, was the sure-fire protection and peace of mind offered by your prophylactics.

I eventually matriculated at Bollerman State College and began dating a terrific young German woman, Rachel Fenztermann. Say what you will about Rachel, but her sexual appetite was almost the death of me. It seemed like I was tearing open a fresh box of condoms each week, as we addressed the relentless urges of young adulthood. Again, Trojan-Enz proved 100% reliable, at least in the cases were Rachel *would* otherwise have become pregnant. Beyond that, your success rate can't be determined, and is (frankly) irrelevant. I *do* know that I did *not* become a father. Yay!

I graduated from Bollerman in 1984, and spent the next five years working as an eyeglass-frame designer at LensCrafters in Greenbelt, MD (pop. 16,000). This period of my life was less sexually active, but my two girlfriends (Kelly and Kim Si Lee) encouraged me to continue my proud alliance with Trojan-Enz. In 1989, while vacationing in scenic Telluride, CO, I met my (future and current) wife, Somatra Kartametra. I must confess, I neglected to buy condoms in 1990 as we attempted (much like Maury Povich and Connie Chung) to produce young. Upon our stunning success -we have a son, Willi- I returned to the pharmacy and purchased a brand new pack of Trojan-Enz's. My proud association with you fine folks continues to this day!

Lastly, I want to know why all the "Early Pregnancy Test" television commercials only feature scenarios where the couples are pleased with positive results or unhappy with negative results! What about the other 70% (or so) who are thrilled with the news of "no baby?" I would very much like to hear your opinion on this matter -I would be angry at this apparent snub if I were you- and would like you to send me all the information you have on condoms (clearly, I find them to be quite interesting). Lastly, an (XL) T-shirt would certainly be a delightful gift...I've earned it! God bless!

97% Successful,

Paul Rosa

Paul C. Rosa

Note: Names of women have been slightly changed to protect their privacy.

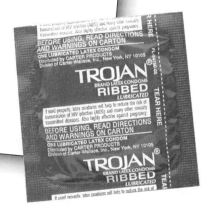

CARTER-WALLACE, INC.

1345 AVENUE OF THE AMERICAS

NEW YORK, N.Y. 10105

TEL: (212) 339-5000
FAX: (212) 339-5100

November 10, 1993

Mr. Paul C. Rosa
117 E. Espanola St.
Colorado Springs, CO 80907

Dear Mr. Rosa:

Thank you for contacting us regarding our product, TROJAN-ENZ
Lubricated condoms.

We value positive feedback from our consumers. Your comments are
important to us and have been forwarded to our Marketing Division.

In further response, we are pleased to enclose a copy of our
brochure entitled "CONDOMS AND COMMON SENSE" which we believe you
will find helpful and informative.

In appreciation of your interest, we are also enclosing a
complimentary package.

Once again, thank you for thinking of Carter-Wallace and for giving
us the opportunity to respond.

Sincerely,

CARTER-WALLACE, INC.

Roxana Montecino
Consumer Relations Representative

19931110009

117 E. Espanola St.
Colo. Springs, CO 80907
November 3, 1993

Consumer Affairs
Oscar Mayer Foods Corp.
Madison, WI 53707

Dear Meal Makers,

Wieners and lunchmeat. Lunchmeat and wieners. I don't know which should be mentioned first, but both need to be paid proper homage to. Only one hour ago (7:00 p.m., Mountain Time), I finished yet another delicious dinner consisting of three Oscar Mayer Wieners, a bowl of Kraft Macaroni & Cheese Spirals, corn on the cob, and a Diet Dr. Pepper. For lunch today, I enjoyed a hoagie made from a generous cross-section of your "Variety Pak." When one places boiled ham (with natural juices), oven roasted turkey breast, and smoked, cooked ham (with natural juices) between two slices of whole grain bread, he/she can be assured that pleasure of the highest order is approaching. Oh yeah, that's living, my friends!

Now, maybe you can help *me*, folks. When I was a boy in Germantown, TN (pop. 20,459), I frequently (and joyfully) observed your lighthearted commercials on my parents rickety black and white television set. I always enjoyed singing along to the catchy tune:

Oh, I wish I was an Oscar Mayer Wiener
That is what I truly want to be...

I would happily sing along to this funny ("feel good") song, and I actually *did* want to be an Oscar Mayer Wiener! I would even dress like a hot dog for Halloween, and my younger brothers and sisters would be the french fries. Oh, when I remember those days I am forced to fight back the "happy tears." But as you can plainly see (above), I only remember the first two sentences of the song! Please send lyrics for the *entire* song, so I can recapture a bit of my spirited youth. Information on the song's origin is welcome as well!

Finally, as a 44-year-old, independently-wealthy sandal manufacturer, I have been seriously contemplating a career change. After months of introspection, I have concluded that I would like nothing more than to be the driver of your world famous "Wienermobile!" Whenever that zany promotional vehicle would roll through Tennessee, I would insist that my parents take me to see it. It is perhaps my fondest childhood memory, and for this reason I would like to pursue employment with Oscar Mayer as a Wienermobile Chauffeur! Please send all available information on your delightful trademark song, and all details on employment opportunities. An (XL) T-shirt would be terrific as well! You are loved.

Still a kid at heart,

Paul Rosa

Paul C. Rosa

P.S. Why are hot dogs sold in packs of ten and buns in packs of eight?

OSCAR MAYER FOODS CORPORATION

November 12, 1993

Paul C. Rosa
117 E. Espanola Street
Colorado Springs, Colorado 80907

Dear Paul:

Thanks for the great letter. As you know, timing is everything. Your request for the lyrics arrived the day we celebrated the 30th aniversary of the wiener jingle.

Enclosed is a copy of an article from a local Madison newspaper and a copy of the music.

You also asked about driving the Wienermobile. Our drivers are hired on a one-year internship, usually recruited from college campuses across the country. They are constantly on the road.

Thanks again for your letter and for being a loyal Oscar Mayer fan.

Sincerely,

Jean Cowden
Manager, Public Affairs Programs

jc161
Enclosures

The Wiener Song

"I Wish I Were An Oscar Mayer Wiener"

Wisconsin State Journal, Thursday, November 11, 1993

State Journal photo/CAROLYN PFLASTERER

Richard Trentlage's family sings along while he performs his enduring "I wish I were an Oscar Mayer weiner" song Wednesday. From left are Jackie (his wife), Tom (his son), Linda Bruun (his daughter) and grandchildren Kris, Brad and Brittany Bruun. Trentlage accompanied the tunes with the same banjo-ukelele he used when he recorded it more than 30 years ago.

Wiener song gold-plated hit

Jingle writer makes a bundle

Rochell Denise Thomas
Wisconsin State Journal

Three decades ago, Richard Trentlage wrote a hotdog jingle that has kept money jangling in his pockets for years:

I wish I were an Oscar Mayer wiener
That is what I'd truly like to be.
'Cause if I were an Oscar Mayer wiener
Everyone would be in love with me.

The song has kept people singing about — and buying — wieners since it debuted in a radio ad in 1963.

The Illinois man, who wrote the music and lyrics, visited Madison-based Oscar Mayer Foods Corp. Wednesday with members of his family to help the company celebrate the catchy tune's 30th anniversary.

"When many people find out that I wrote the song, they instantly sing it to me," Trentlage said. "It's as if they feel a need to prove that they really know the song."

Oscar Mayer officials claim that not only is the tune one of the longest-running jingles in American advertising history, it has also helped the company sell some 38 billion hot dogs.

Trentlage wrote the song in 1961 as part of a jingle competition by Oscar Mayer's advertising agency. He heard about the contest at 2:30 p.m. on the day before the jingle had to be submitted. It took Trentlage a few hours to compose it.

"I was watching my kids and listening to them talk at the kitchen table when I got started on it," Trentlage said. "I began to think, 'Well, everybody loves wieners, and if a kid turned into a wiener then everybody would love him.' "

The idea may sound a bit corny, but you'd be hard-pressed to argue with the results.

The Trentlage family recorded the song in their living room. Two of the children — 9-year-old Linda and 10-year-old David — sang, Trentlage strummed his banjo-ukelele, and his wife played bass fiddle.

A year later, they were told the entry had won, and they've been reaping in the benefits ever since. Trentlage has received more than $60,000 in royalty payments over the years.

"A good jingle can work wonders," he said. "For 30 years, every 13 weeks, I would get a check. Even though I didn't hear it on the local radio or see it on TV, it was always being broadcast somewhere."

The children have gotten a share of royalties, too.

"I never thought it would get to be so big," Linda Trentalage said. "David and I each got about $30,000 apiece."

Linda was with her father Wednesday to sing the jingle and to judge an Oscar Mayer employees' jingle contest. She watched while 13 groups of employees performed what they hoped would be the next big wiener jingle.

"I'm going for the grand prize (a weekend trip to Chicago)," said Beth McConnell, an order processing clerk. "I had my 4-year-old help me out with some of the rhymes. But I wrote it in about 15 minutes at around 11 o'clock last night."

McConnell won the Chicago trip. She had written two jingles.

One, about making an Oscar Mayer sub sandwich, she sang to the tune of "On Top of Old Smoky."

The other, a crowd favorite, was called "I'm a Little Beef Frank." She sang it to the tune of "I'm a Little Teapot".

"Yes, it was a little embarrassing," McConnell said. "But we all have to have a little humility sometime."

117 E. Espanola St.
Colo. Springs, CO 80907
November 4, 1993

Customer Service and Issues
Tyson Foods, Inc.
Holly Farms (America's #1 Brand)
Springdale, AR 72764

Dear Fowl Forwarders,

It's hard to believe that I've never written to you before, but when you are an independent greeting card developer (with a staff of three) there is little time for anything besides "work, sleep, and eat." Oh, don't get me wrong, I wouldn't trade places with anyone -with the possible exception of Richard Gere- but it's difficult to keep in touch with all the folks I'd like to. I've been contentedly dining on your wondrous chicken products for over twenty years, and feel it is now time to extend the wreath of friendship (if you will). What could possibly be more American than Tyson Chicken? Ivory Soap? Street hockey? Doubtful, friends!

It is my earnest goal in this letter to find out as much as possible about chicken in general and your company in particular. I have an **unquenchable** thirst for knowledge, and would appreciate your dedicated indulgence in this matter. My first question involves the tuna company, "Chicken of the Sea." How do you feel about a tuna company insolently "borrowing" your product name for their own selfish gain? And what the hell does chicken have to do with tuna anyway? "Nothing at all," is the answer, I suspect! Your views?

Next, I would like to find out all I can about "the chicken," a misunderstood, often ridiculed bird. Did they once roam free? Do they make good house pets? Do they get along famously with turkeys? Cornish hens? Do they show any *visible* signs of anger when their eggs are confiscated (I sure would!)? Are they *truly* cowardly (i.e. "You're such a *chicken*, Dwight. Bawk, bawk, bawk!")? I urge you to pass along all available, pertinent information.

Thirdly, has the conviction and incarceration of boxing legend Mike Tyson given Tyson Chicken an image problem. I know it borders on insanity to hold a chicken company responsible for the transgressions of a boxer with the same name, but stranger things have happened. You're probably familiar with the public relations nightmare brought upon by the handful of zealots who insist that Procter & Gamble (based on their logo) is "in cahoots" with Satan. Absurd!!

Lastly, I would like to take exception to something printed on your labels. It reads, "98% Fat Free. Contains 2% Fat." Now if you supply the fact that your product is 98% fat *free*, don't you think that the average citizen can perform the math to determine the fat *content*? Unless we're dealing with the baffling 110% that so many athletes wish to "give."

I look forward to your conscientious reply to the four above issues. Also, if such a thing is even available, I would like (nay, **love**) an (XL) T-shirt! I think the world of you folks!

Pass the rib meat,

Paul Rosa

Paul C. Rosa

Tyson Foods, Inc. 2210 Oaklawn Drive • P.O. Box 2020 • Springdale, AR 72762-6999 • 1-800-643-3410

December 27, 1993

Mr. Paul Rosa
117 E Espanola St
Colorado Springs, CO 80907

Dear Mr. Rosa:

Thank you for your letter regarding Tyson Chicken. It is always a
pleasure to hear from our consumers. Please accept our apologizes
for not responding earlier, but we did not receive your first letter
in this department.

First: "Chicken of the Sea" could refer to the white meat or perhaps
they were using the connotation that tuna is as tasty, healthy as
chicken. You might get a truer response from them.

Second: Today's chickens are bred especially for consumption. A
good source of information is the encyclopedia as it is impossible
to detail all the information that you requested in a letter.

Third: There is no correlation between the conviction/incarceration
of Mike Tyson and Tyson Foods sales. The public knows the business and
personal life of Mike Tyson, so there has never been an image problem.

Fourth: Your comments were forwarded to our Director of Nutritional
Labeling who related that the term, % Fat Free, is fat measured by
weight. According to the United States Department of Agriculture (USDA),
% Fat Free may be used only if the product meets the definition for
"Low Fat" or 3 grams fat or less per 100 grams for meals, 3 grams fat
or less per RACC (reference amount customarily consumed) for foods.

Thank you again for your letter. Please be assured that at Tyson Foods
we are committed to producing quality foods for you and your family.

Sincerely yours,

Nancy Lee
Nancy Lee
Consumer Relations

Feeding you like family.™

NL/wdb
Enclosures/

117 E. Espanola St.
Colo. Springs, CO 80907
November 4, 1993

Customer Service
Student Loan Servicing Center
P.O. Box 2461
Harrisburg, PA 17105-2461

Dear Mom,

When I was little and you fought with Dad, was it because of your own unresolved   ...Oops, wrong letter! But as a strict environmentalist and protector of the earth's limited supply of trees, I refuse to blithely toss out this "problem letter" simply because the first paragraph is flawed. So, with the spirit of the mighty sequoia in mind, I start afresh:

Dear loan officers and the like,

I almost feel like I'm talking to family -this probably explains the embarrassing first sentence- since we've "done business" for so long! Since I graduated from the Pennsylvania State University (magna cum laude) with a business degree in 1984, my life has taken a multitude of turns, dips, and flat-out gyrations. But my loan payments were as unwavering as the tide.

From 1984 to 1988 I worked for a small pajama (tops only) business in Washington, DC. I utilized many of the lessons taught to me in my classes at Penn State, including Economics, Accounting, and Finance. In 1988, when the company went bankrupt (the pajama conglomerates devoured us like tater tots!), I packed up my Volkswagen Van and headed west (young man). I was soon in business for myself in Colorado Springs, selling quality fudge-nut brownies and cinnamon sticks. Using my college teachings again, I prospered, as the company doubled in size in 1990, and again in 1992. This year I sold "Sweetness Enterprises" to a Swedish investor for a substantial amount (roughly $275,325), and began to pursue my romantic dream of becoming a militant environmentalist.

Whether it's protesting against the wholesale slaughter of young trees in Washington State or trying to pass legislation to protect the endangered Stuyvesant Beetle (deep south), I have devoted my life to this glorious place we call "*earth!*" For this reason, I have decided to write to you! I had no objection to faithfully sending you $58.05 per month for the past nine years (over $6,000), as I was truly "using" my college degree. Since the diploma *had* value, I felt comfortable sending you monthly checks. But now that I've exorcised myself of all *evil* corporate influences, I realize that my college experience has virtually no merit. Thus my student loan is completely inconsequential. I wish to stop payments.

I welcome your thoughts on this matter, as I am a charitable, God-fearing man. An (XL) T-shirt is welcome as well. Write soon! And recycle!

Aerosolong,

Paul Rosa

Paul C. Rosa (a k a "Windsong")

STUDENT LOAN SERVICING CENTER

P.O. Box 2461

Harrisburg, Pennsylvania 17105-2461

TOLL FREE - 1-800-233-0557

November 9, 1993

91025-0034-024
Paul C. Rosa
117 E Espanola St
Colorado Spng, CO 80907

Dear Borrower:

We received your payment on NOVEMBER 5, 1993.

We applied $58.05 to your student loan account.

Your current unpaid principal balance is $799.62.

If you have any questions or need additional information, contact us at the address or telephone number shown above. SLSC representatives are available to discuss your account Monday through Friday from 8:00 a.m. to 8:30 p.m. and on Saturday 8:00 a.m. to 4:00 p.m., Eastern Time.

Account Research and
Response Department

2MP:TN
S178460771 P A

117 E. Espanola St.
Colo. Springs, CO 80907
November 6, 1993

Consumer Affairs
Exxon Gas Corporation
800 Bell St.
Houston, TX 77002

Dear Doctors and Nurses there at Exxon Gas,

Boy, I can get the gas real bad sometimes to be sure! Whenever my mama cooks up some of them sausages or chili, all I have to do is wait about an hour, and my tummy gets to hurtin real bad. A doctor fella once told me in alabama that I had a shrunken stomach and that's the reason I get gas and indigestion. But I'm tired of the hurting, and my big brother (Bobby Ray) told me that you folks were the experts on gas and what to do about it. Now, I know I'm not the smartest fella around, but I think my brother really gave me some good advice this time. He usually picks on me and calls me "retard" and stuff cause I'm 27 and not so quick, but sometimes he helps me and I think he did that right here. He even taught me how to use his fancy typewriter and about paragraphs! He's a good brother when I think about it.

So I tried all that stuff like Rolaids and Alki-Selzer and Mylanta, but nothing seems to set me right, especialy when I'm eating some of mama's great food. I also like pizza and Mcdonalds sandwiches and chocolate, but the best tasting stuff makes me feel worst of all. That is real unfair in fact it's terrible to me don't you think so? Bobby Ray told me you are the biggest company in the world that knows about gas so I knew I should talk to you. If you can't help me, there's not much more to do, is it? I guess I'll just suffer but I'm pretty tough.

Please write to me fast and tell me some of the medicines and operations that are good for folks like me who get real nasty stomachaches and don't know where to turn. How much would it cost to come on down to texas and get an operation that would fix me right up, good and proper. I have a little extra money from my custodian job, so I can spend it on getting better. Someone said that if you have your health that's evrything you need and I think that's the truest thing ever said by someone. I bet it was that Lincoln president fellow! He looked so good in his beard and coat. Also, do you have any medicines or pills you can send me that would be good for my stomach and put me right? Please send me all information you have in the mail, because my mama won't let me use her phone. She says that I spit on it which is sometimes true but I can't help it that I get so darn excited and all.

I even put an envelope in with my letter that is ready to mail with a stamp. I'm looking forward to hearing from you quickly and getting better and all. if you have a really big teeshirt you could send it would be great too because Bobby rays birthday is in December!

I like this typewriter!

Paul Rosa

117 E. Espanola St.
Colo. Springs, CO 80907
December 21, 1993

Consumer Affairs
Exxon Gas Corporation
800 Bell St.
Houston, TX 77002

Dear Medical People and your coworkers,

When I wrote you my letter six weeks ago I told my brother Bobby Ray that you would answer really fast because I was smart enough to put in one of those stamped envelopes everyones always talking about. Well now it's getting sort of sad that you might not answer at all and that isn't right because I gave you the stamp and every thing! I know you guys are really busy and all that but I think six weeks is a lot of time to answer my letter to you!! But then I thought that maybe the mailman dropped the letter in the bushes or under some stones and you never even recieved the envelopes at all. Then it wouldn't be your fault really, so I decided to write one more time to give you a chance to answer my questions you might never even have seen before this point in time now!

I enclosed my first letter I mean another copy of it, where I asked you what was best for a fellow to do when he had the real bad gas and stomachaches and pains and that. Last Thursday my mama (Jessie) made some rabbit stew that was real good but made by belly feel like a raccoon was fighting with a badger inside of me. I took some Pepto Bismal and it helped me some but I couldn't help but recall the letter I wrote to you asking for advice. If your really a gigantic gas company I think you could make my life a lot more comfortable with some ideas. Maybe I could even quit my job mopping and cleaning and work as a house painter if I felt better. My aunt Lee used to say that a strong stomach is nice or something. That is so true I think too!

Anyway, my brother is calling me retard again because I couldn't get an answer from you even with a stamped letter with my address, so I want you to prove him wrong. PLEASE write back and give me the stomach and gas information so's I can feel better and get Bobby Ray off my back. I thought of slugging him but he always wins in a fight because he does bench-pressing in the attic. I'm going to put in another stamped letter so you can write to me fast and help me out. I put a copy of the first letter next to it too. Thanks a lot and write fast to me!

I'm getting good at the typing!

Paul Rosa

EXXON COMPANY, U.S.A.

POST OFFICE BOX 2180 • 2681EB • HOUSTON, TEXAS 77252-2180

CONSUMER AFFAIRS TEAM
1-800-24-EXXON (243-9966)

January 12, 1994
Reference Number: 529080

Mr. Paul Rosa
117 E Espanola St
Colorado Springs, CO 80907

Dear Mr. Rosa:

Your letter of December 21 was referred to me for handling.

As you know, Exxon Corporation is a a gas and oil corporation for motor vehicles. We regret that we cannot assist you. May we suggest you contact someone in the medical field.

Thank you for your interest.

Sincerely,

Carolyn L. Blackwell
Consumer Affairs Specialist

LFREE1

117 E. Espanola St.
Colo. Springs, CO 80907
November 7, 1993

General Information
American Medical Association
515 N. State Street
Chicago, IL 60610

Dear Physician Organizers,

If someone were to say to me, "American doctors aren't the best in the world," I think I'd laugh so hard that I, in fact, would *require* a doctor! Yes, we have the best physicians on earth, and, regardless of the confusing health-care issues facing us today, you should be darn proud of this fact! Here's what I suggest (and I realize it may sound a bit silly at first): Say to yourselves, "I'm a part of the finest medical contingent this planet has ever seen!" You see, I've always believed that a person should regularly stop and smell the roses. My friends, you are sitting in the biggest bed of roses...I think you get my point (I tend to drift a bit)!

Had I not been encumbered with a *slight* learning disability, I would have become a doctor, following in the sizable footsteps of my father, Dr. Orville P. Rosa (a podiatrist) and my Aunt, Dr. Kate B. Kronsheimer (a cardiologist). Oh, don't get me wrong; I'm proud of the fact that I'm a well-respected producer of fine jams and jellies, but I'd be lying if I said that there's no part of me which isn't "complete." Yet one must take the hand he's dealt, correct?

Anyway, I hope I haven't bored you with my letter thus far, as I assure you there is an important reason for writing. You see, although I have the utmost respect for American physicians, I have a dreadful phobia which simply makes *visiting* a doctor impossible at this point in time. I can't even see a therapist with my problem, as the phobia includes them as well! Thankfully, I am in good physical health, so my "doctor phobia" is not yet a problem. However, I do have one medically-oriented question I would like to ask you. A few minutes of your time devoted to my query would be greatly appreciated. Okay, here we go...

As a highly religious man (ultra-strict Lutheran), it is my fervent desire to be a virgin when (if) I get married. Sadly enough, I "strayed" **once** in high school (fourteen years ago in Rome, NY, pop. 43,826), with an evil girl who tempted me. This was my lone transgression, and it pains me terribly that I am lumped in, as a non-virgin, with every (far worse) sinner in the world! Is there some sort of ritual or ceremony I can perform to *return* me to "virgin status?" I would be willing to engage in any manner of difficult rite to undo the wrong that was done in 1979. Mercy, it was only one violation!

Please write to me at once and let me know my options (if any). As a God-fearing man, this matter is of the utmost importance to me. Thank you and God bless.

Respectfully yours,

Paul Rosa

Paul C. Rosa

American Medical Association
Physicians dedicated to the health of America

Arthur M. Osteen, PhD   515 North State Street   312 464-4677
Director   Chicago, Illinois 60610   312 464-4184 Fax
Office of Physician
Credentials & Qualifications

April 1, 1994

Mr. Paul C. Rosa
117 East Espanola Street
Colorado Springs, CO 80907

Dear Mr. Rosa:

I remember receiving your letter at an earlier time and thought that I had sent a reply.

Unfortunately I do not know of a medical procedure, particularly one that can be undertaken in the absence of a physician, that will solve your problem.

You state in your letter that you are an ultra-strict Lutheran. Perhaps you should take the problem up with a clergyman. The church is far more likely to have a ritual solution to your concern than is scientific medicine.

Yours truly,

Arthur M. Osteen, PhD

AMO:mm

117 E. Espanola St.
Colo. Springs, CO 80907
November 8, 1993

Consumer Concerns, Issues, Comments, and Questions
Advil Pain Reliever
Whitehall Laboratories, Inc.
New York, NY 10017

Dear Ibuprofen Professionals,

I occasionally get headaches so potent that it feels like a thousand tiny centurions are driving their diamond-sharp sabers into my cerebrum. When I am staggered by such an assault, I inevitably turn to Advil Tablets for safe, expeditious pain relief. Within minutes (usually ten to fifteen), those wonderful little pills "do their stuff," dousing the problem area with wonderful, healing medicine! Soon I can efficiently return to my job as a master mechanic, fine-tuning a Porsche or doing a front-end alignment on a classic Plymouth Fury. Frankly, without your remedy my crushing headaches would probably reduce me to rolling around on the floor, clutching my temples, and crying, "This pain is exquisite! For God's sake, somebody help me!" That would be tedious, don't you agree, my friends?

As a voracious reader of product labels and warnings ("You can never be too safe," I can still hear my mother, Erma, gently instructing me), I read that your product is "For the temporary relief of minor aches and pains associated with the common cold, headache, etc." My question to you is: What is the basic difference between an *ache* and a *pain*? I realize that my head aches (head<u>ache</u>), but there is definitely considerable pain involved as well ("I have a pounding head<u>pain</u>," sounds funny though!). Webster's Dictionary defines an ache as, "a dull, steady pain," while pain is defined as," the sensation of hurting." So, it seems that aches are, by definition, a subset of the pain genre (i.e. all aches are pains but not all pains are aches). You can have a pain which is not an ache, like my cousin's stab wound, but you can't have an ache which is "pain-free." Kindly correct me if my research is faulty.

The last remaining question is why you chose to mention the word "ache" at all on the label, since it clearly is included in "pain." Okay, there's another question: Why *isn't* it called a "headpain?" Again, my head doesn't suffer from "dull, steady pains," but from sharp, piercing ones (see first sentence!). It all may seem trivial to you, but when you inhale information like I do, every available fragment of data is consequential!

I look forward to your learned reply on my ache/pain question! Also, as I type, my oldest son (Albert) is requesting an (XL) T-shirt. Do you have them? God bless.

It pains me to say good-bye,

Paul Rosa

Paul C. Rosa

Whitehall-Robins
5 Giralda Farms
Madison, NJ 07940-0871
Telephone (201) 660-5500

December 6, 1993

Mr. Paul Rosa
117 E. Espanola Street
Colorado Springs, CO 80907

Dear Mr. Rosa:

It was such a pleasure to receive your letter regarding Advil
Tablets.

We always enjoy learning that our products are beneficial to
consumers' ailments. It is a wonderful indication that products
are meeting Whitehall Laboratories' performance standards.

We appreciate your taking the time to write about your positive
experience. Under separate cover, we are sending you a sample with
our compliments. Please allow 2-3 weeks for delivery.

Sincerely,

Jennifer A. Johnston
Consumer Affairs Associate

117 E. Espanola St.
Colo. Springs, CO 80907
November 14, 1993

Timex Corporation
P.O. Box 1676
Little Rock, AR 72203

Dear Timekeepers,

"Where would we be without timepieces?" I ask you. For instance, if my friend, Kurt suggested we play basketball at the YMCA at 4:30 today, I'd have to say to him, "4:30? What does that *mean*?" You see, such a statement would be nonsensical if ours wasn't a society chock full of wristwatches, alarm clocks, and the tiny digital read-outs on VCR's which continuously blink "12:00" for years and years. I guess what I'm trying to say (I frequently get sidetracked) is that the very success of our society depends on the fine types of products which your company offers the consumer. You bet your bottom dollar that you make a difference, my friends!

I've been fascinated with "time" since I was a goofy, young kid in Abernathy, TX (pop. 2,904). My father (Kip) bought me a Timex for my eighth birthday, and since then I'm quite sure that I've worn a wristwatch every day, without fail. Over the years, however, I've compiled a list of questions which I hoped could eventually be answered. For this reason, I am compelled to finally write to you.

My first question deals with a common social situation. If you check your wristwatch and, moments later, someone asks you the time, you invariably check the watch *again*. Since the current time should still be fresh in your mind, why does everyone always check again? It has baffled me for some "time" and I thought you may have some answers. Do you?

Secondly, where did the name "Grandfather Clock" come from? Was it invented by an older gentleman? Does it have some of the *characteristics* of grandfathers? Do they traditionally last a long time, like grandfathers? What gives? I'm an information <u>sponge</u>!!

Lastly, I ask you to indulge me with a little conjecture. I believe it was Andy Warhol who suggested that we each get "fifteen minutes of fame." If one's fifteen minutes of fame began two minutes before we set our clocks ahead in the spring, would they be forced to forfeit thirteen minutes of fame? That seems unfair, and I thought you might have some input. Would you offer me your speculation please? I look forward to your reply and will count the hours, minutes and seconds (get it?) until you write. Thank you for your terrific products, and try to send an (XL) T-shirt!!

Punctually yours,

Paul Rosa

Paul C. Rosa

P.S. Are Timex employees frequently late?

TIMEX
CORPORATION

BUILDING 19, ADAMS FIELD
POST OFFICE BOX 1676
LITTLE ROCK, ARKANSAS 72203

April 21, 1994

Mr. Paul C. Rosa
117 E. Espanola St.
Colorado Springs, CO 80907

Dear Mr. Rosa:

Sorry we have not replied to your letter but have been unable to find anyone at Timex who has the answers to the questions you have asked although they did think it was rather humorous that you asked.

We do not know why someone would look at their watch again if someone asked what time it was after only having looked at it a short time ago other than it is force of habit. I had not noticed that people did this.

We don't know who gave the name "Grandfather Clock" to such a clock since we do not make clocks or if the old Clock Company at one time made them, everyone working at the Clock Company has long since gone.

Never heard of Andy Warhol and if I were the one whose fifteen minutes of fame began two minutes before we set our clocks ahead in the spring that it would really matter because nothing changes other than the time on your clock or watch and who says what time you have to make that change. Most people set the clock up before they go to bed on Saturday night but that could be any time during the night or early Sunday morning.

Sincerely,

Ruby L. Harris
Special Correspondent

rlh

P.S.   Timex employees are not frequently late.

117 E. Espanola St.
Colo. Springs, CO 80907
November 19, 1993

Customer Concerns, Ideas, Suggestions and Opinions
General Motors Corporation
3044 West Grand Blvd.
Detroit, MI 48202

Dear Automobile Giants,

Wow, I can't believe I'm actually "talking" with you. I have used your terrific cars for transportation since I was an underdeveloped ragamuffin in Hastings, NE (pop. 23,045). My hulking father (Jimbo) drove an equally hulking Cadillac for many years, and I quickly learned that you don't mess with good results. That car ("The Caddy," my father would affectionately call it) lasted for twelve years and 145,000 miles, and he rapidly replaced it with a Chevrolet Impala. This car lasted "forever" as well, and was inherited by my sister (Kate) when she went off to college (Princeton). I've owned a Pontiac Firebird -It was great for wooing the gals in high school- and an Oldsmobile Cutlass. Complaints? <u>None</u>!

I've noticed for some time that car names generally have nothing to do with the car. The Honda Civic. The Buick Skylark. The Chevrolet Corsica. What does it all mean? Nothing I suppose; it just "rolls off the tongue" effortlessly! No one wants to own a Ford Intestine or a Chrysler Depression (Do I follow your logic, my friends?). In the spirit of this "catchy name" mentality, I would like to offer you some suggestions that I came up with:

- ◎ **The Buick Brain** (It's our most vital organ!)
- ◎ **The Pontiac Pretzel** (Who among us doesn't relish a chewy pretzel?)
- ◎ **The Oldsmobile Opossum** (What a resourceful marsupial!)
- ◎ **The Chevrolet Lady Lay** (Bob Dylan would be proud!)
- ◎ **The Cadillac Cardigan** (Cozy sweaters are back!)

I have many (thirty) more ideas I would like to run by you, but I would like to hear your opinion on these first. What do you think, my friends? Is there a place for me in your vast, sprawling complex? I think I'd fit in nicely, as I've owned nothing but G.M. cars in my life and I'm a very hard worker. In fact, my fifth grade teacher (Mr. Coltass) once said to me, "Paul, you're a very hard worker." Proud? You bet I was!

I look forward to a quick response, as the biggest corporation in the country can surely handle the mail expeditiously. Lastly, if you have an (XL) T-shirt, I'd enjoy wearing it.

A self-motivated type,

Paul Rosa

Paul C. Rosa

North American Operations

February 7, 1994

Mr. Paul C. Rosa
117 E. Espanola Street
Colorado Springs, CO 80907

Ref: N.D. File 255506

Dear Mr. Rosa:

Your correspondence of November 19, 1993 to General Motors
regarding your vehicle nameplate suggestions has been referred to
our New Devices Section. The enclosed booklet will acquaint you
with the responsibilities of our office and the policies under
which General Motors accepts ideas and suggestions.

Unfortunately, as stated on page two of the enclosed booklet,
General Motors does not wish to consider ideas and suggestions
relating to product names.

We regret our reply could not be more favorable. However, we
value you as a customer and truly appreciate your interest in
General Motors. Thank you very much for writing to us.

Sincerely,

R. E. Greib
Assistant Director
GM New Devices Section

jtg

enclosure
booklet

117 E. Espanola St.
Colo. Springs, CO 80907
November 24, 1993

Mr. Mike McNeil
Vice President of Marketing
Hooters Restaurants
4501 Circle 75 Pkwy., Suite E5110
Atlanta, GA 30339

Dear Mr. McNeil,

I love owls. Always have, always will. From the moment I saw my first owl as a youngster in Androscoggin, ME (pop. 99,657), I knew my life would be devoted to the study of this noble creature. I attended the Pennsylvania State University on a science scholarship and received my masters degree in zoology from the University of Iowa. For the past twenty-two years I have diligently learned all I could about (you guessed it) owls! I'm partial to the Great Horned Owl, the Barred Owl, and the Snowy Owl, but I've never met an owl I didn't like (that's a *little* zoologist joke!). I've had articles published in National Geographic, Field and Stream, and a host of other national publications. Married with three children, my life couldn't be any better. But perhaps I should get to the point, my friend.

When I moved to Colorado Springs recently I was delighted to see an advertisement for a Hooters Restaurant, featuring the word "Hooters" and a large picture of an owl. Needless to say, I believed this was a club or diner of some sort devoted to the study of owls. I swiftly dressed in my finest blazer and rushed to the Hooters location, eager to mingle with other owl authorities over cappuccino. I envisioned a lively discussion about the well-publicized plight of the spotted owl or a vigorous debate over which is the "most majestic" owl!

Well, my deceptive friend, imagine my chagrin when I burst into the building and discovered...bimbos and beer! Expecting to see framed photographs of nocturnal birds of prey, my senses were instead assaulted with the odors of chicken wings and processed cheese! Being an educated man, I soon realized that the word "hooters" was in fact a nickname for breasts (how perfectly unrefined!). My hope for an educational evening had dissolved into vapor. Standing in this "den of ill repute" I vowed to respond to your ruse!

How do you justify this blatant example of false advertising? What do owls *really* have to do with scantily clad cocktail waitresses? I think you are sullying the name of God's greatest creatures, and I would like to hear your "defense!" I would appreciate a prompt reply to my letter, sir. I appreciate your time.

Incensed,

Paul Rosa

Paul C. Rosa, M.D.

Paul C. Rosa, M.D.
117 E. Espanola St.
Colo. Springs, CO 80907
December 6, 1993

Dear Paul,

For the record Hooters in addition to being the name of Americas
fastest growing restaurant company also is a nickname for owls and
an innocuous slang expression for a portion of the female anatomy.
I am truly sorry that you were unaware of the "other" meaning that
Hooters has and can assure you that we intend no disrespect for
bird lovers of the world.

Hooters is a wonderful restaurant that over 500,000 people per week
visit and enjoy at one of our 115 locations in 30 states. We wish
you felt differently but will understand if we can no longer count
on your patronage.

Sincerely,

Mike McNeil
Vice President of Marketing

MM/sf

4501 Circle 75 Parkway, Suite E-5110 • Atlanta, GA 30339 • (404) 951-2040

117 E. Espanola St.
Colo. Springs, CO 80907
November 30, 1993

Harley-Davidson Motorcycles
3700 West Juneau Ave.
Milwaukee, WI 53208

Dear Hog Heroes,

I suppose I've always been a "biker" at heart, but for many years I suppressed my natural urges and pursued society's "civilized" things. Oh yes, as my father (Ben) directed, I attended Harvard University and entered the world of business on Wall Street. I drove Cadillacs, Lincolns, and LeSabres as my life became duller and duller and my spirit began to seep from me faster than you can say, "mortgage control strategies." For eighteen years I played the game, married my "corporate wife," and hobnobbed with New York's elite, including Donald Trump. Then six weeks ago (on my fortieth birthday) my view of life snapped like an autumn twig. Get comfortable, my friends, as I continue my tale.

Coming face to face with my own mortality -a mid-life crisis if you will- I began to re-prioritize my life. I told my boss (Philip) to engage in "self procreation," left my egotistical wife (Brenda), and escaped to scenic Colorado. I have secured a fulfilling position as an insect exterminator and am dating a marvelously centered woman (Sage). My tailored suits have been replaced with blue jeans and sandals. Happy? You bet I am!

And now I'm interested in purchasing a Harley! I have been told that yours are the "baddest" bikes on the road, and I wish to complete my amazing transformation by "straddlin' a hog!" Perhaps my Ivy League experience is rearing its ugly head again, but I wish to educate myself before spending thousands on a vehicle. So kindly indulge me...

I have *extremely* sensitive skin and was wondering if you offer motorcycles with protective, tinted domes. Furthermore, I never learned to ride a bicycle and was wondering if this skill was a prerequisite for motorcycle riding. Thirdly, I wish to fit in with the other bikers and get a tattoo, so I was hoping you could inform me which is the most popular (skull and crossbones? American flag?). Do tattoos hurt? Lastly, is it possible to buy a motorcycle with an airbag? Money is no object!

I realize that you must grow weary of questions from the "uneducated," but I assure you that my heart is in the right place! I look forward to a swift reply to my questions and any other information you can offer a changed man (me). An (XL) T-shirt would be valued as well. Thank you so much!

Dreaming of wheelies,

Paul Rosa

Paul C. Rosa

HARLEY-DAVIDSON, Inc., 3700 W. Juneau Ave., POB 653, Milwaukee, WI 53201   414/342-4680

December 13, 1993

Mr. Paul Rosa
117 E. Espanola St.
Colorado Springs, CO   80907

Dear Mr. Rosa,

I am writing to you in response to your letter dated November
30, 1993, in which you requested information on our current
line of motorcycles.

It was refreshing to read of the "transformation" you have
made, and of the adjustments you are now undertaking. Being
truly happy in your work and life is a very worthwhile goal -
congratulations on your achievements!

Harley-Davidson, Inc., does not currently produce vehicles
with the features you requested (protective domes or air
bags). If you are new to the sport of motorcycling, I would
suggest you enroll in a rider safety course to learn the
recommended principles of operating a motorcycle. You may
contact the Motorcycle Safety Foundation at 714-727-3227 to
obtain information on classes nearest your home.

I understand that having tattoos put on your body can be
somewhat uncomfortable. It is probably true that most people
now riding our motorcycles do not have tattoos - that is a
personal choice. Just remember, tattoos are forever.

Thank you, Mr. Rosa, for your interest in Harley-Davidson
products. If you have any further questions, please feel
free to contact the Customer Service Department at 414-935-
4056 between 8:00 A.M. and 4:30 P.M. central time. Ride
Safe!

                              Sincerely,

                              Bob Laubenheimer

                              Bob Laubenheimer
                              Retail Customer Support

2459

117 E. Espanola St.
Colo. Springs, CO 80907
December 2, 1993

Customer Service
Toshiba America Consumer Products
Television Division
5490A East Francis St.
Ontario, CA 91761

Dear Disappointers,

When I was growing up in Mississippi we never owned a television because my daddy (a preacher) said that it was the work of the devil. Now, I was never one to challenge my daddy (his temper was volatile), so the only televisions I ever saw were in the windows of local department stores. Even then I hastened my pace, as I feared "rotting in hell for all eternity." Nevertheless, I remained curious about this wondrous, magical "box!"

Last year I finally moved away from home (I was twenty-six!), settled in Colorado, and began to undo the considerable harm my fanatical father burdened me with. I got a good job as an exterminator, began playing basketball ("hoops") at the local YMCA, and even went out on a few (two) dates. This July, feeling my oats, I took a deep breath, strode into a local electronics shop and purchased my very first television set (Toshiba!). I doubted that "work of the devil" rubbish, and was determined to catch up on what I was missing!

For the past few months I have watched approximately seven hours of television each day. I have witnessed such inferior fiascos as "Full House," "Roc," "Beverly Hills 90210," and "Saved by the Bell." Perhaps television has nothing to do with Satan, but I'm beginning to believe that my daddy was right to forbid such stupidity! That is why I am writing to you.

Why do you put such horrible programs into your televisions? Surely you can try a bit harder to build your sets with *quality* inside! My friend (Akeem) has a Sony television and he says that the programs on *his* unit are quite good. Why can't you be more like *them* and offer enticing presentations?! Perhaps I should have done more research and discerned which are the most stimulating televisions, but I was naive! If your programs don't get better soon, I will be forced to trade in my set for a Sony or a Magnavox (I've heard their programs are good too). I'm willing to pay more for better entertainment!

So why *are* your shows so faulty? Can't you *afford* top-notch offerings? I would truly like to hear your explanation for the poor performance before I abandon my Toshiba set - That's the least I can do! I look forward to your reply. Lastly, do you offer (XL) T-shirts?

I like Dave Letterman though,

Paul Rosa

Paul C. Rosa

TOSHIBA

TOSHIBA AMERICA CONSUMER PRODUCTS, INC.
5490 E. FRANCIS STREET
ONTARIO, CA 91761
PHONE: (909) 988-5303

April 28, 1994

Mr. Paul C. Rosa
117 E. Espanola Street
Colorado Springs, CO 80907

Dear Mr. Rosa:

I'm sorry I didn't respond sooner. I'm sure you understand
that the holiday season is a very busy time for us. The holidays
coupled with employees taking time to be with their families made
it very easy for your first letter to get lost. The recent
earthquakes added a significant workload to our department, which
also contributed to a less timely response.

I found your letter very interesting. It was obvious that you
were not aware of who was responsible for TV programming or how the
programming was selected for view by the user or consumer. For
this reason I have enclosed a diagram to help you better
understand. Secondly, I believe that after studying the diagram
that you will realize that you have access to the same programming
seen by your Sony and Magnavox friends.

As requested I have enclosed a T-Shirt **(XL)**. Please study the
enclosed diagram as I am reasonably confident that you will find it
to be your ticket to many hours of video entertainment.

                    Yours truly,
          W. Zone Service Department

enclosure

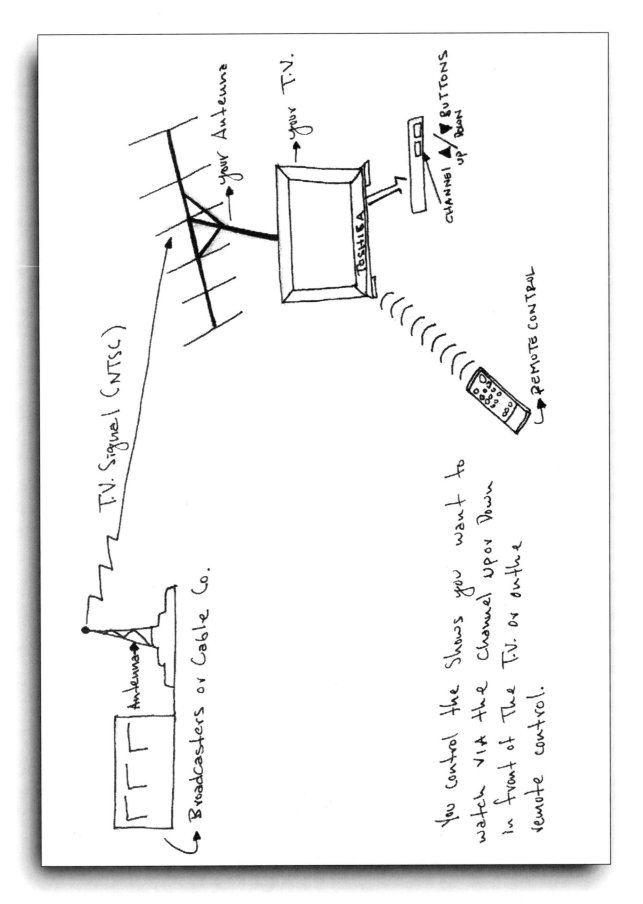

117 E. Espanola St.
Colo. Springs, CO 80907
December 5, 1993

Consumer Issues, Topics, and Questions
Eveready Battery Co., Inc.
801 Chouteau St.
St. Louis, MO 63102

Dear Power Brokers (If you will),

As a zoologist with over twenty-seven years of experience in the field of fur-bearing mammals, I have been consistently delighted and amused with the "Energizer Bunny" in your superb commercials. When that wonderful little creature promenades across my Sony Trinatron screen, beating his little drum, I inevitably turn to my wife (Grace) and declare, "Now *there's* a commercial!" Since your organization has a clear interest in rabbits and hares, I thought I would provide some information you may not have already known. This additional knowledge may serve to increase the credibility and entertainment value of your (already terrific) commercials. Let us begin, shall we?

The tradition of the "Easter Bunny" began in the year 1768, in Philadelphia, PA. Benjamin Franklin, a man who has been credited with countless other "inventions" would amuse his young relatives at Easter time by covering himself in fur and playfully growling at them. Apparently this scared the children a bit, so the tradition evolved into one featuring a good-natured hare who blesses the holiday and brings the "word of God" to earth from the heavens. How and why the creature began bringing *eggs* is apparently a mystery still! Frankly, it makes me a bit uncomfortable, my friends. But alas, what can one do?

The story of the "Playboy Bunny" is another interesting one! In the 1950's, when a young chap by the name of "Hugh Hefner" was planning the release of his now-famous publication, he was trying to choose an animal which best exemplified the "spirit" of the modern American woman. Hysterically, the wolf, cheetah, pheasant, and dolphin were considered before the rabbit was chosen as the official "mascot." Imagine a woman on the cover of Playboy dressed in a pheasant costume! Absurd!! Anyway, Mr. Hefner decided that the rabbit combined many of the qualities he was looking for in the "perfect woman" (softness, vulnerability, etc.) of the 50's. Clearly the ideal woman stereotype has changed (she's more independent!), so a new mascot should be considered. I've written to Playboy, but my letters have gone unanswered.

The final nugget of data I will pass your way concerns the myth of rabbits procreating like...well, rabbits. Since rabbits often have litters in excess of twelve sucklings, it is widely believed that they are "oversexed." There are simply no facts to support this, in fact many animals (geese, sparrows, and bison to name a few) "indulge themselves" far more frequently, yet aren't saddled with such an unsavory reputation.

Well I hope I haven't bored you. Please write to me and let me know if these facts are useful to you. I look forward to your prompt reply! An (XL) T-shirt is requested as well.

I own a Volkswagen Rabbit,

P. Rosa

Dr. Paul C. Rosa

Eveready Battery Company, Inc.

February 15, 1994

Dr. Paul C. Rosa
117 E. Espanola St.
Colorado Springs, CO 80907

Dear Dr. Rosa:

Thank you for the interesting information about the Easter Bunny and Playboy
Bunny. Your thoughtfulness is appreciated. However, we are not in a position
to utilize these facts.

At one time Eveready ran a T-shirt promotion, but the offer expired and stock
has been depleted. We will keep your name on file and send you a certificate
when the offer comes available again.

Thank you for your interest and for taking the time to write.

                                    Sincerely,

                                    S. Michael Mazva
                                    Manager-Consumer Relations

SMM:SK

Checkerboard Square
St. Louis, Missouri 63164 • • • • • • • • • • • •

117 E. Espanola St.
Colo. Springs, CO 80907
December 8, 1993

Mr. Walter Shipley, CEO
Chemical Bank
270 Park Avenue
New York, NY 10017

Dear Safe Keeper,

Calcium Pyrophosphate. Abietic Acid. Garnierite. Hydroflumethiazide. Sodium Diuranate. Even Octamethylcyclotetrasiloxane! You name the chemical, I've got it! Ever since I was a thin teenager in agreeable Payson, AZ (pop. 5,068), I've been fascinated with the world of chemicals! As a college student, majoring in (you guessed it) Chemistry at the University of Alaska (Fairbanks), I earned a perfect 4.0 grade point average. Although I had to abandon my dream of becoming a chemist due to a mild personality disorder, I have continued to faithfully study and collect chemicals from around the globe. In the past fourteen years I have accumulated over 275 bins, containers, vessels, and drums of specimens in my modest two-story Victorian home. I have samples of the above chemicals as well as Erucic Acid, Thiophosphoryl Chloride, Zinc Permanganate, Diphenylmethyl Bromide, and a host of others. "Good gracious, I'm running out of room!" I declared last week, as I added a remarkably pure portion of Methylmercury-2,3-dihydroxypropylmercaptide to my already-cramped attic.

Due to the crowded quarters in my residence, I feared I would be forced to move! When I heard (last week) about the Chemical Bank, I was fairly beside myself with delight! At last I can house my valuable collection in a licensed and bonded institution while "reclaiming" the rooms of my home. Not since I studied the works of Louis Pasteur (1822-1895) and Sir Robert Boyle (1637-1691) have I been this excited. But before I place the cart before the horse (as the saying goes), I would like to learn more about your bank. Please indulge me while I "bend your ear" with a few pivotal questions:

⇒ Do you offer checking *and* savings accounts?
⇒ What about interest (i.e. seven ounces per one hundred ounces of acid yearly)?
⇒ Will automated tellers ("drive-thrus") be available soon? That would be wonderful!
⇒ Are you an F.D.I.C. member?
⇒ What does "F.D.I.C." stand for?

I'll probably have a million more questions in the coming months, but wanted to rush this letter to you! I urge you to write to me and let me know **everything** about your institution. Frankly, it seems too good to be true! A self-addressed, stamped envelope (SASE) has been thoughtfully enclosed for your convenience. Lastly, do you offer (XL) T-shirts?

With compounding interest,

Paul Rosa

Paul C. Rosa

Chemical Bank
Consumer Affairs
270 Park Avenue
New York, NY 10017-2070
212/270-9300

April 25, 1994

Mr. Paul C. Rosa
117 E. Espanola Street
Colorado Springs, CO 80907

Dear Mr. Rosa:

There seems to be some misunderstanding about Chemical Bank. We are a <u>financial</u> institution, the fourth largest bank in the United States. In the late eighteenth/early nineteenth centuries, chemical manufacturing was a part of our business; but the connection to the chemical industry ended long ago. Only the name hearkens back to that part of our corporate history.

"Reclaiming" the rooms of your home sounds like a very good plan. Perhaps you can find a local warehouse that will permit you to store your collection. Good luck in your search!

Sincerely,

Ronald Werdann
Assistant Treasurer

117 E. Espanola St.
Colo. Springs, CO 80907
December 9, 1993

Management
Cheyenne Mountain Zoo
4250 Cheyenne Mountain Zoo Rd.
Colo. Springs, CO 80906

Dear Animal Displayers,

I've always loved animals! Whether it was my Grandma Bain's Collies or an aggressive male Blue Jay in the Iowa woods, I've always treasured and respected God's creatures. I even owned an ant farm as a kid, and gave each ant a special name (Louie, Karen, Skeeter, Ramone, Lee Anne, Agnes, Kurt, Ben, etc.). I've been a subscriber to National Geographic for over twenty-five years, and I never miss an "animal special" on TV. Never. As I mentioned earlier (first sentence), I've always loved animals! I will now dedicate myself to the crux of the letter, as I realize you have busy schedules.

I've passed my love for animals on to my young son (Kip), and he will be celebrating his fifth birthday on January 8, 1994. Nothing would give him greater joy than to be surprised with a back yard full of animals. That's where you come in (hopefully), my friends! I was wondering if I could borrow some animals from the Cheyenne Mountain Zoo for one evening (1/8/94). I could pick up the beasts after the zoo closes and return them before it opens, thus eliminating any customer dissatisfaction. My brother (Henry) owns a fleet of enormous trucks, so transporting the creatures wouldn't be a problem. I don't know what your "inventory" is, but I was hoping to "rent" the following:

√ 3 giraffes (two adults, one baby)
√ 4 peacocks (2 males, 2 females)
√ 1 hippopotamus (either sex)
√ 3 monkeys (preferably chimpanzees)
√ 5 goats and/or gnus
√ 1 male lion (with cage, of course)
√ an assortment of lizards (gila monsters, iguanas, etc.)

I am willing to pay top dollar for the use of your animals for one night, say $10,000 for the assortment outlined above. I'm willing to offer a $75,000 security deposit as well. Money isn't an object, as I am a successful oil magnate. Again, this would certainly make my son's birthday special, so I hope you can help. Even if only a few animals are available to me, I'd be interested. As Kip's "big day" is only a few weeks away, I urge you to write to me as soon as possible! If my plan is not possible, I will ask the Denver Zoo for assistance. Thank you! Finally, do you offer (XL) T-shirts?

How about that Marlin Perkins?

Paul Rosa

Paul C. Rosa

CHEYENNE MOUNTAIN ZOO

4250 Cheyenne Mt. Zoo Rd.
Colorado Springs, CO 80906
(719) 633-9925
Fax: (719) 633-2254

BOARD OF DIRECTORS

OFFICERS
Dennis A. Weber
   Chairman of the Board
Gary D. Whitlock
   Vice-Chairman
Sherry Clarkin
   Treasurer
Jane Emery
   Secretary

DIRECTORS

Mary G. Armour
Jo Boddington
Bernice E. Brister
Sherry Clarkin
Tim L. Cobb
Lewis A. Cryer
Joan C. Donner
Jane Emery
Margaret F. Hillman
Freita F. Keluche
Donald T. Kramer
Margot Lane
Dorothy A. Lavick
Terence Lilly
Geoffrey E. Lind
Katherine H. Loo
Mary Ellen McNally
Becky L. Medved
Leota J. Roads
Peter R. Spahn
John W. Street
Dennis A. Weber
Gary D. Whitlock
Jon R. Whitney
Richard R. Young

Susan M. Engfer
   President & C.E.O.

Accredited by

December 13, 1993

Mr. Paul Rosa
117 East Espanola Street
Colorado Springs, CO 80907

Dear Mr. Rosa:

Thank you for your letter of the 9th. With regard to
your request to rent several of our animals for your
son's birthday, I'm afraid I must inform you that the
Cheyenne Mountain Zoo does not rent or loan animals to
anyone for any purpose. There are several reasons for
this, not the least of which is that situations outside
their normal routine can be extremely stressfull on the
animals, and we try to avoid that at all costs.

Once again, thank you for your inquiry, and I hope you'll
consider bringing your son to the Zoo to visit the
animals in the near future. I've enclosed applications
for our membership and Adopt-An-Animal programs for your
use...a membership or adoption will make a great gift for
a birthday or any occasion!

Best Regards,

Paul Montville
Marketing & Development Director

117 E. Espanola St.
Colo. Springs, CO 80907
December 11, 1993

Ken-L Ration Dog Hero of the Year
P.O. Box 1370
Barrington, IL 60011

Dear Pooch People,

When I read that you were having a "Dog Hero of the Year" contest, I let out a whoop of excitement that could be heard blocks away! You see, I have a dog (Galileo) who performed an act of heroism this year which was so selfless that I've been shaking my head in wonder for months! Since his playful puppy days, my best friend, a glorious "Chinese Crested," was special. Children naturally flocked to his side, as if he were -I mean no disrespect here- touched by the Lord. And then, just when I had decided Galileo couldn't surprise me further, he saved my life. The story I am about to tell you is so amazing that you may decide to end your little contest with this entry. But perhaps I should get off my high horse and tell my tale!

I was vacationing in Nashville, TN last February with Galileo, when I decided to drive several hours south to explore Lynchburg and the Jack Daniel's Distillery. While driving through Tullahoma, TN on Route 41, I swerved to avoid a badger carcass which was spread (cream cheese-like) across my lane, and soared into a ditch. Upon regaining consciousness I discovered that both my legs had been fractured and my Plymouth Duster was submerged under eighteen inches of fresh snow! Galileo was (miraculously) unharmed, exhaling his warm, damp breath onto my body to keep me comfortable until aid arrived. After an excruciating five-hour wait, a man (with his Labrador Retriever) arrived, offering to help. The powerful man, John "Bo" Culbertson, hoisted my crippled body across his powerful shoulders and took us (Galileo trotted along with the dog, Sparky) to his nearby cabin. But soon the rescue turned sour.

Mr. Culbertson knew that I was a famous cookbook author and decided that he would be the perfect consultant on my next volume, which he insisted I begin at once. As he forced morphine down my throat, I painfully pecked away on the ancient typewriter he provided. But this awful man was never satisfied with my recipes, screaming such things as, "no cinnamon!" or "more butter!" It was soon apparent that I would *never* be allowed to leave, so Galileo (it turns out) devised a plan. One night my dog leapt through the second-story window, ran to a nearby phone booth, and dialed 911 (with his nose, I assume). When the emergency official answered, Galileo, using Morse code barks (I have no idea where he learned this), described the grim situation. Within minutes the police stormed Mr. Culbertson's home and whisked me away to a hospital. Mr. Culbertson and Sparky are now serving a twenty-year sentence for kidnapping.

So you see, my pal is "Dog Hero of the Year," hands down! I initially thought the prizes ("National recognition, a silver-plated engraved bowl, and a year's supply of Kibbles 'n Bits dog food") were a bit...stingy, but *then* I realized it's worth <u>seven times</u> as much to a dog! Please let me know if Galileo has won - a self-addressed, stamped envelope is enclosed with a photo! Lastly, please send an (XL) T-shirt.

Barking up the right tree,

Paul Rosa

Paul C. Rosa

National Photo Service, Inc.

Ken-L Ration is sniffing out winner for dog hero contest

Do you know a dog that has performed a heroic deed? Whether it was your dog, the dog next door or one you've read about, that act of canine bravery could earn a reward.

Ken-L Ration is accepting nominations for the Ken-L Ration Dog Hero of the Year Contest to honor ordinary dogs for outstanding bravery, intelligence and loyalty.

You may remember reading news stories about last year's winner. Sparky, a yellow Labrador retriever from Tullahoma, Tenn., dragged his owner, John "Bo" Culbertson, nearly 200 yards home after Culbertson suffered a heart attack.

The 1993 Dog Hero of the Year will receive national recognition, a silver-plated engraved bowl and a year's supply of Kibbles 'n Bits dog food. To nominate a dog, send a detailed description of its heroic deed, with your name, address and telephone number, to Ken-L Ration Dog Hero of the Year, P.O. Box 1370, Barrington, Ill., 60011. Heroic acts must have occurred after Oct. 1, 1992; entries must be postmarked Dec. 31.

FYI

MYSTERY PHOTO: The Children's Museum has a bit of a mystery to solve. Museum staffers recently found what appears to be a family portrait of a man

Sparky, Ken-L Ration's 1992 Dog Hero of the Year, "is worth millions to me," says owner John "Bo" Culbertson of Tullahoma, Tenn. Sparky saved Culbertson's life.

"GALILEO"

Dog Hero of the Year

February 22, 1994

Dear Ken-L Ration Dog Hero Nominee:

Thank you for participating in our **1993 Ken-L Ration Dog Hero of the Year** contest. Although your nominee has not been named a finalist, we hope you will enjoy the enclosed coupon for a FREE 4 lb. bag of Kibbles 'n Bits Dog Food in appreciation for sending in your story. You might be interested to know this year's winners. They are:

1993 Dog Hero of the Year: *Weela*, Imperial Beach, CA: She saved 30 people, 29 dogs, 13 horses and one cat in repeated heroic efforts during large scale flooding which struck parts of Southern California last winter.

Runners-up:

● *Papillon*, Trotwood, OH: Alerted owner that her infant daughter had stopped breathing while napping.

● *Rosie O'Grady*, Garden City, SC: Saved 36 condos and many lives from being lost to an act by arsonists.

● *Poudre*, Johnstown, CO: Pulled master from river after he slipped down a steep bank while fishing and broke his arm in two places.

● *Ruby*, Medina, OH: Alerted family to a serious carbon monoxide leak in their home.

Special Recognition Awards:

● *Two Bears*, Shohola, PA: Born with a disability, this Newfoundland pup is a constant companion to her young master with Down's syndrome.

● *Buffy*, Mission Viego, CA: Serves as a constant, devoted companion to owner who suffers from Alzheimer's disease.

Thank you again for taking part in our program. We hope you'll continue to be on the lookout for dog heroes!

Sincerely,

Steve Willett

Steve Willett

Sponsored by

KEN-L RATION Kibbles 'n Bits

© 1991 The Quaker Oats Company

117 East Espanola Street
Colorado Springs, Colorado 80907
December 22, 1993

Lysol Toilet Bowl Cleaner
L & F Products
Montvale, New Jersey 07645

Dear Nice People,

Hello my name is Paul and I am now twenty years old. I live with mother and father in a big house and I like to be friends with people. My friend Kurt came over to my house yesterday and we made paintings and bowls from clay. It was fun and my mother said I was good and maybe I could have Kurt over again soon. I love my parents because they treat me like anyone else not mean like my neighbor Scott. My mother lets me help in the house and since I am very good at cleaning things she lets me wash the kitchen and bathroom. I like to scrub and scrub until the stains and mildew go away for a long time. They come back in a week or two but I scrub them again! My mother says you should stay one step or two in front of the dirt if you want a shiny home. I think she is right so I do my best! I use your toilet bowl cleaner in our two toilets and it works well and smells good. I think the angle neck bottle is such a good idea that I wish it was mine! Then I could make a lot of money and laugh at Scott. That would be fun do you agree? My father says that Benjamin Franklin was a great inventor. Do you know some more? Tell me the ones you know and what they did please. I have questions about the Lysol bottle and my parents said I could use their computer to ask you. I am getting pretty good at typing so I decided to write to you! My first question is about the top of the bottle. It says Lysol in big letters and then there is a little R next to it like this ®. What does that mean? I think it stands for rust because there are rust stains in toilets but I am not sure. Then there is a sentence at the bottom of the bottle that looks like this 16 FL. OZ. (1 PT.) 473 ml. I do not know any of these words so I looked them up in the big dictionary my father has and could not find any of them in there at all. I am getting better with my words but I can not figure this sentence out. I do not want to ask my parents and seem dumb so could you tell me please? On the back of the bottle is a pretty drawing with a lot of lines and numbers that looks like what I put at the bottom of this page. Why did you put this on the bottle? I think maybe more people will buy something that is pretty than ugly is that true? I have more questions but my mother said I should not take too much of your time because you are busy people. Please write to me soon and send it in the envelope I am giving you. Thank you very much and I really like your product because it is easy to use.

I like to write letters,

Paul C. Rosa

117 East Espanola Street
Colorado Springs, Colorado 80907
February 3, 1994

Lysol Toilet Bowl Cleaner
L & F Products
Montvale, New Jersey 07645

Hello again to you,

It is Paul again and I am sad that you never sent me a letter when I sent a letter to you in December. That was two months ago and my mother tells me that I should get a letter within four weeks or it is rude! When I am nice to my friend Kurt it seems like everyone should be nice too, so I wish you could finally send me the letter that I asked from you back then. I told you that my mother lets me do a lot of the scrubbing in the house and I think that your Lysol is really a very good product that does what it should do. I wrote to you with some questions like do you know any inventors and what does this ® mean (rust?) and what does that one funny sentence mean with those words and why is there a pretty painting on your bottle? I don't think that I asked too many questions and my father said that I should write to you again and send the first letter again if you don't want to answer me. He fought in Korea and says that every American deserves to be treated well and fairly and things such as this. That is so true don't you think, Lysol people in New Jersey? Anyways, I don't want to take too much time because I know you have busy things to do, but I would sure like that answer. When I wrote to you before I also sent you one of those stamped envelopes so it makes no sense to me that you couldn't write! If you are worried about more letters I promise you here and now that I won't ask more questions. I don't even like to have to write because my neighbor Scott says that means I'm dumb. I am not dumb I am special my mother tells me. Please write today to me!!!! And if you have really big T-shirts, please send me some too right away!

Please treat me nice!

Paul Rosa

Paul C. Rosa

117 E. Espanola St.
Colo. Springs, CO 80907
December 27, 1993

Customer Dealings
The d-Con Company
L&F Products
Montvale, NJ 07645

Dear Vermin Assassins,

Mice and rats. Rats and mice. They are all around us and boy are they pesky! They help themselves to our food (uninvited), leave little "pellets" behind our cabinets, and make annoying squeaking noises. For these reasons, along with many others I choose to presently ignore, the awful rodents <u>should</u> be annihilated. That's where the proud men and women of d-Con (proudly) step in! Your various traps and poisons are the envy of the entire trap and poison community. I tend to believe that your unofficial motto is, "Death to the cursed rodents!!" But I am gallivanting away from the very skeleton (if you will) of this letter. It's refocusing time!!!

Living in a "high rodent zone" (HRZ), I use your fine line of products to kill an average of 9.31 rats and/or mice per week (figure rounded off). In the past two years (1992/93) I have discarded more than 960 whiskered pests, blithely tossing them in my (side yard) garbage canister. Given that the average weight of each creature I slay is 3.37 ounces-I keep detailed records-I have tossed more than 200 pounds of rodent carcasses into the aforementioned container. That's a lot of meat, my aggressive friends!

Last night, while I was enjoying dinner with my wife of twenty-two years, Magda, it occurred to me that I may be wasting a lot of *edible* meat (when properly handled)! If thoroughly cooked, should I feel comfortable preparing "rodent meals" for my family? Mouse and rat bacteria are certainly no match for powerful American-made ovens set at 425°F, wouldn't you agree? I have several ideas for tasty rodent stews, soups, and pastries! Do you offer recipe books? I am convinced that I could reduce my monthly food bills by 15-20% if you give me the (knowledgeable) go-ahead to serve cooked rodent flesh! Inform me!

I am also eager to hear any ideas you may have on the possibilities of *wearing* rodent fur. I imagine that a full length mouse jacket would be "toasty warm" and pleasing to the eye as well. Even the animal rights activists would cheer my clever idea! Please write to me as soon as possible and let me know what the food/clothing possibilities are for mice and rats. Your conscientious response could make a big difference in my (upper) lower class family! Finally, an (XL) T-shirt would be wonderful!

Say cheese,

Paul Rosa

Paul C. Rosa

117 E. Espanola St.
Colo. Springs, CO 80907
February 7, 1994

Customer Dealings
The d-Con Company
L&F Products
225 Summit Ave.
Montvale, NJ 07645

Dear Response Defaulters,

It has now been exactly forty-three days since I sent my "fact-finding" missive. Forty-three days! I certainly believe that six weeks (plus change!) is enough time to mentally formulate a retort, transcribe it on quality paper, and send it to a faithful consumer! My wife (Magda) urged me to switch my affiliation with d-Con and substitute a more courteous outfit. "After pumping all that money into their swelling coffers, you should expect *more*, honey!" she elaborated while fixing Belgian waffles last week (Wednesday, I think). Frankly, she has a fairly good point, but little capacity for pardoning others, possibly *my* strongest emotional feature. Therefore, in the spirit of forgiveness, I have decided to re-submit my original letter, and also offer additional information.

As my first correspondence meticulously reported, I have access to roughly two pounds of rodent flesh per week, as a result of your devastatingly efficient poisons and traps. I asked if this meat was edible, and, if so, are recipes available (stews, soups, pastries, etc.). I have begun saving carcasses, and to date have accumulated 11.18 (figure rounded off) pounds of "beef." Needless to say, with all of this "food" lying around I am extremely anxious to learn the possibilities of future ingestion!! I have also collected fifty-two rat and mouse pelts (enough for a coat) and would like to learn the applicable health risks, if any!

I must confess that my curiosity was so resolute yesterday that I removed a diminutive rat from a d-Con trap and proceeded to grill it (skinless) on my imported hibachi. Served with au gratin potatoes, French bread, and Coors Light Beer, I was duly impressed with the rodent's delicate flavor, not unlike chicken's. Realizing the main course was *free*, it somehow tasted even better (retroactively)!

I have felt no unpleasant digestive reactions, but would certainly like to hear your views on vermin consumption before also serving my family. Your views on rodent apparel are encouraged as well. Finally, my cousin ("Sindi") would certainly enjoy an (XL) T-shirt. Please write promptly this time. Remember what my father said: "Work hard but always be respectful!"

A creative cook,

Paul Rosa

Paul C. Rosa

encl: Self-addressed, stamped envelope ("SASE" for short)

*Author's note: After sending the previous letter, I realized d-Con was owned by the same organization -L & F Products- as Lysol (I wrote to *them* in December). Since the two letters had conflicting information, I wrote the following message, desperate to explain the disparities and get a reply. ☺It worked!

119 E. Espanola St.
Colo. Springs, CO 80907
April 29, 1994

Customer Situations
L&F Products
225 Summit Ave.
Montvale, NJ 07645

Dear Rodent-Destroyer and Toilet-Cleaner Professionals,

I have grown angrier and angrier over the past four months as you have *repeatedly* ignored my letters concerning rodent flesh ingestion (and other topics). Perhaps my letters are a bit...peculiar, but our country grew and prospered on the rugged shoulders of those once considered peculiar themselves (Ben Franklin, Abe Lincoln, etc.)! However, my ire graduated to rage last night when my wife, Jenny (affectionately nicknamed "Magda") explained that I wasn't the only one in the family to be treated disrespectfully by a company (L & F Products) we once supported proudly and without reservation (damn it, our house is chock-full of your goods!). Allow me to explain.

Apparently on December 22, 1993-a mere five days before I initially wrote-my developmentally-disabled son (Paul Jr.) innocently requested some information as well (coincidence!) from L & F, concerning Lysol, which the "average" person could handle with ease on their own. Be assured, typing two letters on our computer was no small task for a grown man who tests at a fifth grade reading level! Your contemptuous lack of effort (reply) has made him somewhat sullen and withdrawn. And when Jenny explained that she herself <u>politely</u> re-submitted Paul's letters with absolutely no luck, I decided to boycott your organization and urge my community to do the same. But *then* I realized a final letter, requesting a reply (to both correspondences), is in order. You see, as a passionate Lutheran, I was raised to treat people with mercy and dignity!

Again, I urge you not to dismiss my family as "weirdos" or "goof-balls!" *This* particular goof-ball served this country proudly (in Korea) and is a model, tax-paying citizen. It would mean the world to my son if you responded to his letters (copies enclosed), and I certainly expect the courtesy of a response to my letters (enclosed) as well! Two convenient "SASEs" (for father *and* son) have been included, and I encourage replies <u>within</u> <u>one</u> <u>week</u>. I certainly feel my family (especially Paul Jr.) deserves that, friends. God bless and good day to you!

Requesting courtesy and such,

Paul Rosa

Paul C. Rosa

P.S. My cousin (Sindi) still requests an (XL) T-shirt!

May 5, 1994

Mr. Paul Rosa
117 E. Espanola Street
Colorado Springs, CO 80907

Dear Mr. Rosa:

Thank you for your letters and for your interest in our product
line.

The reason we have not responded to your letters is that many of
your questions and concerns are not areas which we can expertly
advise you such as the edibility of rodents. We would suggest you
consult a physician, nutritionist or a dietician.

The circled R after the name Lysol indicates that Lysol is a
registered trademark. A trademark legally restricts the use of a
name or symbol to the owner or manufacturer.

Enclosed are your postage-paid envelopes (4). Once again, thank you
for your interest.

Sincerely,

Consumer Relations

9400018920

enc. 4 ppe

117 E. Espanola St.
Colo. Springs, CO 80907
December 25, 1993

Consumer Affairs, Issues, Concerns, Questions, and Topics, etc.
TV Guide Magazine
100 Matsonford Rd.
Radnor, PA 19088

Dear Viewing Shepherds,

Lord almighty, I certainly enjoy my television set! I simply can't get home from work swiftly enough -I am a dog groomer-to renew my love affair with the fine entertainment offered by ABC, NBC, CBS, MTV, CNN, FOX, HBO, TNT, and the many other superb networks that have catchy three-letter names! Why, just last night (Christmas Eve), while visiting my parents (Nancy and Santiago) in Pittsburgh, I enjoyed the following splendid offerings: "Full House" (Fox; 6:00-6:30p.m.), "Designing Women" (IND; 6:30-7:00p.m.), "Hard Copy" (ABC; 7:00-7:30p.m.), "Disney's Christmas Fantasy on Ice" (CBS; 8:00-9:00p.m.), "The Harry Connick, Jr. Christmas Special" (CBS; 9:00-10:00p.m.), "Mama's Family" (FOX; 10:00-11:00 p.m.), "Unsolved Mysteries" (LIF; 11:00-12:00a.m.), and, finally, "Love Connection" (FOX; 12:00 a.m. - 12:12a.m.). Mind you, 12:12 is only an *estimate*, as I fell asleep on the sofa, only to awaken at 3:05 a.m. (exactly!) with my hand still steadfastly clutching the remote.

Clearly, I pass a lot of quality time in front of my Sony Trinatron-my parents have one too-so I feel that I am somewhat of an expert on programming (if you will). But the shows are actually of secondary importance to me. You see, my friends, I am someone who could be (loosely) described as a "commercial nut!" When I see a "presentation" featuring the Energizer Bunny (he keeps going and going...), Ford Trucks (like a rock!), The Pillsbury Doughboy (cute!), or Coors Beer (such magnificent physiques!), I give the "Volume+" button on my trusty remote a few urgent clicks. "One can never be *too* informed!" my half-sister (Louise) always says, moments before reading a consumer journal of some sort. She's 100% right, so I embrace television commercials with unfettered enthusiasm!

For the reasons I have concisely outlined (above), I would like to urge TV Guide to begin listing all television *commercials* along with the television programs! Each product being advertised should be detailed, as well as the exact time of airing (i.e. "Lemon Pledge"; 10:12.00-10:12.15a.m or "Campbell's Soup"; 3:22.30-3:23.00p.m.). This will give (the many) folks like me a chance to "fire up" the VCR and save valuable data for posterity. Also, I would like to see more commercials. I realize that you simply "report the facts," but a little pressure from the world's most influential magazine (you) would certainly give the cocksure network honchos reason to reevaluate their outdated priorities! So, faithful colleagues, please let me know what you think of my idea of increased commercials-I would suggest a 25% addition-and detailed *listings*! I would be thrilled to receive a written response, as it will one day surely serve as a collector's item! Finally, if you have (XL) T-shirts, I'd be overjoyed to receive one. Have a robust 1994!

With a television in (almost) every room,

Paul Rosa

Paul C. Rosa

Radnor, Pennsylvania 19088 • 610-293-8500

April 18, 1994

Mr Paul Rosa
117 E Espanola St
Colorado Spgs CO 80907

Dear Mr. Rosa:

   Thank you for your suggestions regarding TV GUIDE's
programming content. Most of our subscribers indicate they would
prefer less advertisement.

   Your suggestion would not be practical considering all prime
time national shows have advertising according to their area. When
we also consider the number of advertisements per commercial break,
it would not be possible to include them and still have a usable
book. Most viewers prefer no commercials and that is why premium
channels on cable are doing so well.

   Thank you for your interest in our publication.

                              Sincerely,

                              Paul Davis
                              CUSTOMER SERVICE DEPARTMENT

PD/hc/aez
cf

117 E. Espanola St.
Colo. Springs, CO 80907
December 26, 1993

The Pillsbury Company (Consumer Topics)
2866 Pillsbury Center
Minneapolis, MN 55402-1464

Dear Dough Distributors,

Frankly, it is **amazing** to me that I have never written to you before! You see, my friends, dough is (was, and always will be) vital to me! Call me "dough crazy" if you wish, but if you like biscuits, croissants, scones, or any of the other delicacies requiring (you guessed it) dough as an ingredient, then you are "dough crazy" as well. Most folks are too uptight to describe themselves in such a flashy manner, but my godfather (Kwon Chai Lee) always said, "Paul, never be ashamed to portray yourself in a candid, forthright fashion!" He clearly led a rich, full life-he died in 1989-so I've chosen to adhere to his passionate philosophy. But just look at the way I am meandering from the very heart and soul of this meaningful correspondence! I shall now rededicate myself to a concentrated course of written action!

As I mentioned, dough is vital to me (it *seems* as though I am straying again in my letter, but as you shall soon see, this is *not* the case!), so choosing a superior flour company was pivotal as well. In 1981, I decided to stop leaping from one flour brand to another and stick with the finest available. An entire weekend (in April) was devoted to a flour study, and Pillsbury was the clear winner! Occasionally I still repeat the rigorous competition, but your brand consistently prevails. Frankly, *no one* offers bleached, enriched, pre-sifted, all purpose flour in a five pound (2.26 kg) sack the way you do. Bravo! I am also a big fan of your delightful mascot, "The Pillsbury Doughboy." I'd rank him right up there with Ultra Snuggle Fabric Softener's "Snuggle Bear" and Eveready's "Energizer Bunny!" They are all cute, informative, and concise. I especially enjoy the way the Doughboy giggles when his tummy is playfully poked. My entire family titters right along with the mischievous scamp, especially my youngest daughter, Agnes! In fact, she begs me again and again to bring the Doughboy *home*. It breaks my heart to have to tell her that you probably don't permit such a loan, but she is becoming increasingly insistent.

With Agnes' sixth birthday and kindergarten graduation rapidly approaching (May, 1994), I decided to finally try and grant her wish. I know it is probably not your practice to "rent" out the little mascot -he must be priceless!- but I am willing to pay a tidy sum. How does **$20,000** sound, to borrow the Pillsbury Doughboy on May 28 and 29 (weekend!), with a deposit of **$200,000** to protect against accidental injury, trauma, etc. I am a successful manufacturer of quality aircraft, so money is plentiful. I am also prepared to follow strict guidelines in order to protect the Doughboy's (no doubt) fragile constitution. He will certainly not be allowed within twenty feet of an oven; we will treat him with kid gloves!

Please let me know what the possibilities of renting your mascot are. He will be well protected and well insured, not to mention unconditionally loved! Please make Agnes ecstatic by granting her this wish. I look forward to your swift response. Two T-shirts (Child S and Adult XL) would also be welcome!

Making plenty of bread,

Paul Rosa

Paul C. Rosa

MICHAEL BONGO
DIRECTOR
COMMUNITY RELATIONS

TELEPHONE: 612/330-4976
FAX: 612/330-4923

February 8, 1994

Mr. Paul Rosa
117 E. Espanola St.
Ohio Springs, CO 80907

Dear Rosa:

Thank you for the opportunity to have the Doughboy participate in your daughter Agne's birthday and kindergarten celebration.

We receive many such worthwhile requests for the Doughboy to appear but, unfortunately, it is our company policy to participate only in events hosted by non-profit organizations in which Pillsbury contributes to.

In recognition of Agne's birthday and graduation, we would be glad to contribute our lovable Doughboy doll along with a personalized photograph.

Would like to extend our sincere wishes for a successful event.

Sincerely,

Mike Bongo
Mike Bongo
Director
Community Relations

enc.

A Grand Metropolitan PLC Company

117 E. Espanola St.
Colorado Springs, CO 80907
December 29, 1993

Customer (Patron, Buyer, User) Issues
Roget's International Thesaurus
Harper Collins Publishers, Inc.
10 E. 53rd St.
New York, NY 10022-5299

Hello "Word Alternative" Suppliers!

I am a man who can't *comfortably* make up his mind about **anything**! *Nothing*, my informative, helpful friends! Ever since I ran (dashed, raced, sprinted) headlong into my family's sturdy elm tree during a 1974 pick-up football game in serene Cordaville, MA (pop. 1457), I have had a hard time with...choices. When faced with a puzzle (a problem, a dilemma, a quandary) I instantly visualize every (EVERY!) possible solution and/or approach to the situation, often taking fifteen to twenty minutes before making my eventual decision (choice, selection. pick) "That sounds *incredibly* frustrating!" you may say to yourself as you stroll evenly (with my letter in hand) to the coffee machine. Well, yes it is, but things could be worse. "How?!" you may bellow (clamor, thunder, roar) as you casually return to your office. I think it's better than failing to grasp *any* eventualities, thus remaining "stuck" indefinitely. Don't you agree (acquiesce, concede, allow)?

You may now be wondering why I decided (after much contemplation) to write to you. Well, that's the crux (basis, axis, essence) of the current paragraph. Before I continue, I wish to tell you that I have now been typing for over two hours, carefully agonizing over each strike of the computer keyboard. Since being rudely "dismissed" by the Xerox Corporation several months ago, I have been unable to secure gainful employment, spiraling downward into a quagmire (swamp, mire, bog) of Pepperidge Farm Cookie wrappers and...more Pepperidge Farm Cookie wrappers. Just when my spirits had apparently reached their lowest possible point, a stupendous (superlative, profound, exceptional) idea came to me like a thunderbolt from the heavens!

"Okay, what's the idea, 'Mr. Indecisive?'" you may sigh, as your patience ebbs from your very being. Okay, here it is: **I should work for Roget's Thesaurus!!!** My personality would perfectly complement your company's relentless pursuit of synonyms (alternatives, if you will)! For instance, when I hear the word, "howl," I also <u>instantly</u> *see* the words, "wail," "yowl," and "bellow!" Can't you see how perfectly (flawlessly, matchlessly, purely) I would fit into your organization (establishment, association, league)? Note: I have *now* been typing for nearly four hours!

Please write to me concerning my job possibilities with Roget's Thesaurus! I look forward to your speedy answer. Finally, please send an (XL) T-shirt (jersey, pullover, undershirt).

Hopefully (longingly, expectantly, optimistically) yours,

Paul Rosa

Paul C. Rosa

January 7, 1994

Paul C. Rosa
117 E. Espanola St.
Colorado Springs, CO 80907

Dear Paul,

Your letter arrived today and delighted everyone who read it. It is always a
pleasure to hear from literate and amusing fans of **Roget's Thesaurus**.
Roget's is updated every five to six years and we have just published our
latest edition this past year. I will be delighted to keep your letter on file and
when we are in the process of hiring free lance help for the next edition I
hope you will be available to interview.

Thank you again for your charming and clever letter.

Pat Bear
Assistant to Carol Cohen

117 E. Espanola St.
Colo. Springs, CO 80907
December 29, 1993

Consumer Relations, Points and Procedures
American Airlines
P.O. Box 619612
DFW Airport, TX 75261-9612

Dear Soaring Supporters,

Mercy, another Christmas has come and gone, and I just returned from my annual holiday visit to Pittsburgh, PA. "Why Pittsburgh?" you may ask, as you comfortably recline in your plush office chair(s). Well, that's where my parents (Jenny Lee and Sulaam Anrathek Rosa) live, so my choices are clearly limited. Granted, *they* could come out *here*, but it simply doesn't make much sense from a fiscal standpoint to transport two persons rather than one. Therefore, my annual pilgrimage shall no doubt remain a tradition until one of them passes on. I don't mean to sound grim, but *then* it would certainly make sense for the surviving parent to board a plane and fly west. But perhaps I am boring you.

As is often my custom, I chose to fly American Airlines. On December 24, I took flight 1070-seat 9A-to Dallas and flight 296-seat 15A-to Pittsburgh (where I was picked up by my childhood friend, Mark "Boomer" Gessler). Today I traveled from Pittsburgh to Dallas on flight 1867-seat 32F-later arriving in Colorado Springs on flight 345* (I drove myself home). Typically, these flights were punctual, the food tasty, and the "accommodations" pleasant. However, since I absentmindedly packed my book (a spirited Jackie Collins novel), I was bored, so I passed the time by compiling *dozens* of "Airline Questions." As I realize you must answer tens of thousands of letters each day, I have chosen my "top three" queries for your review. They appear immediately after this sentence, so you can't miss them:

1. *Why* must the seats be "upright" before the airplane lands?
2. Why (and when) did "stewardesses" become "flight attendants?"
3. Why are there no showers in the restrooms?

When I arrived in downtown Colorado Springs ("Colo. Spgs.," the street signs indicate), I met my girlfriend of seven months, Sue Ellen Constantisky, at the Subway Submarine Shop, where I enjoyed a "Seafood Sub" while she devoured a "Turkey Sub." As we munched on tasty chocolate chip cookies (later), I posed the three (above) questions but Sue Ellen had no information or data to lighten my load (if you will). I was satisfied calorically but not informationally (Question #4: Is that a word?).

As I am a virtual "fact magnet," I decided to contact you and politely request the above information. A fleet response and an (XL) T-shirt would be appreciated. Enjoy 1994!

Pass the pretzels please,

Paul Rosa

Paul C. Rosa

*I don't know the seat number.

AmericanAirlines

January 19, 1994

Mr. Paul C. Rosa
117 East Espanola Street
Colorado Springs, CO 80907

Dear Mr. Rosa:

We are pleased your enjoyed your trip and thank you for your interest
in American. I welcome the chance to respond to your questions.

While safety requires seats remain in the upright position during
take-off and landing, it is for economic reasons that we cannot
sacrifice passenger seating space to provide room for showers on
board.

Since the 1960's we have employed a number of men as cabin crew
members. Rather than calling a male cabin crew member a "steward"
and a female cabin crew member a "stewardess," the term
"flight attendant" became more appropriate and generic. It is now in
the dictionary, along with the word "calorically."

Mr. Rosa, although we have no T-shirts to offer you, please feel free
to call 800-289-3462 and request a catalogue from which you may order
the item of your choice. We welcome every opportunity to serve you.

Yours truly,   .

Ms. K. J. Lindenberger
Staff Assistant
Executive Office

117 E. Espanola St.
Colo. Springs, CO 80907
December 31, 1993

Patron Information
The J.M. Smucker Co.
Orrville, OH 44667

Dear Jelly Personnel,

Your motto is, "With a name like Smucker's, it *should* be good," or something like that. You'll receive no argument from me, as I have enjoyed your (sinfully) delicious offerings for over twenty-seven years! My favorite Smucker's delicacy is surely "Strawberry Preserves," but I have explored each of your varieties with innocent enthusiasm and anticipation. I devour roughly fifty-four ounces (3 jars) of your jellies each week, smearing the dreamy "spread" on everything from bananas to cheese. I don't care how revolting a food may be, when it is adorned with Smucker's it becomes appealing. My devotion to jelly is so complete that I've embarked on a truly unique undertaking. But let's first backtrack a bit, shall we?

When I was a child, my family frequently vacationed at various eastern beaches, where we would customarily have a "rip-roaring good time" (to quote my father, Shamus). However, our plans were occasionally sabotaged by the most awful creatures ever to clutter the earth. The *jellyfish*, with its hideous, hanging tentacles and stinging cells is one of the few animals I would like to discuss with God. "God," I would say, "what is the purpose of these awful free-swimming marine coelenterates, with bodies made up largely of a jellylike substance and shaped like an umbrella?" Perhaps he (she?) would offer a reasonable reply, but I doubt it, my gelatinous heroes! Many times these repugnant organisms would sting my sister (Naomi) or mother (Meg) on the leg(s), and our good times were delayed as we rushed to the pharmacy (for ointment). I'll now explain why I am confessing these details to you.

As I mentioned, I've loved jelly since my early childhood, so it infuriates me that my least favorite creature (the jellyfish!) contains the word "jelly." It is certainly a disservice to all jelly manufacturers to be associated with this miserable, evil animal. Furthermore, when customers (like me) select a jar of jelly from the supermarket shelf, they invariably are forced to visualize a slimy, menacing jellyfish! Let me tell you, it is very difficult to contentedly make a choice with this image in one's mind! For this reason, my patient friends, I have decided to petition the U.S. Government (Wildlife Division) to change the name from "jellyfish" to "oozingfish."

I have already gathered over 1,400 signatures and I would be honored if you would join my noble movement! If you agree with the following statement, I urge you to sign the lines at the end of this page: **The name "jellyfish" is unfair to jelly lovers and workers alike, so the name "oozingfish" is humbly suggested as a replacement.** There is room for several signatures, so please pass this memorandum around the office and return it promptly! An (XL) T-shirt would be nice too!

Signatures:

_____

_____

_____

_____

Ignoring honey,

Paul Rosa

Paul C. Rosa

Established 1897

January 21, 1994

Mr. Paul Rosa
117 E. Espanola St.
Colorado Springs, CO 80907

Dear Mr. Rosa:

Thank you for your recent letter and your kind comments
about our products. Consumers like you are the very
foundation of our business.

Your campaign on behalf of jelly is very interesting and we
wish you success with this venture. However, due to our own
policy, I did not circulate your petition.

We do appreciate your taking the time to write to us,
Mr. Rosa. Please accept the enclosed complimentary product
coupons along with our best wishes.

                              Sincerely,

                              Vickie Limbach

                              Vickie Limbach
                              Manager of Communications

VL/ph
Enc.

THE J.M. SMUCKER COMPANY • STRAWBERRY LANE, ORRVILLE, OHIO 44667-0280 • TELEPHONE (216) 682-3000 • FAX: (216) 684-3370

119 E. Espanola St.
Colo. Springs, CO 80907
May 25, 1994

Ms. Vickie Limbach, Manager of Communications
The J.M. Smucker Co.
Orrville, OH 44667-0280

Dear Ms. Limbach,

On December 31, 1993 I wrote to Smucker's, implying that jelly was my all-time favorite food. I detailed that I consume roughly fifty-four ounces of your incomparable offerings each week, favoring "Strawberry Preserves." As you recall, I also confessed my displeasure with the jellyfish and its use of the word "jelly." I simply feel it is unfair to associate (fabulous) jelly with this miserable, evil creature that harms many and makes many *more* simply itch!

I explained that I was circulating a petition to have the name of the jellyfish changed to "oozingfish," and that I had (at that point) already gathered 1,400 signatures! It saddened me that Smucker's was unwilling (due to an internal policy) to join my cause, but I understood your position and relished the valuable ($3.00) jelly coupons you sent! By April I had gathered roughly 17,000 signatures from concerned citizens in my cross-country travels as a new-zoo advisor. My signed papers (along with my passionate suggestion) have been forwarded to the U.S. Government (Wildlife Division) and my idea is currently being handled by a "Mr. Ostrosski," a helpful chap, to be sure. As you are clearly involved in a closely related area, I felt it would interest you to learn of the progress in my battle for jelly respectability. Ms. Limbach, I shall keep you posted! Since I appreciate how terribly busy you must be, a copy of our earlier communications have been forwarded as a "refresher."

With one of your valuable coupons, I obtained a 10 ounce (284g) jar of Smucker's Simply Fruit Boysenberry Spreadable Fruit (100% fruit sweetened with concentrated fruit juices). Well, ma'am, it was absolutely heavenly, a taste sensation unlike any I've experienced before. As this is one of the few Smucker's offerings I hadn't tried, I must (again) say "Kudos to you and yours! You've outdone yourselves!!" Although I am *thrilled* that this product name has <u>no</u> connection with the repulsive *jelly*fish, it saddens me that spreadable fruit is (in fact) not, technically, a "jelly item." You see, Ms. Limbach, my devotion to jelly is so complete that I am constructing a small <u>JELLY MUSEUM</u> on the third floor of my roomy Victorian home. I plan to offer (for a small fee) extensive jelly literature (history, etc.), along with jelly-container viewing possibilities (antique and current containers, vessels, and urns). With my modest income, much of this ground-breaking museum will remain unrealized without proper funding. This is where I hoped Smucker's (the jelly giants, if you will) would step up to the mike (so to speak) and invest in their heritage! I am sure this outlay will pay for itself ten-fold due to added jelly awareness and appreciation!

Please discuss my proposal with the Smucker's higher-ups and send your thoughts. At the very least, I would certainly cherish an (XL) Smucker's T-shirt, as requested in letter number one. Fare thee well!

Let's jam,

Paul Rosa

Paul C. Rosa

Established 1897

June 1, 1994

Mr. Paul Rosa
119 East Espanola Street
Colorado Springs, CO 80907

Dear Mr. Rosa:

We have received your most recent letter and appreciate your
keeping us apprised of your efforts to rename "jellyfish".

Thank you for the invitation to support the establishment of a
Jelly Museum. Unfortunately, we must decline. However, under
separate cover, we are pleased to send you a Smucker T-shirt. We
trust you will wear it in good health.

                            Sincerely,

                            Vickie Limbach
                            Manager of Communications

VL:kd

117 E. Espanola St.
Colo. Springs, CO 80907
January 2, 1994

Administrative Offices
Denver Nuggets Professional Basketball Organization
1635 Clay St.
Denver CO 80204

Dear Dribblers,

Well, this is my first letter of the new year, so I'll try to make it as enthusiastic as possible. You see, communicating with others is (to me) the single most important aspect of successful human relations. A lack of communication is no doubt the "thorn" which causes the vast majority of today's divorces. And, speaking of marriages, isn't it ironic that a synonym for "communication" is "intercourse," another pivotal area for couples as well? But enough of my cerebral conjecture and full steam ahead with this letter!

I attended a Denver Nuggets game last Thursday evening (December 30) and had the time of my life! Accompanied by my buddies Leroy (he drove), Paul, and Bob (he told jokes), we drank beer, devoured pizza and enjoyed a thoroughly competitive contest. With the Nuggets prevailing (barely!), we left McNichol's Arena with songs in our hearts and pepperoni in our bellies. The athletic prowesses exhibited by such players as Dikembe Mutombo (he's so tall!), LaPhonso Ellis, and Chris Mullin were inspirational! I returned to work (I'm a fragrance consultant) on Friday with renewed fervor. Thank you, Nuggets!

As a fan of the NBA, I have noticed that many of the contests are decided (for all intents and purposes) by the midway point of the fourth quarter or earlier. Since it seems foolish to keep the high-priced stars (thoroughbreds if you will) in such a game, risking injury, wouldn't it be adroit to substitute players of "lesser" talents? For instance, if the Charlotte Hornets were leading the Indiana Pacers by twenty points with four minutes to play in the game, why not take Alonzo Mourning out and insert John Q. Public? The rules stipulate that five players must be on the court, but they needn't be (and shouldn't be) <u>talented</u>!

If it interests you, I am willing to offer my services to the Denver Nuggets. For $22,500 per year, I would be willing to play in the very situation described above. If Reggie Williams injures a knee at the end of a "decided" game it would be terrible for the team (talent-wise and money-wise), but *my* injuries could be greeted with an indifferent shrug of the shoulders! As a former high school (church league) player, I will not embarrass your organization either, as I still have a deft shooting touch and crisp bounce pass. In 1977 my coach (Mario Gessler) compared my set shot favorably with Bob Cousy's. So, why not protect your valuable investments and hire a few gentlemen who are expendable? Please write and let me know your thoughts on my ground-breaking idea. Leroy, Paul, and Bob are interested as well. And, if it's not too much bother, an (XL) T-shirt would be truly appreciated. Good luck on the "hardwoods" in 1994, my friends!

Shooting from the hip,

Paul Rosa

Paul C. Rosa

Dear Nuggets fan:

Thank you for your letter. It's nice to see you're a Nuggets fan!

Please find enclosed some souvenir items which we hope you enjoy.
As you could imagine, we receive a tremendous amount of letters
each week; therefore, we may not be able to fulfill each specific
request. We hope you enjoy the enclosed items.

However, to request autographs from players please send a self
addressed stamped envelope to each individual player to avoid being
lost.

If you wish to purchase official items with the Denver Nuggets logo
or that of other NBA teams, the NUGGETS LOCKER ROOM is located on
the Sixteenth Street Mall.

> **NUGGETS LOCKER ROOM**
> **303 16TH ST.**
> **DENVER, CO 80202**
> **(303) 446-2830**

If you are unable to make it to our store, please contact the
address below for a NBA gift catalog .

> **NBA GIFT CATALOG**
> **10812 ALDER CIRCLE**
> **DALLAS, TX 75238**
> **1-800-635-4438**

Media Guides are available by mail order please send check or money
order payable to the Denver Nuggets for the amount of $8.00 dollars
to cover our cost plus postage. Send to the address below.

> **DENVER NUGGETS**
> **1635 CLAY STREET**
> **DENVER, CO 80204**
> **PLEASE DO NOT SEND CASH**

Once again, thank you for your letter and we appreciate your
support of the Denver Nuggets!

McNichols Sports Arena • 1635 Clay Street • Denver, Colorado 80204-1799 • (303)893-6700

117 E. Espanola St.
Colo. Springs, CO 80907
January 2, 1994

Consumer Communications
Heinz Ketchup (Catsup?) Company
1062 Progress St.
Pittsburgh, PA 15212

Dear Condiment Creators and Distributors,

I am sick and tired of all the violence being depicted on television and in the movie theaters! Apparently it is mandatory that each show or film contain a minimum of ten deaths per hour before being released. With our nation's murder rate growing by leaps and bounds each year, perhaps it is time we turned our attention to the entertainment industry and its influence on society as a whole. "But what does any of this have to do with Heinz Ketchup (Catsup?)?" you may ask, as you scratch your heads in a befuddled fashion. Plenty.

I have heard that when we are subjected to a "dramatic" death or injury by Hollywood, the blood we see isn't blood at all, but ketchup (catsup?)! Since Heinz is the leading producer of ketchup (catsup?) in the United States, I feel your organization has a responsibility to try and decrease the violence. I know that you probably make $1,700,000 or more each year from violent shows/movies, but the impact on society must now be considered as well! For God's sake, think about our children's futures!! Perhaps the directors and producers will simply open their fat wallets to other ketchup (catsup?) companies like "Town House" or "Hunt's," but that is beyond *your* control, isn't it? By acting quickly and decisively you can sleep well at night, knowing that you have done your small part to make a "dent" in the violence of America!

As the father of four young children (Jessie, Paul Jr., Leroy, and Bob), I am trying to take a more active role in shaping their fragile futures. I am waging a personal war against crime and violence by attacking them in the small, lesser known areas such as yours (blood substitutes). Please do your part by declaring all Hollywood ketchup (catsup?) contracts null and void in this new year, 1994. Your delicious topping enhances the lives of the tens of millions of people who enjoy French fries, hamburgers, tater-tots, etc. You mustn't spoil this image by hopping on the violence bandwagon, regardless of how lucrative it may be! Act now, friends!

I would certainly appreciate a letter expressing your feelings and attitudes on the above topic. Sometimes it is good to hear the convictions of others and allow *them* to continually refine and shape one's own views! I look forward to your reply and hope to continue to support your company. I am also requesting an (XL) T-shirt. God bless you and happy new year!

A Pittsburgh native,

Paul Rosa

Paul C. Rosa

P.S. Is it "ketchup" or "catsup?!"

Heinz U.S.A.

Division of H. J. Heinz Company

1062 Progress Street
Pittsburgh PA 15212-5990
Telephone: 412 237 5757

January 28, 1994

Mr. Paul C. Rosa
117 East Espanola Street
Colorado Springs, CO 80907

Dear Mr. Rosa:

Thank you for your recent letter regarding Heinz Ketchup.

In response to your concerns regarding television violence and the possible correlation between "on-screen blood" and Heinz Ketchup, please be assured that neither the H.J. Heinz Company nor any of our products reinforce violent depictions in television or movies.

In speaking with a representative of the Pittsburgh Film Office as well as the Screen Actor's Guild, it was confirmed that the special effects blood used in broadcast is not ketchup, but rather a gel-like, chemical solution that features a consistency similar to syrup...rather than thick, rich Heinz Ketchup.

While many people mistakenly associate ketchup's role in Hollywood, the movie industry does <u>not</u> rely on the condiment for special effects.

In response to your second question regarding the difference between catsup and ketchup, Heinz has maintained the "ketchup" indentifcation since 1895. Heinz Ketchup was first introduced in 1876 and at that time the Company did refer to the product as "catsup" as a common product name. However, nearly 20 years later, Heinz changed its labels to "ketchup" in order to distinguish the Heinz brand from competitors who produced a lesser-quality product. Today, as the leading manufacturer of ketchup in the U.S., Heinz is proud to be America's #1 choice for ketchup!

Thank you for your inquiry, and I hope you enjoy our quality products for many years to come.

Sincerely,

Deb Magness
Manager - External Communications

117 E. Espanola St.
Colo. Springs, CO 80907
January 3, 1994

Customer Objections
Ford Motor Co.
1 American Rd.
Dearborn, MI 48121

Dear Car Higher-ups,

It happened over half a century ago and it changed our country forever. From that point on, getting from point A to point B was rearranged and reshaped. You probably agree, the car is one of the top inventions of this (or any) century! And I've fully enjoyed the concept of a car, owning four models in the past two decades. The finest of the bunch? Fords! They're handsome, rugged, and dependable. Congratulations on your work. I'm pleased that American cars are making a comeback, meeting the powerful challenge of the overseas corporations in Japan, Germany and Sweden.

I'm also a big fan of car *commercials* because they can be very informative and exciting. The Ford commercials are generally quite good but I simply don't like the slogan you've used in the past few years. **"Like Iraq"** is the worst, most insulting motto I've ever heard. As a veteran of the United States Marine Corps (honorable discharge), I think it is outrageous that you compare your products to a country whose butt we just kicked three years ago! Perhaps Saddam "Insane" Hussein is flattered, but U.S. citizens are definitely not impressed. Furthermore, I don't even *understand* the comparison. In what way are your cars like Iraq? Do they regularly overheat?

I had hoped to continue owning Fords until I was an old man (I own a "Bronco" now), but my principles won't allow it. I have been described by friends as "fiercely patriotic," and I can't support a company who compliments an enemy of our country. Please respect all the brave men who liberated Kuwait and change your motto at once. "Like Hercules" or "Like The Grand Canyon" would be much better without insulting *anyone*! Give it some thought.

Please write to me promptly and let me know what you think of my notions. I am not closed to the opinions of others and truly welcome your input. As a final note, I would prize an (XL) Ford T-shirt. God bless you and have a profitable 1994. Good-bye.

Nationalistically,

Paul Rosa

Paul C. Rosa

Marketing Strategies and Plans   Ford Motor Company
North American Automotive Operations   17101 Rotunda Drive
                                                        P.O. Box 1517-B
                                                        Dearborn, Michigan 48121

                                                        March 3, 1994

Mr. Paul C. Rosa
117 E. Espanola St.
Colorado Springs, CO 80907

Dear Mr. Rosa:

This is in reference to a recent letter you sent to **Ford Motor Company** which has
been forwarded to this office for review and reply.

The slogan is **"LIKE A ROCK..."** <u>not</u> "Like Iraq" and it is used by **General Motors**
for advertising its Chevy Trucks. Ford's popular slogans include, "Have You
Driven a Ford... Lately," and "Quality is Job 1."

Thank you for your letter. Unfortunately, we do not have a supply of Ford T-
shirts. As employees, we must purchase all Ford products from the same catalogs
as the general public.

                                        Sincerely,

                                        S. A. Nicholls
                                        North American Advertising

117 E. Espanola St.
Colo. Springs, CO 80907
January 12, 1994

Consumer Considerations
KFC Corporation
P.O. Box 32070
Louisville, KY 40232

Dear Chicken Czars,

Wings and breasts. Legs and other parts. You name the cut of chicken, and it's a safe bet that I enjoy eating it, my friends! In one way or another, chicken is represented in ten to fifteen of my meals each week (47.62%-71.43%). Oh, don't get me wrong, I enjoy an occasional steak or lasagna dinner with corn, but I inevitably return (like the sparrows of Capistrano) to my beloved chicken feasts! As you are the *absolute, undisputed champions* of the chicken solar system, I decided it was time I finally (humbly) wrote to you. Frankly, I am a bit awed and I am literally trembling as I peck tentatively at my modest keyboard. But press on I must!

For years I have enjoyed dining at your terrific establishments (they're nationwide!), and have always been a big fan of "The Colonel" (Sanders). I plunged into a modest depression when he died but was lovingly nursed back to health by my girlfriend (Soyeta) with a meticulous combination of love and chicken dinners. Clearly, this man's (The Colonel's) unwavering devotion to chicken touched me deeply, and there's no shame in that, is there? For years I have kept a detailed scrapbook on the life of this noble gentleman, collecting any newspaper clippings I could lay my hands on. Yes, I consider myself a "Colonel Connoisseur," but one nugget (appropriate word) of data has doggedly eluded me. What branch of the armed forces did The Colonel serve in!? I believe that he was a Navy man while my best friend (Manny) claims he was in the Marine Corps. Please settle this argument once and for all by sending information on your founder's military career. I would be tremendously grateful if you made my scrapbook complete!

Finally, why did you change the name from "Kentucky Fried Chicken" to "KFC?" Do you think The Colonel would have approved of this questionable alteration? Was it smart to modify the name *completely*? Perhaps you could consider the name **"K Fried C."** This would provide a sleek, streamlined new name while acknowledging the proud heritage of the restaurant. Please let me know your feelings on my suggestion.

I look forward to your letter as well as my next visit to a K Fried C (tomorrow). Please keep up the good work while considering my notions. Finally, I would enjoy an (XL) T-shirt. Remember, you are very important to many citizens in this great land of ours!

Rarely balking (get it?),

Paul Rosa

Paul C. Rosa

P.O. Box 32070
Louisville KY 40232-2070
502 456 8300

January 27, 1994

Mr. Paul C. Rosa
117 E. Espanola Street
Colorado Springs, CO 80907

Dear Mr. Rosa:

Thank you for your clever letter and your devotion to KFC!

If you and your friend Manny have a bet, there is no winner. The Colonel
was not in the Navy nor the Marines. He was recruited as a 16-year old
country boy by what he called a "fast talker", a recruiter for Teddy
Roosevelt's Army. The recruiter told him that since he was a husky lad,
"tell them you're twenty-one and they'll take you." The Colonel said this
was probably the first time he ever lied, but it surely taught him the
serious consequences of not telling the truth! Soon he was on a cargo
ship headed for Cuba, with 1500 mules on board. The smell of the mules,
combined with seasickness, produced a young man who arrived in Cuba some
forty pounds lighter than when he left the U.S. This explains why Mrs.
Sanders was never able to interest the Colonel in a cruise.

In answer to your second question, changing our name and logo was a very
serious business decision. The newly-introduced logo features "KFC" to
reflect our new, broader, more convenient menu and our plans to offer
products which are non-fried. Of course, research proved that the
Colonel's likeness says more about who we are to consumers than any other
indicator. Therefore, his likeness remains in the new logo. Our new logo
was featured this past year in a <u>Wall Street Journal</u> article that tested
customer recognition of corporate logos. We were pleased with the results
indicating KFC was one of the most recognized.

Thank you again for your interest in KFC.

Sincerely,

Shirley Topmiller
Group Manager - Consumer Affairs

enclosure

117 E. Espanola St.
Colo. Springs, CO 80907
January 14, 1994

Consumer Headquarters
Wardley's Aquarium Products , Inc.
Secaucus, NJ 07094

Dear Fish Friends,

Since I was fourteen years old I have owned aquariums. At first it was only a (trial) five-gallon variety with goldfish, but over the years I consistently graduated to bigger tanks with "better" fish. Presently I own a fifty-gallon aquarium with Tiger Barbs, Zebra Danios, Kissing Gouramis, and several Plecostomuses, the "vacuum cleaners" of the ichthyological world. If it interests you, my fish each have names: Kurt, Agnes, Zipster, Mike, Felicia, Rowdy, Turbo, Matilda, Carmen, Bela, Nicki, Holger, Astrid, Kip, Jesse, Jayne, and Tipi (in order of decreasing size). Now you may be whispering to yourself, "This fellow has too much free time on his hands," but my love for animals is something I will defend to the grave...if this (unlikely) necessity arises. Anyway, let's move on, shall we?

I recently treated my underwater pals to some of your "Freeze-Dried Tubifex Worms," and was amazed when they attacked the cubes with a voraciousness I've never seen (in my living room)! A layman might have concluded that I hadn't fed the little critters in *weeks*, but that would simply be an aberration of the truth, my friends! The fact is they are fed twice daily, but your tasty concoction simply drove them into a feeding frenzy (if you will). I could almost hear big Kurt shouting to me through the glass, "Paul, we'd all appreciate it if you dropped this delicious stuff into the tank on a regular basis!!" And you know what? That's *exactly* what I have done! Every Monday, Wednesday, and Saturday, at 3:00 p.m. sharp, I give "the gang" their much-anticipated treat. Perhaps it's only my (fertile) imagination, but there seems to be a tranquility and a sense of love and respect in the "ol' aquarium" that never existed before! For this reason, I cry, "Hats off to the selfless workers of Wardley's!"

But this letter wouldn't be complete without a few (well-meaning) questions! Here we go:

1. Is it "okay" to cook and eat my deceased fish? My religion suggests that "ingestion of a departed pet furthers spiritual evolution." What are your educated thoughts?
2. Having been convinced (by a pet store owner) that fish do indeed sleep, I was wondering if they dream too. If so, about what? Tubifex worms? The Bahamas?
3. Do fish ever long for beverages other than water? They must get frightfully bored consuming the very substance they *live* in! I'd hate to be forced to eat *air* constantly!

Well, that's all for now. I hope the Wardley's Company has continued success. I encourage a speedy reply in the enclosed SASE (Self-Addressed, Stamped Envelope). And how about an (XL) T-shirt?

Swimmingly yours,

Paul Rosa

Paul C. Rosa

the wardley corporation

P.O. BOX 2687, ONE AQUARIUM DRIVE, SECAUCUS, NEW JERSEY 07096-2687 U.S.A.
(201) 348-4040   FAX NO. (201) 348-9201   TELEX NO. 640130

Paul Rosa   January 19, 1994
117 E. Espanola St.
Colo Springs, CO 80907

Dear Paul,

I would like to thank you for your recent letter. In customer service, I spend most of my time dealing with complaints and problems. We found your letter rather creative and entertaining. Unfortunately, we can not provide you with a T-shirt unless, you send us at least two more entertaining letters including photographs. Once, this goal is accomplished we would not have any problem with issuing you a T-shirt.

It is not recommended to consume your pet fish due to the fact that they may have been treated with Malachite Green which has been determined to be a cancer causing agent according to the FDA.

The pet store was correct fish do sleep. Do fish dream? Well, that will probably remain one those unsolved questions in life such as if a tree in the forest fell down would it make noise if no one was there to hear it? If fish could I'm sure they would dream about girl fish, boy fish, when is this guy going to feed us?, and what type of new furniture are they going to get in there new aquatic townhouse by the lake?.

Do fish ever long for beverages other than water? Well, that's a good one! I guess that's one that will have to join the list of unsolved questions of life but if you ever find out please pass the information along to me.

Once again, thank you for your letter and thank you for your continued interest in Wardley Products.

Sincerely,

Shemya Bryant
Customer Service

119 E. Espanola St.
Colo. Springs, CO 80907
May 23, 1994

Ms. <u>Shemya</u> Bryant, Customer Service
The Wardley Aquarium Corporation
P.O. Box 2687
One Aquarium Drive
Secaucus N.J. 07096-2687

Dear Shemya,

You have a wonderful name!! It's sort of a combination of Sheila (my aunt's name) and Enya (the musical genius from Portugal). It's been a while since I wrote to you, as I have been busy with a truly arduous task. You see, my friend, I have been overseeing the construction of the largest complex of squash courts in southern Colorado, and time is at a premium! But finally I have a few free moments and I felt compelled to finally return your splendid, heartfelt missive of January 19, 1994.

As you recall, my first letter complimented Wardley for their tremendous Tubifex Worms, which my seventeen fish devour with unfettered ecstasy. You were also considerate enough to "tackle" my difficult queries concerning human fish-consumption, fish dreaming possibilities, and fish drinking urges. Most corporations would dismiss me as a "crackpot" or "goof-ball," misunderstanding my curious nature as a "problem" of some sort. You were learned enough to cut to the chase (so to speak) and afford me the courtesy I (and all folks) deserve. For this, I trumpet, "God bless you, Shemya!"

Shemya (what a name!!), you promised me a T-shirt if I sent two more letters and photographs, but I passionately urge you to settle for only *one letter and **one photograph. Given my aforementioned time constraints, it would be at least Halloween before I could send another note! Besides, I only have one more subject to discuss with you: the Wardley *Weekend* Pellet Fish Feeders. I am delighted that each pellet feeds my beautiful fish automatically for two days, but, you see, I rarely travel during the *weekend*. My typical "ramblin' days" are Wednesdays and Thursdays, and I feel remorseful when I must ask my sister (Meg) to feed my slippery pets. I am somewhat dismayed that Wardley has failed to manufacture an automatic feeder that can be used on days other than Saturday and Sunday (i.e. "weekends"). In today's age of convenience, such a product is *long* overdue, so <u>what</u> <u>gives</u>, Shemya (☺Shemya☺)?

Having faithfully composed a (*one) letter, I am now enclosing a (**one) photograph. It features Bill Eastman and Andy Anderson, my memorable roommates from 1986-1987, when I resided in Washington D.C. Bill (on the left), ironically enough, was born only one day before me, on November 16, 1961! Shemya, Shemya, Shemya, I am enclosing a copy of my first letter (for convenience) and urge you to respond as swiftly-to my above question-as you did in January! And how about that (XL) T-shirt?!

Shemya,

Paul Rosa

Paul C. Rosa

the wardley corporation

P.O. BOX 2687, ONE AQUARIUM DRIVE, SECAUCUS, NEW JERSEY 07096-2687 U.S.A.
(201) 348-4040   FAX NO. (201) 348-9201

October 14, 1994

Mr. Paul Rosa
117 E. Espanola Street
Colo. Springs, CO 80907

Dear Paul:

I sympathize with your frustration since you have fulfilled your end of the bargain with Shemya. However, Shemya still requests you send a photograph, not your old chums, but yours. She was very disappointed.

Nevertheless, I apologize for the delay of our "freebies" because we are understaffed. Please feel free to send a resume. We thank you for writing to remind Shemya. This expedited your request.

Yes, Shemya has sent your T-shirt and the food samples enclosed as per your request.

As to your query about Automatic Fish Feeder, The Wardley corporation is a manufacturer of "food and aquatic remedies" not an aquatic hardware manufacturer. There are various automatic fish feeders available manufactured by Pen Plax, Hagen, and others. We use the "Nutra-matic" in our laboratory. Nutra-matic is a battery operated automatic fish feeder distributed by Rolf C. Hagen Corporation, Visit your local Pet Dealer and ask for this product if you wish. We are very good at meeting our customer needs, even if it means recommending our competitors products.

Though I may not be as candid as you were in your letters, please do send a photograph of your self. Address it directly to Shemya, she will be very pleased.

Again, we apologize. If you have further queries please do not hesitate to write or call our 800 number.

Sincerely Yours,

Chuchi R. Coble
Quality Control

117 E. Espanola St.
Colo. Springs, CO 80907
January 14, 1994

Mike Daniels, Weatherman
Eyewitness News, KOAA-TV
530 Communications Circle
Colo. Springs, CO 80905

Dear Mr. Daniels,

"What is it about weather that brings us all together?" is an often-asked question. The answer? You guessed it; it's the undeniable effect it has on *everyone* who chooses to venture from their homes. Since this group encompasses roughly 97% of the population -invalids and the severely mentally ill comprise approximately 99% of the remaining 3% who are "shut-ins"- we're talking about a tremendous amount of people (roughly 291,000,000 in America alone!). Therefore, weather is one of the most important factors in most folk's lives. But I certainly don't have to tell *you*, and I certainly don't mean to patronize. I merely want to "set up" this letter in a proper, well-meaning fashion. Shall we commence with the essence of this correspondence?

I think it is safe to say that most of the public prefers sunny skies and temperatures in the 60°F-75°F range. Also, the majority no doubt favors minimal snowfall (less than twenty inches yearly) and winds which are consistently calm. I would venture to guess that humidity, rain, and clouds are generally viewed with disfavor and resignation. Finally, barometric pressure is of no consequence to the layman.

Given these statistics, Mr. Daniels (is that Scottish?), why on earth are you consistently "forecasting" days that are bitterly cold or plagued with high winds or depressing rainfall?! Perhaps some citizens enjoy a variety, but I challenge you to find the individual who desires all the cold evenings you've brought us recently! Also, the amount of rainfall this past summer was distressing, so I am forced to ask why you don't give us better weather, sir.

When I visited my half-brother, Cyrus, in Oceanside, CA (pop. 76,698) last October, he gloated that southern California consistently enjoys the very temperate conditions I outlined above! What do the weathermen there know that you don't know? How are they able to "deliver the goods" (if you will) on such a consistent basis while *your* well-meaning efforts produce mediocre results at best?

Now Mr. Daniels, I'm not a "grumble-bunny," but I would certainly like to know why none of the local weathermen can yield more agreeable conditions? Is it that the personnel in California, Hawaii, Arizona, etc. are simply more accomplished? I would appreciate a response to my questions and look forward to your speedy reply! Lastly, do you offer (XL) T-shirts?

Forever seeking the truth,

Paul Rosa

Paul C. Rosa

P.S. *Does* anyone really care about barometric pressure?!

MIKE DANIELS
EYEWITNESS
WEATHER

1 - 31 - 94

Dear Paul,

I Enjoyed your letter,
very humorous. Keep in mind

I Am Trying To give you

Better weather than what we've
had Recently - Those Guys in
California and Hawaii, Are Just
The Best, I can only hope, To
Reach Their status soon.
Sorry no T-Shirts
Thanks for watching MIKE

NBC THE PLACE TO BE

117 E. Espanola St.
Colo. Springs, CO 80907
January 15, 1994

Consumer Protests and Accusations
3M Audio and Video Markets Division
905 Highway 22S
Hutchinson, MN 55350-2927

Dear Careless Ones,

Most folks would characterize me as a "simple man." *Simple*, <u>not</u> naive! I was raised by a proud suspender salesman in tiny Cloverdale, VA (pop. 850) and was taught to respect the earth and all of God's creatures who inhabit it. "There is simply no shortcut for hard work," my father (Clarence) would consistently preach. "If you put in the hours, the success will follow," he'd continue as he helped me with my Little League batting practice. When I hit .422 for my baseball team (The Ravens) in the summer of 1972, I decided it would be prudent to forever mind his learned advice.

I began mowing lawns in the summer of 1975, and by 1982 owned the largest landscaping business in southwestern Virginia. Forever seeking new challenges (another "law" of my father's), I moved to Colorado Springs several years ago and immersed myself in the expanding field of realistic, adobe lawn ornaments. "What an odd career path," you may be mumbling to yourselves, but our 1993 worldwide sales topped $1.75 million! And now I'll address *your* firm.

Although extremely successful, I simply have never had a knack for things...scientific. Several weeks ago my loving wife (Leeza Banchoff Rosa) surprised me with a snazzy Panasonic VCR for Christmas. I was a bit intimidated by the confusing device but soon learned how to record my favorite television programs (Roc, Dateline, etc.). Last Wednesday I decided to venture to the store and purchase a movie for the first time. At K Mart I scanned a selection of films from Polaroid, JVC, Memorex, and Maxell, but decided to concentrate on the 3M possibilities. As your company created those terrific "Post-It Notes," I assumed your movies would be top-notch as well. I chose a motion picture titled, "Scotch High Standard T-120 VHS." I am a big fan of the science fiction genre, and this certainly sounded like a futuristic offering. The price was right ($3.00), so I rushed home to enjoy the tape-and a bowl of buttered popcorn-with Leeza.

After supper, we slid your tape into the VCR, settled into our respective recliners, and pressed "play" on the remote control. Nothing happened. I pressed "Fast Forward" to search for the movie, but it simply wasn't there. The tape was completely blank! How can you allow such a defective item to slip past inventory control? Has this happened before? I know the film was very inexpensive, but I would like to hear a (prompt) explanation for this disappointment!

Ejecting my feelings,

Paul Rosa

Paul C. Rosa

Customer Service
3M Audio and Video Technology Division

905 Highway #22 South
Hutchinson, MN 55350-2927
612/234 1779

January 26, 1994

3M

Paul C. Rosa
117 E. Espanola St.
Colorado Springs, CO 80907

Dear Paul:

Thank you for your recent letter telling us about your experience with one of our
Scotch™ brand T-120 High Standard videocassettes.

The tape you purchased was a BLANK TAPE to be used for recording from either
your VCR or camcorder. 3M does not produce any pre-recorded videocassettes.

So, although you were disappointed, the tape you purchased appears to have
worked as it was designed to.

If I may be of further assistance, please feel free to contact me.

Sincerely

Scott K. Johnson
Customer Service Coordinator

SKJ/bpk

June 8, 1994

Mr. Paul C. Rosa
117 East Española Street
Colorado Springs, CO 80907

Dear Mr. Rosa:

Your letter to 3M (copy attached) caused some stir among the folks at 3M. They weren't
sure whether you expected a motion picture to appear on the tape you had bought and were
truly disappointed, or if you simply were poking fun at them out of your heightened sense
of playful camaraderie.

In any event, as a curious third party who occasionally provides public relations advice to
3M, I'm interested in your point of view. Were you poking fun? And did you receive a
reply? If so, I'd be interested in receiving a copy — I also teach business communications
at a local college and I'm certain their reply will be interesting fodder for my class.

You may send your reply to:

    Greg Smith
    PACE Instructor
    1644 Oak Avenue
    St. Paul, MN 55112

Wishing you the very best.

Sincerely,

Greg Smith
Vice President and
Account Manager

117 E. Espanola St.
Colo. Springs, CO 80907
January 18, 1994

Citizen Inquiries
American Birding Association
P.O. Box 6599
Colo. Springs, CO 80934-6599

Dear Flight Fanciers,

I love owls. Always have, always will. From the moment I saw my first owl as a youngster in Androscoggin, ME (pop. 99,657), I knew my life would be devoted to the study of this noble creature. I attended the Pennsylvania State University on a science scholarship and received my masters degree in zoology from the University of Iowa. For the past twenty-two years I have diligently learned all I could about (you guessed it) owls! I'm partial to the Great Horned Owl, the Barred Owl, and the Snowy Owl, but I've never met an owl I didn't like (that's a *little* zoologist joke!). I've had articles published in National Geographic, Field and Stream, and a host of other publications. Married with three children, my life couldn't be any better. But perhaps I should get to the point, my friends, as this paragraph is all too...familiar.

I am interested in hearing your feelings on the topic of Hooters Restaurants. This corporation blithely exploits the image of an owl in their advertisements, linking this meritorious animal with (and I quote Mr. Mike McNeil, Vice President of Marketing at Hooters) "an innocuous slang expression for a portion of the female anatomy." Indeed. As they are unwilling to part with this insulting motto, I feel it is the responsibility of bird lovers nationwide to boycott this barbaric bastion of bimbos and beer. When they feel the devastating economic impact of our wrath they will solemnly (and respectfully) choose a more dignified slogan. I am willing to coordinate the offensive, but your thoughts on this sensitive topic are heartily encouraged, my earthbound friends!

Finally, I wish to address an item that has confused me for some time. As somewhat of a mechanical wizard (if you will), I utilize a great deal of *duck* tape in my labors. About once a month I venture to Ace Hardware where I purchase my customary 2 inch x 1620 inch (45 yards) roll of duck tape, but I always feel...ignorant. I have been tempted to ask a salesperson the origin of this name, but I legendary pride stands in the way. For this reason I have chosen to contact you, the ornithology experts, about this mystery. My personal theory is that, since the duck is such a powerful, strong-willed bird (proudly flying south each year), it makes sense to honor this creature by naming a "robust" tape after it. Am I close? Inform me! Data is my passion!!

I appreciate your time and politely request a response in the enclosed self-addressed, stamped casing (SASC). I would encourage a phone call, but I am often away on business (I frequently serve as a "zoo consultant"). Frankly, I find letters more "rewarding" anyway! Godspeed!

(Whippoor)will you please write?

Paul Rosa

Paul C. Rosa

American Birding Association, Inc.

Gregory S. Butcher, Executive Director
PO Box 6599, Colorado Springs, CO 80934
Tel: (719) 578-9703 • Fax: (719) 578-1480

March 30, 1994

Dear Paul Rosa:

Thank you for your letter, and I apologize for taking too long to respond to it. I, too, am often away on business, which causes me to get behind in my correspondence.

I have never been to a Hooters Restaurant, and as the father of three boys (8, 10, & 13), I do not plan to take them to the restaurant. However, I do not expect to lead or even to take part in a boycott or public protest of the restaurant. If sex and sexism sells, my protests will do little good. My favorite causes at the present time are promoting the use of volunteers to census bird populations and the renewal of the endangered species act. These are issues that I feel are important and for which my expertise is useful.

On the topic of duck tape, I have always thought that the word was "duct" tape and that the tape was used primarily to keep heating ducts from leaking air. Let me know if you find out differently!

I would love to talk to you about owls some time. Colorado Springs seems to be a super place for owls, and I would love to see Spotted Owl, Pygmy Owl, and Flammulated Owl in the wild (plus all the other native owls).

Sincerely,

Greg Butcher

Greg Butcher

---

117 E. Espanola St.
Colo. Springs, CO 80907
January 18, 1994

Amway Corporation
7575 East Fulton Rd.
Ada, MI 49355

Dear Distributors,

"When you have questions and/or concerns about *anything*, go straight to the top!" my father would consistently exhort his children, as he meticulously built a humble vacuum cleaner "fix-it" shop into the second largest repairers of small-to-medium-sized appliances in southwestern Kentucky. His logic? When you approach the "highest authority," they simply can't send you elsewhere, claiming ignorance. "If the top banana doesn't have the answers, *no one* has them!" he'd chuckle as he mischievously winked at me with his one good eye (note: he lost the sight in his right eye in a tragic fishing accident). But perhaps you grow weary of my self-centered chatter, so I will graduate to the nucleus of my missive.

After months of painstaking introspection I have arrived at the conclusion that I would like to pursue a career with Amway. As a chronic asthmatic, it behooves me to spend as much time as possible in the clean outdoors, and a "door-to-door" career seems...fitting. But I am the type of person who must respect, nay *love* a product before trying to convince others to do the same. After thoroughly researching all corporations of your ilk, I must say that I was truly impressed with Amway's sparkling credentials:

√ Over 750 products in more than 55 countries worldwide.
√ Largest vitamin corporation in America (65 years old).
√ 250 quality cosmetic items.
√ Creators of the remarkable "bagless" vacuum cleaner.

As you can plainly discern, I am a man who does his research, but it was the final "factoid" that caught my eye (I can't help but think of my father when I say, "caught my *eye*," nor when I hear about vacuum cleaners!). Yes, all the facts are in and Amway is my distinct, number-one choice.

But what choice doesn't have its obstacles? As I mentioned, I am an asthmatic, and as such I strive to avoid germs and dust at all costs. As doorbells are quite possibly the filthiest items on the face of the earth, I avoid them like the plague. I merely have to *think* about doorbells and I am forced to joylessly reach for my trusty inhaler. Since selling Amway door to door requires alerting the homeowner of one's presence, I was wondering if it is acceptable to simply *knock* on doors rather than risk certain health problems. I realize that doors aren't much more sanitary than door*bells*, but an Amway salesman can't stand outside a home and shout...can he? Please write to me at once and address my fears so I can pursue my new career with the vengeance I inherited from my father. Also, please send an (XL) T-shirt.

Fresh air and sunshine for me,

Paul Rosa

Paul C. Rosa

Amway Corporation, 7575 Fulton Street, East, Ada, Michigan 49355-0001

June 21, 1994

Paul Rosa
117 E Espanola ST
Colorado Springs, Co 80907

*** Resending note of 06/21/94 16:56
From: ****DEBRA MOORE***
****NATIONAL DISTRIBUTOR RELATIONS***
We appreciate your taking the time and interest to contact Amway Corporation
regarding "door to door" selling. Our goal is be the "Most Admired" business.
We are happy you made Amway Corporation your number (1) one choice.

With our ever changing modern technology and innovation, "door to door"
selling, can take on a whole new meaning. No longer are you required to "ring
door bells" you can knock on doors, contact prospects by telephone and also by
facsimile, etc......

As you requested a "T-Shirt" is being sent to you under separate cover.
X-Large "T-Shirts are no longer available, I am sending you the next available
size (Large).

Also, to become an Amway Distributor you would first need to be sponsored into
the business by an authorized Amway Distributor. Please check your "yellow
pages" in your local telephone book or contact our Distributor lead telephone
number 1-800-544-7167 to locate an Amway Distributor in your area.

Paul, please accept my apology for the lengthy response to your letter. I am
sure you will find this information helpful. Should you have additional
questions, please call me.

Best Regards,

Debra Moore

Amway®

Amway Corporation, 7575 Fulton Street, East, Ada, Michigan 49355-0001

July 28, 1994

Paul C. Rosa
117 E. Espanola St.
Colorado Springs, CO 80907

Dear Paul:

I apologize for the fact that you have not received a response to your numerous letters to Amway Corporation. Apparently, these letters have been bounced around until one finally found its way to International Inquiries. Because we respond to all letters received here, I am writing this response to you today.

To answer your concerns, Amway Corporation does not encourage distributors to become door-to-door sales people. Our preferred method of starting and developing your distributorship is to contact friends and relatives using this as a natural progression.

Paul, if you are interested in becoming a distributor, you can call our 800 number for customer leads. They can attempt to locate a distributor within your area that you may contact. This number is 1-800-253-6500.

Again, I apologize for this late response. In my heart I remember reading your letter over a month ago but, I cannot find a copy of my response. If you have already received a response from me, I apologize for this second letter. My only intent is to make sure that you have received a response. I hope this information will be of benefit to you.

Sincerely,

Bill

Bill Southworth
International/Offshore Coordinator
International Inquiries
Office Phone (616) 676-7552

BS/jkp/jidr28

117 E. Espanola St.
Colo. Springs, CO 80907
January 19, 1994

Public Considerations
Lenscrafters
P.O. Box 429580
Cincinnati, OH 45242-9580

Dear Vision Visionaries,

"Four eyes." "Nerdling." "Poindexter." "Doofus." "Paul." I've been called every name in the book, my optical friends! The first four I mentioned (Four eyes, Nerdling, Poindexter, and Doofus) were brought on by my decision to wear eyeglasses. Oh sure, I could have folded under the peer pressure to "fit in" at high school but I've never been one to pay homage to my vanity. Along those lines, Radial Keratotomy (barbarically slicing the cornea to correct near-sightedness!) has been equally dismissed with a stately wave of my self-assured hand. I wear my Lenscrafters frames with a mixture of pride and humility, while recognizing and enduring the unfair social stigma that accompanies my bold decision. I may not have attended my senior prom last May, but I am secure in the knowledge that I am an *"eyeglass man,"* damn it!

I was surprised that, when I visited a local Lenscrafters (April, 1993) to fill my prescription (20/400), I received the fitted frames in one hour and eighteen minutes. Granted this is not long to wait, but your advertisements consistently trumpet, "Glasses in about an hour." What does this mean exactly? If the product is ready in fifty-five minutes or one hour and two minutes, it is certainly "about an hour." However, I believe that beyond one hour and fifteen minutes it is no longer "about an hour." Granted, there is an indisputable "gray area" here, and that is one of the reasons I chose to write. What *do* you mean when you declare, "Glasses in *about* an hour?" I hate to nit-pick, but I am a fierce defender of truthful advertising and fair play (if you will). Kindly address this issue and let me know if I'm entitled to compensation.

Secondly (and lastly), I wish to address a complaint I have concerning a product which you manufacture. The Lenscrafters "Lens Cleaner" (eight ounces, in a convenient pump format) certainly cleans my lenses well, but the drawbacks are simply unacceptable. Every time I "spritz" some of the liquid onto my glasses I invariably burn my face and (particularly) my eyes. After stumbling about my (one bedroom) apartment shrieking in agony for a few minutes I proceed to efficiently clean the lenses, but the entire experience can best be described as "daunting." When distributing a product that stings sensitive body parts when sprayed in the face, wouldn't it make more sense to first dilute it somewhat?! Your thoughts are encouraged.

I don't mean to sound overly critical because (all told) I find your organization impressive indeed. But a response to my "trouble areas" and an (XL) T-shirt is encouraged. Good day.

Lucidly yours,

Paul Rosa

Paul C. Rosa

LENS CRAFTERS
VISIONCARE SPECIALISTS

Helping people see better. One hour at a time.

July 15, 1994

8650 Governor's Hill Drive
P.O. Box 429580
Cincinnati, OH 45242-9580
513 583-6000

Mr. Paul C. Rosa
117 E. Espanola Street
Colorado Springs, CO 80907

Dear Mr. Rosa:

Thank you for your letter and persistence. Please accept our
most sincere apology for the delay in responding to you. You are
a very creative writer and we have shared your letter and
information with our communications and marketing groups.
However, it has taken a great deal of CREATIVE effort on my part
to acquire the enclosed shirt for you - Please enjoy!

The comments stated in your letter are appreciated. We always
enjoy hearing from our customers sharing with us how they feel
about our products and services. To address your concern
regarding our statement "in about an hour", LensCrafters is
required to provide documentation to the FTC indicating the
percentage of glasses which are made within an hour. I apologize
that we were 18 minutes short of meeting your expectation in the
one hour process.

Again, we would like to thank you for your comments and your
creative letter. Please enjoy wearing the enclosed shirt. Mr.
Rosa, we truly value you as a customer and look forward to
serving you in the future.

If you have any additional comments or concerns, please do not
hesitate to call me through Customer Service number 800-283-5367.

Sincerely,

Bonnie Volz
Customer Service Coordinator

Printed On 100% Recycled Paper

117 E. Española St.
Colo. Springs, CO 80907
January 20, 1994

Consumer Revelations
Frito-Lay, Inc.
Dallas, TX 75235-5224

Dear Crispness Kings and Queens,

For years I was "satisfied" with the taste of potato chips, crackers, and corn curls. Corn curls, potato chips, and crackers. Crackers, corn curls, and potato chips. Potato chips, corn curls, and crackers. Corn curls, crackers, and potato chips. Crackers, potato chips, and corn curls. No, the sequence wasn't particularly relevant because the same three snack foods (potato chips, crackers, and corn curls) were my only selections! Month after month, year after year, ever since I was a young stripling in Mexico City (pop. 23,000,000), these were the only foods I ingested when I craved something "less than a meal." I moved to the United States in 1985, but my routine (sadly) didn't waver one iota.

This all changed during last year's Super Bowl (Cowboys over Bills). My second-best friend, Kermit, hosted a medium-sized gathering and favored us with a variety of party favors and food possibilities. In a bowl that would typically contain (you guessed it) potato chips, crackers, or corn curls there was a generous supply of Frito-Lay (multigrain, harvest cheddar-flavored) Sun Chips. My life instantly changed forever. Since this time -almost one year ago- I've embraced your delicious chips with the enthusiasm of a lad receiving his first Communion! As you so proudly declare, "These wholesome grains make a delicious chip with the golden goodness of corn and the nut-like flavor of wheat." Amen! I don't know what Extractives of Turmeric, Disodium Inosinate, or Disodium Guanylate are, but with taste like that, who cares?! I will continue to purchase this tempting nine ounce (225.1 gram) delight until I come home to heaven! And this segues nicely into the zenith of the letter, my friends.

This afternoon, while contentedly munching on my second bag of Sun Chips of the day, I paused when I happened upon a remarkable chip. Turning the delicate fragment over in my hands, I was amazed to comprehend that I was holding the image of our Lord (Jesus Christ!) in my trembling left hand. It was <u>clearly</u> the son of God, and his brow was (is!) furrowed, as though considering the imminent Last Supper. My brother (Poyoto) soon rushed to my house and verified that it was, without a doubt, what I had fervently described! He sagely advised that I proceed with utmost care.

At approximately 4:22 p.m. today I secured a safety deposit box (I won't say where) and tenderly placed the "Divine Chip" within, on a velvet pad. Several hours later, quivering with reverence and awe, I realized that I was uncertain of my next move. After arduous introspection I decided to contact Frito-Lay, as I "believe" in you, without reservation. Please tell me what I should do next!! Is it typical in such situations to approach a clergyman or government official? I am truly confused and urge you to *write* (for security reasons) to me at once with your learned advice. God bless you!

A true confession,

Paul Rosa

Paul C. Rosa

Frito-Lay, Inc.

Mr. Paul C. Rosa
119 E. Espanola St.
Colorado Springs, CO 80907

Dear Mr. Rosa,

Thanks for contacting Frito-Lay. We're sorry you were dissatisfied
with a recent purchase of SUNCHIPS® brand French Onion Flavor
Multigrain Snacks. We sincerely regret any inconvenience this may
have caused. We strive to satisfy all our consumers and are
disappointed when our efforts fall short in any way.

We'd like to forward your comments along with a sample of the
unsatisfactory product to our manufacturing facility for a more
thorough investigation. In order to do so, we have enclosed for your
convenience in mailing, a clear plastic bag and a self-addressed,
stamped envelope. Upon receipt, the sample will be reviewed and
tested by our Quality Assurance staff.

We are sorry you were dissatisfied and hope you will give our snack
products another chance.

If you have any questions or additional comments, please call
toll-free 1-800-352-4477 Monday through Friday 9:00 a.m. - 4:30 p.m.
Central Time.

Sincerely,

Heather Hemby
Consumer Affairs

Enclosure: 1 Small Self-addressed, stamped envelope

400950

117 E. Espanola St.
Colo. Springs, CO 80907
January 22, 1994

Duraflame Logs, Inc.
California Cedar Products
Stockton, CA 95201

Dear Lumber Substitutes,

For many years I would chop down trees on my two-hundred-acre ranch on the outskirts of Colorado Springs, load the (cut) yield onto my flatbed truck, and stack the logs near my house. Here I would labor to build customized cabins for the tedious "yuppie types" who have infiltrated the hills of this town. Chopping was a perfectly acceptable method for many, many years until two things happened:

1. I became older (68 on my last birthday, August 4).
2. I ran out of trees and, with God's help, embraced nature.

Some folks would suggest that I am seeking a "log alternative" merely because I've depleted all the natural resources on my land, and they would have been correct...last year. However, after then illegally chopping trees on some neighboring property for several months, my conscience got the best of me and I allowed Jesus Christ to triumphantly enter my life. One evening (November 17) he advised me to "embrace God's work and seek new ways to build cabins"...or something like that. You see, I was so amazed to be in the presence of the handsome, confident Son of God that my mind was somewhat impaired. Be assured, however, that the important message "hit home."

Consequently, I have been researching various log options, and my friend (Gene B. Waylonski) suggested I give Duraflame a try. He patiently explained that Duraflame is gentler to the environment because you utilize incense cedar sawdust, a by-product of wood manufacturing. After sipping calmly on his apple juice, he continued by elucidating that your logs are *then* mixed with petroleum wax to complete the miraculous process. The final products, he stated, were called "Extruder Logs." I understand very little of this (I have only a sixth-grade education because my father insisted that I help out in the fields, maintaining that an education really "wouldn't do me any good anyway." Well, he was a fool, and I have spent a lifetime cursing his evil intent and undoing the substantial damage done to my psyche by voraciously reading the classics. However, I digress.) but Gene, a good fellow, convinced me to write for more information. Clearly that is what I am doing now, my friends! I'll skip a space before concluding this memorandum.

Is it indeed possible to build a home entirely of Duraflame Logs? Given a modest three-bedroom, two-bath home, roughly how much would the raw materials cost? Is a fire-proofing fluid available to coat and protect the exterior? Do you have any photographs of Duraflame Log cabins? Please send all available building information in the enclosed envelope. And please hurry! Bless you!

You're <u>never</u> too old to learn,

Paul Rosa

Paul C. Rosa

June 14, 1994

Mr. Paul C. Rosa
119 E. Espanola St.
Colorado Springs, CO 80907

Dear Mr. Rosa,

Thank you for your interesting letter. To the best of our knowledge it is not possible to build a home of duraflame logs. As you are aware, our firelogs are made of a combination of incense-cedar sawdust and petroleum wax. Since this results in a moldable mixture, the resulting firelog is not strong enough to withstand the pressure that would be exerted by having multiple logs placed upon it to form a wall, not to mention the addition of a roof. Our logs are also quite flammable, and we do not think they would be a suitable building material accepted by fire departments or building code officials. We therefore strongly recommend that duraflame firelogs not be considered for use in building a home, but they are great for providing no hassle entertainment when burned correctly within your home's fireplace.

Sincerely,

Chris Caron
Marketing Manager

CC/pjs

117 E. Espanola St.
Colo. Springs, CO 80907
January 24, 1994

Public Affairs Division
Robitussin-DM Cough Medicine
Whitehall Robins Co.
P.O. Box 26609
Richmond, VA 23261-6609

Dear Phlegm Fighters,

Since I was a spirited youth growing up in Gooding, ID (pop. 11,874), I have faithfully combatted my coughs with your magnificent suppressant/expectorant. In February of my sophomore year in high school (1972), I began to acquire a nasty, hacking cough and retaliated with the best product on the market (yours). You see, I was developing a fascination with the young ladies, and embracing a moist, hacking cough clearly wasn't in my best interest. Two teaspoonfuls of your healing, *delicious* elixir every four hours quickly returned me to good health. Consequently, I began dating Maureen and we were married ten years later! We are now happily raising our seven girls (Becky, Shilsa, Lila, Toni, Kipo, Ray Anne, and "Sam") on my twenty-acre spread in south-central Colorado Springs. Perhaps it is naive to give Robitussin much credit for my well-rounded life, but your organization provided a "launching point!" And for this, I say, "Thank you!" However, *now* I have a a few questions for your corporation!

Today I noticed that the label of your bottle reads, ***"Keep out of reach of children."*** Well, *all* of my children (ages 7-16) benefit from regular, healthy doses of Robitussin. How is the potion to be administered if it is "out of their reach?" It seems to me that <u>reaching</u> it is an unavoidable prerequisite! Maureen and I have ignored your advice and dispense your product liberally when a troublesome cough interferes with their young lives. But we are a little worried that we are missing something. Are we? Why shouldn't children be able to reach it? Is it bad for their tongues or something? Can it stunt their growth? If so, why are there instructions for child dosages printed on the bottle?! Please get back to me quickly and let us know if we are uninformed (it's all so confusing!). You are very kind.

Lastly (and this is *most* unusual), I have a query concerning the "way" I cough. I have heard that it is impossible to keep one's eyes open when sneezing, but my reaction has always been, "Who cares?!" However, I have experienced a "similar" phenomenon and I hope *your* reaction won't be, "Who cares?!" Whenever I cough, I inadvertently clench my right hand into a fist! It is neither intended nor controllable and I have done this since I was a lad! Isn't that odd? And it's always my *right* hand, never the left! Have you heard of this "condition" before? Does it have a name? Should I be concerned? Please send all available data (if any) on this unusual situation as well as the above ("keep out of reach of children") predicament! Farewell, friends!

Have you thought of making soda?

Paul Rosa

Paul C. Rosa

Karen Brown
Director, Consumer & Public Affairs

Whitehall-Robins
5 Giralda Farms
Madison, NJ 07940-0871
Telephone (201) 660-6923

April 27, 1994

Mr. Paul C. Rosa
119 East Espanola Street
Colorado Springs, CO 80907

Dear Mr. Rosa :

This is in response to your entertaining and creative testimonials detailing your experiences with Preparation H and Robitussin products.

We are always pleased to hear that our products are beneficial to consumers.

Thank you for your interest in our products. We are enclosing a free product coupon for Robitussin Cough Drops.

Sincerely,

Kathy Van Steenwyk
Consumer Affairs Associate

117 E. Espanola St.
Colo. Springs, CO 80907
January 25, 1994

Consumer Eventualities
St. Ives Swiss Formula Hair Conditioner
9201 Oakdale Ave,
Chatsworth, CA 91311

Dear Shine Bringers,

I'm an efficiency expert! Simply put, my wife (Winnie Ellen) and I run our large family (kids: Nicki, John, Lisl, Jesse, Rudi, Sigfried, Fritz, and Mitzi) with *extreme* efficiency. Let's face it, when you have eight children, each in school, you'd be a damn fool not to approach life in a "scientific" fashion. I try to never waste a moment, and this outlook has served me well, whether the discipline is child-rearing or "buckling down" at the Hewlett Packard laboratories, where I serve as an electrical engineer. I have been awarded seventeen patents, mostly for devices used in submarines and oil rigs. Some of these projects utilize Secret (or Top Secret) data, so forgive me for not continuing with this line of conversation.

While I try to always be as productive as possible, I also consider one's personal appearance to be a powerful commodity in today's competitive environment. Given this fact, I take great pride in my meticulous grooming habits. Every day, for fifty to fifty-five minutes, I shower, shampoo, condition, and apply a European styling gel to my (full) head of hair before blow-drying. I also (still within the aforementioned time constraint) clip my nails, shave, administer after-shave, coat my underarms with anti-perspirant/deodorant, swab my ears, brush and floss my teeth, and, finally, soothe and replenish my skin with Nivea Creme (Cream?). At this point you are probably squirming uncomfortably in your chairs, asking aloud, "Paul ,what has this got to do with *us*, for heaven's sake?" I will explain.

My hair conditioning product of choice is "St. Ives Swiss Formula Hair Repair Intensive Conditioning Treatment." Aside from the fact that the name is quite long, perhaps *too* long, your product is without equal! For this I offer my unfettered congratulations! If I lived in California, I would visit and give you each "high-fives," like my kids are so fond of doing! As an efficiency expert, however, I have trouble with a peculiarity of the directions on the back of your product. St. Ives stipulates that one must "leave the Hair Repair on the hair for two minutes, then rinse thoroughly." Since nothing angers me more than idle time, I am always uncomfortable with this aspect of my rigid morning routine. I have no idea how this two minutes can be spent productively, and it pains me to merely stare stupidly at the front of the shower until the time has passed. Some conditioners actually require a *five* minute wait before rinsing, and I'm amazed they can stay in business! It's so...inefficient, my friends!

Can you offer any suggestions for productively passing the two minutes? I've tried reading a novel (encased in plastic) but it's quite tedious. Are your chemists working on a product which requires "no waiting?" That would be super! I look forward to your response and would welcome an (XL) T-shirt.

With exceptional stylability,

Paul Rosa

Paul C. Rosa

ST. IVES LABORATORIES, INC.

February 15, 1994

Paul Rosa
117 E. Espanola Street
Colorado Springs, CO 80907

Dear Mr. Rosa:

Thank you for your interest in St. Ives Swiss Formula®.

May we suggest that you shampoo, then apply the Hair Repair Intensive Conditioner while still in the shower. While it is working, you can proceed with your other morning routines.

Your name has been included in the drawing for a trip to the St. Ives facilities in Switzerland. This exciting drawing will take place in November, 1994. Good luck to you! At this time, we do not carry any T-Shirts for they were part of a promotion which has expired.

Thank you again, and we welcome your comments and any future questions you may have about our products.

Sincerely,

Ann Taylor
for St. Ives

AT/rd

117 E. Espanola St.
Colo. springs, CO 80907
January 25, 1994

Consumer Inquisitions
Royal Velvet Towels
Fieldcrest Mills, Inc.
1271 Avenue of the Americas
New York, NY 10020

Dear Dryers,

Towels. I love em'! You step from a luxurious, steamy shower (or bath), wrap yourself in a 100% cotton towel, and suddenly, miraculously, the world seems like a pretty good place! I don't know (or particularly care) what people used *before* towels, but I'm certainly glad they're available to every man, woman, and child in America today, given they have sufficient funds. I estimate that I use towels about seven times daily, which is about average. My point? Towels are a vital, vibrant part of nearly everyone's life and it's high time someone "reached out" to the towel industry and said, "You <u>are</u> appreciated, good people!" But what letter wouldn't be more interesting without queries? As Fieldcrest Mills is the makers of the finest towels in America-they're so absorbent!-I felt it would be resourceful to contact you with my probing, weighty questions and comments.

Towels consistently come with washing instructions (i.e. "Wash with like colors. Deep colors bleed. Wash before first use. Only non-chlorine bleach when needed."). I think it makes good sense to wash a towel before using it (to remove harmful factory oils or dyes) but we *then* enter a hazy, confusing, gray area, my friends. Since towels (bath towels in particular) are only used on squeaky-clean skin, usually after bathing, why is it necessary to wash them at all? I only wash my towels once a year, around Christmas, and I have experienced no unpleasant side effects whatsoever! My point? Since towels are generally used by immaculate folks, it is unnecessary to toss them in the washing machine on a regular basis because, simply put, they never get dirty! I am not implying that towel manufacturers are scheming with the various laundry-oriented industries to make "dishonest" money through kickbacks, but I *am* lost for an explanation for the excessive washing suggestions! Since I trust Fieldcrest, Inc. without reservation, it seemed prudent to write. Your thoughts?

My final inquiry concerns the issue of towel "shapes." As a teacher of high school geometry (grades nine and ten) I think it would be wonderful if corporations could encourage mathematical learning by offering towels in a wide range of shapes and sizes. A lad who dries himself off with a large pentagonal towel is a fellow who will embrace the day with an inquisitive demeanor! A gal who towels off with a small isosceles triangle would, similarly, be more inclined to learn the mysteries of a spider's web. Now, you may be saying to yourselves, "Look, Paul, we're simply in the business of getting people dry!" But this is a tragic, shortsighted view at best! A concise, conscientious reply to *this* idea is welcome as well!

Between showers,

Paul Rosa

Paul C. Rosa

FIELDCREST CANNON, INC. 1271 AVENUE OF THE AMERICAS · NEW YORK, N.Y. 10020 · Tel: (212) 957-2500 · Fax: (212) 957-3384

March 14, 1994

Paul Rosa
117 E. Espanola St.
Colorado Springs, CO 80907

Dear Mr. Rosa:

Thank you for your letter regarding our care labels. You are
correct in the assumption of why we state washing before use.
Whenever an individual decides to wash their towels, once a day or
once a year, is completely up to them. However, we do not
recommend washing a red towel with a white towel - hence "Wash with
like colors. Deep colors bleed." Also if you used a chlorine
bleach with those red towels, they would turn a very pretty pink,
that is why we suggest only non-chlorine bleach.

We appreciate your suggestion regarding the sizing of our towels
and your idea has been passed to the Vice President of our Towel
Department. However, the decision to purchase our products is
the department buyers and we only manufacture merchandise which
they will order.

Sincerely,

Cathy Sharkey
Consumer Relations Manager

117 E. Espanola St.
Colo. Springs, CO 80907
January 28, 1994

Cliffs Notes, Inc.
P.O. Box 80728
Lincoln, NE 68501

Dear Condensers,

Your study aids are useful.

In a nutshell,

Paul

Paul

P.O. BOX 80728 • LINCOLN, NE 68501-0728 • TELEPHONE: (402) 423-5050 • FAX: 800-826-6831

March 10, 1994

Mr. Paul Rosa
117 E. Espanola St.
Colorado Springs, CO 80907

Dear Paul:

Thank you for writing to say you find Cliffs Notes useful.

Your envelope should have been returned to you as our standard package for response to mail is a Study Tips brochure which is mailed in a 6 x 9 envelope.

Some information is enclosed for you. If there is any thing else we may do, please let me know.

Sincerely,

Connie J. Brakhahn
Director of Advertising

Enclosure

CJB/src

117 E. Espanola St.
Colo. Springs, CO 80907
January 31, 1994

Consumer Details and Particulars
I Can't Believe It's Not Butter
Van Den Bergh Foods Co.
Lisle, IL 60532

Dear 70% Vegetable Oil Spread Friends,

One month ago I declared (to some friends) that jelly was my all-time favorite food. "Mercy, it tastes good on everything, from bananas to cheese!" I rambled as we played Pictionary on my imported Portuguese rug. Well, that is still the case, but I wanted *you* folks to know that my second-favorite food is surely vegetable oil spread (made with sweet cream buttermilk). And my favorite brand? You guessed it: "I Can't Believe It's Not Butter!" With your handy squeezable container I'm known to "liven up" virtually any food (as with jelly). Occasionally I'll put I Can't Believe It's Not Butter! on a muffin *with* jelly, and <u>then</u> I'm in absolute heaven, allow me to assure you. But all is not settled (emotionally) with your product, and it's time I addressed these issues. Okay, here we go.

Last April 6, craving 70% vegetable oil spread (on a biscuit) I removed a container of I Can't Believe It's Not Butter! from my fridge (refrigerator). Since the receptacle was nearly empty, I gave it a mighty squeeze, yielding the desired portion. However, while aggressively clasping the receptacle I felt a slight pain in my shoulder which felt not unlike (i.e. *like*) a moderate bee sting. Nevertheless, I enjoyed the tasty treat and put the incident out of my mind for a short while, but the ache persisted! Well, to make a long story slightly longer, the discomfort has come and gone (and come again) over the past ten months, and it has been suggested (by my basketball buddy, Bob) that I have a torn rotator cuff! I'll begin the true "fiber" of my letter now, patient friends.

Given that it's nearly impossible to extract the final few ounces of vegetable oil spread from a squeezable container, I suggest that the sixteen ounce container be priced the same as fourteen ounces of "free standing" butter, which you can easily consume in its entirety. Had I known the last two ounces were free, this injury never would have happened (I would have discarded it!). Furthermore, as you offer an "unconditional guarantee," am I entitled to a refund? Actually, am I not *always* entitled to a refund when the guarantee is <u>unconditional</u>? If I ask for a refund and you ask for a *reason*, aren't you betraying the spirit of the word "unconditional?" Certainly!

Please respond briskly to the topics of: My injury, my refund possibilities, and the nature of the excerpt, "unconditional guarantee." You diligence is appreciated. As a final request, please send me an (XL) T-shirt. And now it's time for some "buttered" scones!

With unconditional respect,

Paul Rosa

Paul C. Rosa

VAN DEN BERGH
FOODS COMPANY

Consumer Services
390 Park Avenue
New York, NY 10022-4698
800 735 3610

February 15, 1994

Mr. Paul C. Ross
117 E. Espanola St.
Colorado Springs, CO 80907

Dear Mr. Ross:

We have received your letter concerning a squeezable container of "I
Can't Believe It's Not Butter!".

I am sorry that you have had difficulty in using the container. Our
packages are designed to be sturdy enough to protect the contents, but
should not be too difficult to use. We are always concerned with any
report of dissatisfaction with one of our products and we will share
your comments with the persons responsible for "I Can't Believe It's
Not Butter!".

Thank you for taking the time to bring this matter to our attention. I
am enclosing your refund, along with a few coupons which we hope you
will enjoy.

Sincerely,

Terry Barlowe
Consumer Representative

TMB/cl

117 E. Espanola St.
Colo. Springs, CO 80907
February 1, 1994

Consumer Interests and Discoveries
AMTRAK Trains
60 Massachusetts Ave., NE
Washington, DC 20002

Dear "Choo Choo" Center (Principal Station),

I'm a collector of *everything* having to do with trains, even remotely! Frankly, I like the clothes* of the engineer, the sound of the whistle, the romantic mystery of the tracks, and the thunder of the proud locomotive. Oh yes, if it's "train related" you can bet I'm interested. I have the largest collection of train paraphernalia in southern Colorado, and my accumulation grows almost daily. Over 1000 feet of track criss-cross my cavernous home, at any given time carrying one of my twelve glorious (faithfully accurate to the tiniest detail) toy trains. I've even take to wearing the clothes of an engineer (*typically overalls and the "big hat") as I travel the country in quest of my next find. Oh sure, by day I'm a mild-mannered tuna executive, but that all changes at 5:00 p.m. sharp (and weekends). Then I attack my hobby with all the resolve of a cornered infantryman! Okay, but why have I written?

As a true train aficionado, I was somewhat depressed to hear the various bits of bad news concerning AMTRAK in recent years. When I learned that several of your engineers had smoked marijuana (and inhaled) before guiding their glorious trains to disaster, I almost slipped into a clinical depression. Only the love of my wife (Birnella) and generous portions of KFC Chicken (extra crispy) averted a psychological "crash." Recently, when one of your trains plunged off a bridge into a murky swamp in the deep south, I almost shared the despair of the passengers...on an equal level! After much introspection though, I concluded-and I'm not proud of this-that my *major* concern was for those glorious trains! To see the twisted wreckage of all those magnificent "cars" was almost too much for my fragile heart to bear, my friends. Lord, to think of those contorted remains now rusting in some impersonal junkyard is (and I'm actually crying now) excruciating!

Now that I have explained my unprecedented devotion to trains, I would like to sincerely ask if some of the damaged cars from the aforementioned wrecks are available *for sale.* I simply can't blithely allow them to forever rot in some Godforsaken landfill! I can't!! Given my formidable skills as a craftsman and my almost unlimited budget (I'm a lottery winner), I think I can return the trains to their original flawless appearance. I would like to turn one of your cars into a guest room which I will connect to our family room. The thrill of sleeping in one of your trains far from any track is an exciting possibility, to be sure! I would also like to purchase 20-30 more impaired train cars to "decorate" my 500-acre ranch (imagine the beauty!). Please write to me at once (SASE enclosed) and let me know the possibilities of purchasing your discarded trains, along with suggested prices! An (XL) T-shirt would be terrific too!

All Aboard!!

Paul Rosa

Paul C. Rosa

National Railroad Passenger Corporation, 30th and Market Streets, Philadelphia, PA. 19104

April 26, 1994

Mr. Paul C. Rosa
117 E. Espanola Street
Colo. Springs, CO 80907

Dear Mr. Rosa:

Thank you for your letter dated February 1, 1994, expressing
your interest in obtaining surplus Amtrak equipment.

Unfortunately, I have been advised by our Legal Department
that the specific equipment you mentioned in your letter is not
for sale at the present time. Periodically, other used or
damaged railroad equipment are offered for sale on a competitive
bid, "As Is - Where Is," basis. I have taken the liberty of
giving your name and address to Ms. Elizabeth A. Hastings,
Manager Material Disposal, so she may contact you when we have
these sales.

Thank you for your interest in Amtrak.

Sincerely,

F. L. Kemerer
Assistant Vice President
Materials Management

cc: Elizabeth A. Hastings

AN EQUAL OPPORTUNITY EMPLOYER

622 North Sheridan Ave.
Colorado Springs, CO 80909
February 2, 1994

Consumer Education
Oil of Olay
Procter & Gamble
P.O. Box 599
Cincinnati, OH 45201

Cream Friends,

I have <u>incredibly</u> smooth skin. Friends of mine have dubbed my complexion "creamy," "radiant," and "sumptuous." Well, as a narcissistic, self-centered teenager and young adult (1974-1989) these words were *necessary* to fuel the raging furnace that was my ego! Since my entire self worth was centered around others' opinions of me, I naturally craved compliments and attention like an underfed housecat craves tuna. Sadly enough, I neglected my studies in high school (barely graduating) and eventually secured an unrewarding position as an insect exterminator. Naively, I continued to focus on my "nice" appearance, firmly believing that I required nothing more to achieve eventual happiness. Oh, how wrong I was, my friends!

In the 1980's I married three times (Kurt, Waylon, and Chester), gave birth to four children (Sarah, Lou, Pipi, and Riley), and bounded from low-paying job to low-paying job. As long as my husbands found me attractive, I felt my lot in life was secure. My skin remained remarkably pliant and wrinkle-free, so I blithely chose to neglect my education, instead comforting myself with the knowledge that I had "fine skin." Yes, *because* of this skin my life became increasingly shallow and uninspired. In 1989 (at age 28) I decided that my complexion was standing in the way of my happiness. Outrageous? I think not! I decided to go about "aging" my epidermis by spending many hours in the sun (and at sun tan salons), avoiding moisturizers, and using an industrial strength soap ("LAVA"). But alas, *nothing* worked and my skin remains absolutely flawless. Consequently, my life continues to flounder as I focus extensively on my comely visage. This year I decided to write to cosmetic companies and inquire if there is a cream available which *adds* wrinkles. I am convinced that, once I begin to get "crow's feet," I will be able to go to college and realize my full potential. Sadly enough, until this time I am doomed to be an underachieving, trailer-park-dwelling washout! Granted, mine is an unusual tale, but it is the unfettered truth!

Please let me know if Procter & Gamble offers a skin care line devoted to the "graceful aging" of its customers. The overemphasis on youthfulness in this society is exceedingly destructive and I shall no longer buy into this atrocity! Nothing is more pathetic than watching the captain of the high school cheerleading squad as she leafs through her dusty yearbook (fourteen years later), bemoaning her numerous, tragic decisions. I await your fleet reply!

I'm ready to wrinkle!

Rosa Paulson

Mrs. Rosa G. Paulson

Procter&Gamble

The Procter & Gamble Company
Public Affairs Division
P.O. Box 599, Cincinnati, Ohio 45201-0599

March 14, 1994

MS ROSA PAULSON
622 NORTH SHERIDAN AVE
COLORADO SPRINGS CO 80909

Dear Ms. Paulson,

Thank you for writing to Procter & Gamble. We appreciate your
interest in Oil of Olay.

Many enthusiastic people tell us they would like to have their
favorite product available in other forms. We routinely consider
other versions of our brands, and sometimes do introduce different
product forms. However, we have no product which adds wrinkles.

Our consumers are important to us at Procter & Gamble, and we want
to keep in touch. The toll-free phone service is available for
questions or comments, and you'll find our phone number on every
consumer product we make. If you have any product questions in the
future, remember we're just a phone call away.

Thanks again for letting us hear from you. We hope
Procter & Gamble products will continue to be your favorites.

Sincerely,

Wanda G. Kuyper

Wanda Kuyper
Consumer Relations

117 E. Espanola St.
Colo. Springs, CO 80907
February 6, 1994

Corporate Advertising Department
Coors Brewing Co.
Golden, CO 80401

Dear Image Conveyors,

Mercy, there certainly are plenty of Coors Beer commercials on the television, especially during sporting events (i.e. football, basketball, bowling, golf, hockey, baseball, horse racing, and soccer). Designed (naturally) to sell beer, these commercials ("presentations," if you will) convey colorful images which many sympathetic viewers can identify with. Emotional connection effectively made, folks routinely proceed to the local liquor store where they purchase six-packs, twelve-packs, cases ("twenty-four packs"), or kegs of Coors Beer. Needless to say, the last eventuality (kegs) is the most attractive to Coors as these receptacles cost the most! None of this is news to *you* folks, since advertising "blurbs" are your business! So, let's proceed to paragraph two.

Here we go! I have noticed that your commercials regularly feature spectacularly attractive women and men, often clad in nothing more than bikinis and volleyball shorts. Consequently we routinely view voluptuous bosoms (women), rippling muscles (men), flawless complexions on lovely faces (women), dapper, chiseled profiles (men), and firm buttocks (both). These incredibly healthy individuals are consistently shown enjoying invigorating, beneficial activities, often at the beach. The titillating promise of sex is the ever-present mood of your smart offerings. That's fine, but something *doesn't* sit well with me, my indefatigable friends. Let's move on to paragraph three.

Okay! I *am* perplexed that your commercials never (never) feature any plain (or ugly) citizens. No immense beer bellies, no sagging teats, no balding domes, no rotten teeth, no goiters. Never. No huge, hooked noses, no facial tics, no bulbous eyes, no irregular spines. Never. ___Why?!___ Just as many unsightly folks enjoy beer as gorgeous folks, probably significantly more! Wouldn't it be prudent to occasionally feature the aged, the sedentary, or the physically repulsive? I'd say so! For goodness sake, these people drink beer too and they need "role models" on the screen. Perhaps you can be pioneers in this clever scheme of mine, friends! Let's end with conviction.

Home stretch! As a visually offensive man, I would like to audition for a Coors commercial. With my sparse, wiry hair, tiny, pug-like nose and forty-five extra pounds on a 5'1" frame, I feel that I would be an ideal actor for the aforementioned discipline. I asked my friends (Lewis, Kay, Pika, Willifred, and "Big Ben") if they approved of my idea and the majority (80%) sided with me wholeheartedly! Please forward your ideas quickly along with an (XL) T-shirt. Let's adjourn.

An "SASE" is enclosed!

Paul Rosa

Paul C. Rosa

Coors Brewing Company
Golden, Colorado 80401-1295

April 27, 1994

Mr. Paul Rosa
119 E. Espanola St.
Colorado Springs, CO 80907

Dear Mr. Rosa:

Thank you for your recent letter. We appreciate your taking the time
to send us your idea. For legal reasons, we are unable to consider
unsolicited ideas. Therefore, we are returning your proposal.

We receive a great number of ideas from consumers and realize that most
letters like yours are written in the spirit of friendship and
goodwill. We wish to emphasize that although we cannot consider your
suggestion, this is not a reflection on its quality or purpose.

Thank you again for contacting us. We very much appreciate your
interest in our company and hope you will continue to enjoy our
products.

Sincerely,

Lisa L. Knipp
Consumer Information Assistant
Corporate Communications

LLK/dbw
0017407B

Enclosure

Recycled Paper

117 E. Espanola St.
Colo. Springs, CO 80907
February 6, 1994

Consumer Offices
Creamette Enriched Spaghetti
Borden, Inc.
428 N. First St.
Minneapolis, MN 55401

Dear Noodle Makers, Marketers, and (finally) Distributors,

Bear with me a moment or two while I detail a fantasy scenario: Okay, I'm on death row with only fifteen hours to live. Scheduled for execution the following morning, the warden (a pockmarked Mr. Olafsen) snidely asks what I would like for my last meal. Well, many sumptuous delicacies dance through my mind (including lobster, steak, and roast beef with Yorkshire pudding). However, after much introspection, I choose spaghetti with meatballs. And the brand of pasta? *Creamette* by Borden, by cracky! Yes, your superlative spaghetti would be firmly requested, served with a crisp garden salad (ranch dressing), garlic bread, and a tart Chardonnay. Finally, for dessert, I would relish a German Sachertorte. This glorious meal would *almost* allow me to fully forget the reality that I would soon feel the full fury of the American justice system via tens of thousands of volts of electricity surging through my immoral person. Awful crime aside, this is a playful "fantasy drama," friends...and you are the major players. Nobody combines Semolina, Ferrous Sulfate (Iron), Niacinamide, Thiamine Mononitrate, and Riboflavin as effectively as Borden. Nobody. Congratulations are in order!

Whew, sometimes I tend to saunter all over the page with my creative musings, but I'll now try to fully draw you into the true spirit of this dispatch! For years I have purchased (and enjoyed) Creamette Brand Spaghetti and it never occurred to me to write. Until now. You see, since I was a thoughtful youth in the late 1970's I have been attracted to the pretty gal featured on the Creamette box. This woman (pictured below) seems to embody all the features I am looking for in a wife! She appears confident, mischievous, industrious, and (clearly) attractive. I am now a thirty-two-year-old piano repairman who would like to meet this woman in the worst way. I am financially secure, emotionally healthy, and eager to father children. As the Borden woman (what *is* her name?!) seems so appealing, I would like to request a meeting. Surely she is swamped with such propositions, but I am ready to face any rigorous "weeding out" process necessary!

In the meantime, please send me any available information on this female. I look forward to learning the possibilities of meeting her and (possibly) romancing her. Finally, I would like to procure a Creamette (XL) T-shirt, if available. May the good Lord be with your establishment!

But what's Semolina?

Paul Rosa

Paul C. Rosa

CONSUMER
RESPONSE
DEPARTMENT

IF IT'S BORDEN-IT'S GOT TO BE GOOD

180 EAST BROAD STREET, COLUMBUS, OHIO 43215-3799

Mr. Paul C. Rose   April 1, 1994
117 E Espanola St
Colorado Springs   CO   80907

Dear Mr. Rose:

We have received your letters regarding the woman pictured on CREAMETTE pasta
packages.

Borden purchased the CREAMETTE company in 1979. The founder of the CREAMETTE
company is James T. Williams. Mr. Williams began marketing elbow macaroni in
1916. The woman pictured on CREAMETTE boxes is the founder's daughter. I am
sorry but we do not know her name.

We appreciate your interest in our product and regret that we cannot be of more
assistance.

                                        Sincerely,

                                        Neil Thompson

                                        Neil Thompson
                                        Consumer Representative

                                                                    94015964

117 E. Espanola St.
Colo. Springs CO 80907
February 7, 1994

Customer Dilemmas
Pearle Vision Center
750 Citadel Drive, East
Colo. Springs, CO 80909

Dear Eyeglass Forgers,

As you can clearly deduce, my eyesight is abysmal. After eschewing eyewear for nearly a decade, I've finally decided to...evaluate the possibilities. I've never had my eyes examined (you see, I'm painfully shy), but would consider a "covert" visit to your establishment, perhaps after normal business hours. Is this feasible? If not, what are the options, my tolerant friends?

Finally, I wish to confess that I have only one ear, having lost the other in a brutal Alaskan Kodiak Bear attack (summer of 1989). Are glasses available that employ only *one* ear? Mercy, I hope so!

I have enclosed a handy "SASE", as I avoid the telephone in all instances, save emergencies. I look forward to your retort (in *large* print please!). Lastly, do you carry (XL) T-shirts? God bless you!

Tired of squinting,

Paul Rosa

Paul C. Rosa

mar. 1, 1994

Dear Paul,

Again in response to your letter about coming in after business hours. It would be more convenient for myself, as well as my doctor to do this before we open for business. It would be helpful for me if you could make an exception, and call me so we can talk in more detail to try to take care of this for you! I look forward to your response.

Sincerely,
Cindy

our phone # is (719) 550-0302

117 E. Espanola St.
Colo. Springs, CO 80907
February 9, 1994

Kraft, Inc. (Cheese Division)
801 Waukegan Rd.
Glenview, IL 60025

Dear Dairy Squad,

I've long been fascinated with cheese but never thought to write to Kraft. Until now. You see, moments ago I finished a hoagie, featuring turkey and ham slices, mayonnaise, lettuce, tomato wedges, and <u>Kraft Natural Shredded, Low-Moisture, Part-Skim, Mozzarella Cheese</u> (packaged in a convenient resealable container). All of the aforementioned ingredients were worthy but your cheese product towered above the others, head and shoulders (so to speak). It simply provided "closure" to a sandwich that otherwise would have been merely "tasty." I don't mean to be overly dramatic, but your cheeses routinely turn the ordinary into the sublime! And in the vast cheese realm, Kraft reigns supreme! That's no small shakes!

Given that you are the "cheese specialists," I feel comfortable trusting you with my pointed queries (see sentence one). To begin with, I was wondering why folks, when being photographed, are encouraged to say, "cheese." Of all the hundreds of foods/words to choose from, why is cheese inextricably associated with cameras? For instance, why not say, "yams!" when a Nikon is pointed your way? Or, "soup!?" Or, "bean!?" Be advised, I have no complaint with this use of the word "cheese," but (as an "information hound") I wish to be educated on the *reason*! That's rational, isn't it? Any ideas, chums?

Next-and this is most uncomfortable-I would like to learn the origin of the expression, "Who cut the *cheese*?" Since cheese is my favorite food (along with jelly), I am outraged that it is linked to...flatulence. Isn't Kraft concerned that their peerless offering is insulted in such an unrefined fashion? Bathroom functions shouldn't be mentioned in the same breath with cheese, damn it! I also object to cheese being associated with inferior items (i.e. "What a <u>cheesy</u> gift!" or "He has a <u>cheesy</u> grin!"). I apologize for my passion, but I *am* sincere. What is going on here?! Your learned views?

Finally, I wish to thank you for declaring (as many corporations do), "Satisfaction guaranteed or your money back." That is a selfless gesture, but I have trouble with the *wording* of the above phrase. The word, "or" implies a *choice* between two or more selections. But customers don't choose their money back *instead* of a satisfaction guarantee. For example, if I am displeased with your cheese and receive a refund, I would have experienced "Satisfaction guaranteed *and* your money back." I could only choose a refund in *addition* to guaranteed satisfaction, but your phrase implies this isn't possible (it certainly is!). You see, the guaranteed satisfaction always remains "intact," so this sentence makes no sense! To cover all eventualities, it should read simply, "<u>Satisfaction</u> or your money back!" Do you follow? Your comments on all the above topics are encouraged along with a snazzy (XL) T-shirt. Good day to you!

Lactose <u>tolerant</u>,

Paul Rosa

Paul C. Rosa

 CONSUMER RESPONSE CENTER

February 21, 1994

Mr. Paul C. Rosa
117 East Espanola Street
Colorado Springs, CO 80907

Dear Mr. Rosa,

Thank you for taking the time to tell us how pleased you are with KRAFT
cheeses. Your compliments let us know that we are meeting our goal of
providing consumers with quality food products.

We are proud of our reputation for excellence and work hard to maintain
it. We are continually exploring new food developments and are very
optimistic about the future of food production. Our pledge is to
continue to successfully build on our past achievements far into the
future.

Your comments regarding the wording of our satisfaction guarantee have
been forwarded to our marketing and packaging specialists for their
benefit and review. Thank you again for your thoughtful comments.

Sincerely,

Sandy Meyer/th
Consumer Representative

Enclosure
Your Comments Count (1)
Consumer's Remittance (1)

117 E. Espanola St.
Colo. Springs, CO 80907
February 15, 1994

Consumer Queries
Armitron Wristwatch Co.
29-10 Thomson Ave.
Long Island City, NY 11101

Dear Wrist Adorners,

Time keeps on slipping, slipping, slipping into the future. Time keeps on slipping, slipping, slipping into the future. I want to fly like an eagle, to the sea. Fly like an eagle, let that spirit carry me! Since the mid 1970's I've enjoyed that poignant song by The Stephen Miller Group. My "gang" in high school (Joe, Lisa, Sue, and myself) would dance to those cool, smooth sounds on tepid Pittsburgh evenings. Let me assure you, we were *nothing* like the notorious gangs of today; no guns, no "colors," no fancy cars, no disrespectful attitudes. Oh sure, occasionally we would crack open a few Keystone Beers and soap windows, but it was just good-natured foolishness. Who among us doesn't have skeletons in our closets, however infinitesimal? But it's the *first* sentence (above) that reveals the pivotal element of my remaining sentences (below)!

Time. It's elusive, it's romantic, and, above all, it's mysterious. My fascination with time is so profound that I've already posed some questions to the Timex Corporation, but I felt that my education wouldn't be complete if I didn't contact you as well. I own an Armitron watch and have been consistently amazed by its pinpoint accuracy...with two annual exceptions. On April 4 of 1993 I arose from bed and discovered that my watch was a full hour *behind* the accurate time. Six months later, on the morning of October 31, I noticed that my watch was exactly an hour *ahead*! This phenomenon seems to occur (without fail) on regular six month intervals, and I'm completely baffled! This watch is *never* off by more than a few seconds yearly, *except* for this bi-annual (maddening) occurrence. No amount of brain-storming provided the "spark" required to ease my confused mind. As I am at a dead end, it felt prudent to ask you for your learned input. Any ideas? I urge you to forward them to me at once!

With perhaps 34% of the space on this page remaining, I choose to "shift gears" and discuss an unusual topic: Poetry! As a professional poet who regularly submits his work to Hallmark and other greeting card corporations, I am consistently impressed with the "rhyme-ability" of the word, "time!" I know it's a bit irregular to share this fact with you, but I'm betting that you're "information nuts," just like me. So, without further ado, I'm now going to reveal all the words I know that rhyme with "time": Dime, lime, rhyme (ironic!), crime, thyme, climb, I'm, slime, mime, and (of course) time. Since you are "time experts," I was hoping you could provide some additional words which rhyme with time. Can you help a passionate poet? Please send all pertinent data concerning the aforementioned "vanishing and appearing" hours, as well as the poetry topic. A swift reply is expected, and, if it's not too much trouble, kindly forward an (XL) T-shirt. Good day, God bless, and keep on tickin'!

I also liked, "Jet Airliner!"

Paul Rosa

Paul C. Rosa

Paul C Rosa
117 E Espanola st
Colo Spring, Co 80907

E. GLUCK CORPORATION
29-10   Thomson   Avenue
Long Island City, N. Y. 11101
718-784-0700

Fax Number: 718-706-6326
              718-786-4153
              718-784-2155

Dear Mr Rosa

        Twice a year all watches
and clocks are to be adjusted to
Daylight saving Time (Spring) and
Standard Time (Fall)
In the spring we advance the time
one hour and we turn back one hour
in the fall.
This would appear to explain the
bi-annual maddening occurence

                    very Truly Yours
                    Joan England
                    Customer Service

117 E. Espanola St.
Colo. Springs, CO 80907
February 17, 1994

Customer Queries and Such
Hugo Boss (A Fragrance)
49 W. 57th St.
New York, NY 10019

Dear Aroma Masters,

For many, many years I dismissed men's fragrances as unnecessary, pointless indulgences. "I smell fine without the stuff," I would say again and again as I dolefully passed another Saturday night alone in front of my television (a Toshiba). I never made the connection between successful human relations and embracing (as you put it) "the enduring warmth of amber and musk in a freewheeling splash or convenient natural spray."

Then one evening, as I sulked about my studio apartment (utilities not included in rent), my friend, Petra Ove, suggested I try his personal fragrance to lift me from my doldrums. Well, I was decidedly skeptical but allowed him to "spritz" me with a bit of his "Boss Eau De Toilette." We proceeded to a nightclub on the south side of town and I was delighted when several attractive women passed by me before turning and demurely smiling. I can only surmise that they were pleased with my musky smell, a "quintessential statement of independence and individuality" (again, I quote you). I flirted with "Susan," "Lee Anne," "Naomi," and "Cindy," before passing the balance of the evening in the company of "Moonstar," a full-blooded Comanche Indian. We danced the night away, and, at 2:00 a.m., promised to meet again.

Three months have passed and we are hopelessly in love. A wedding is tentatively planned for August and I've never felt so alive and vital. Now you're probably asking yourselves, "Can a personal fragrance be *solely* credited with this man's successful courtship?" I suppose that *would* be a bit naive, my friends, but Moonstar *did* say that my scent was what attracted her to me initially. Furthermore, I believe it was Keats who said, "Every great journey or hike begins with a simple footstep." So I wish to thank you for helping transform a shy (almost reclusive) thirty-year-old into a poised, confident "man about town." In short, Boss *is* the boss! Three cheers to the "designers of casually elegant fashion for today's man!" That's quote #3!

Finally-and this is a bit delicate-I would like to confess another amazing benefit of your product. I recently spilled a tiny amount of Eau De Toilette onto my...manhood, and was delighted to achieve the grandest erection of my life that night. Even Moonstar recognized the difference, although I am no slouch in the bedroom. I have continued to dab your product onto my "nether regions," and the results have been consistently stupendous! Have you received other reports similar to mine? Do you discourage such applications? Please send all available data on this subject as it is pivotal to me. I encourage a swift reply. Lastly, do you have merchandise for sale? An (XL) T-shirt is my desire.

It makes "scents" to me,

Paul Rosa

Paul C. Rosa

Procter&Gamble

Cosmetic and Fragrance Products

11050 York Road
Hunt Valley, Maryland 21030-2098

August 18, 1994

Mr. Paul C. Rosa
119 E. Espanola Street
Colorado Springs, CO 80907

Our Reference # E50048

Dear Mr. Rosa:

This is to acknowledge receipt of your recent letter regarding Hugo Boss
Eau de Toilette.

This product has been thoroughly tested for safety when used as a
fragrance product applied to skin. It has not been tested for use on
mucous membranes such as the one you describe in your letter. Such
misuse could be irritating and is not recommended.

Sincerely,

Joan E. Doyle
Consumer Relations Safety Specialist

119 E. Espanola St.
Colo. Springs, CO 80907
February 19, 1994

New Sporting Event Consideration Department
United States Olympic Committee
One Olympic Plaza
Colo. Springs, CO 80909

Dear Aerobic Encouragers,

Wow, I'm enjoying these 1994 Winter Olympics from Lillehammer (Norway, I think)! Moments ago, I watched those dynamic lads (Brian Boitaning, Victor Potrenko, Kurt Brownig, Elvis Strojko, etc.) leap, soar, and spin through the air on that slick, icy, figure-skating surface! I've also enjoyed watching Dan Jansen, Bonnie Blair, and Tommy Moe capture gold medals (in speed-skating, speed-skating, and skiing, respectively), but the two-man luge is clearly my favorite event. For sheer thrills and drama, this competition is without equal! My entire family (wife, Soo-mi, and kids, Ed, Rainbow, Sharci, Quaylan, and Naomi) is passionately using these Olympics to renew our love for our country (U.S.A.!) and each other, as we gather nightly in front of the Sony Trinatron (color)! It's a majestic experience, friends!

As I've mentioned to countless other "contacts" and corporations alike, I'm an "idea man!" Whenever I see something done poorly, adequately, or (even) superbly, I think to myself, "Now, Paul, how can this be *bettered*?" Even a happening as seemingly perfect as the Olympics invariably comes under my meticulous, precise scrutiny. After much introspection–and let me tell you, this wasn't easy-I have come up with a noteworthy list of suggestions for possible future, *new* Olympic competitions. Since it's clearly too late to add sports to these winter games, I will now offer my fresh list of <u>summer</u> possibilities (with explanations!):

1. **Slightly-Greased Balance Beam Competition** - A little "spritz" of Pam® would make this event so much more interesting!
2. **10K Run with Liquor** - Three mandatory "shots" of Jack Daniel's Whiskey for the competitors, after each kilometer, would prove amusing!
3. **Relay Race with Pets** - A squirming tabby cat or toy poodle would certainly add an exciting new dimension to the "hand-off" juncture of any race!

Granted, these are unusual proposals, but I would sincerely like to hear your views on the above recommendations! I have notions for some winter events too (Blind-Folded Ski Jumping, etc.), but hope to learn how open you are to public opinion first! Please consider my above ideas for the 1996 Atlanta games, and respond in the enclosed "SASE." Finally, do you have (XL) T-shirts? Jesus saves!

Bravely,

Paul Rosa

Paul C. Rosa

P.S. Joke: What do you call a lifelong luge racer? A **"Born Luger!"** Ha Ha!

Dear Olympic Supporter:

Thank you for your letter expressing your desire to see your favorite sport added to the official program of the Olympic Games. The International Olympic Committee has established criteria for the inclusion of new sports as follows:

Rule 52

"1.1   To be included in the program of the Olympic Games, an Olympic sport must conform to the following criteria:

1.1.1   only sports widely practiced by men in at least seventy-five countries and on four continents, and by women in at least forty countries and on three continents, may be included in the program of the Games of the Olympiad;

1.1.2   only sports widely practiced in at least twenty-five countries and on three continents may be included in the program of the Olympic Winter Games;

1.1.3   sports are admitted to the program of the Olympic Games at least seven years before specific Olympic Games in respect of which no change shall thereafter be permitted."

Once a sport meets this criteria, the International Federation which governs the sport internationally, must petition the International Olympic Committee for inclusion on the program. This process may take several years, as the IOC is concerned about the large number of sports currently on the official program.

For more information, you may wish to write directly to the International Olympic Committee, Chateau de Vidy, CH-1007 Lausanne, Switzerland.

Sincerely,

USOC Public Information
and Media Relations
One Olympic Plaza
Colorado Springs, CO 80909

119 E. Espanola St.
Colo. Springs, CO 80907
February 20, 1994

Consumer Letter Receiving
Sinton Dairy Foods Co., Inc.
3801 Sinton Rd.
Colo. Springs, CO 80907

Dear "Cowpokes,"

We've all seen the commercial: "When you know where you're going, it *shows*! When you feel good, it *shows*! And when you drink milk, it *shows*!" Well, my pasteurized friends, you'll get no argument from this bright-eyed, resolute teenager (honor student)! When I drink milk, I can fairly *feel* the healthful liquid speeding nutritious "goodness" to the furthest regions of my (still-growing) person. By consuming roughly 1.75 gallons of that delectable "cow yield" each day, I can be sure that I am receiving adequate doses of Vitamins A & D, Protein, Thiamine, Riboflavin, Calcium, Iron, Zinc, and a host of other ingredients that I don't fully comprehend (i.e. Pantothenic Acid). The fact that I have an attractive smile and an attractive girlfriend (Jesse) tells me that my milk-drinking zeal is fully justified! Amen!!

So all-consuming is my devotion to (2% milkfat) milk and, naturally, cows, that I felt it was necessary to pen you a missive! I recently received considerable bovine data from the good people of Omaha Steaks (Omaha, NE) and the National Cattlemen's Association (Denver), but decided my research wouldn't be complete without a letter from my favorite dairy (yours!). When my "cow scrutiny" is complete, I hope to use my knowledge to write a senior thesis on this noble (often misunderstood) creature and its influence. The aforementioned corporations provided information from a slaughterhouse perspective, so it seemed logical to presently pursue the "dairy angle," your particular expertise. So, without further ado, here are my queries:

1. Do cows enjoy being milked? Do they make "contented" sounds during milking?
2. Why is milk always recommended after ingesting poison? Why not juice or syrup?
3. Why are consumers only able to open milk cartons on one end? Why not both?
4. Are the "best-milking" cows rewarded with additional hay, oats, or beverages?
5. When cereal companies use milk in their commercials, must they pay residuals to the American Dairy Association (ADA)?

As I know you are absorbed with many other (more important) dairy-oriented issues, I shan't take any more of your valuable time. Thank you for sending all available material on the above (and related) issues, plus an (XL) T-shirt! While I await your speedy reply in the enclosed "SASE," be advised that I shall continue to consume generous quantities of...**MILK!** ☺ Jesus walks with you!

With strong, healthy bones,

Paul Rosa

Paul C. Rosa

Sinton DAIRY FOODS COMPANY, INC.

P.O. BOX 578 • COLORADO SPRINGS, COLO. 80901 • PHONE 719/633-3821

March 10, 1994

Mr. Paul C. Rosa
119 E. Espanola Street
Colorado Springs, Colorado 80907

Dear Paul:

Here are the answers to all your questions. I called on the people at the Western Dairy
Council for assistance to some of your questions.

1.   Do cows enjoy being milked? Do they make contented sounds during milking?

Answer: Yes, cows enjoy being milked. Though they do not make contented sounds during
milking, we know that cows enjoy being milked by the fact that during milking
they appear relaxed, spending the time chewing their cud which is an indication
of contentment. Further, milking relieves their udder pressure, providing them
with comfort.

2.   Why is milk always recommended after ingesting poison? Why not juice or syrup?

Answer: According to the Rocky Mountain Poison Center, milk or water is recommended
in certain kinds of poisoning situations. When appropriate, milk or water acts to
dilute the ingested poison which helps to decrease the irritation to the stomach
lining. Especially with children, milk is often recommended over water because
children like milk so much and, therefore, will drink more diluting fluid.

3.   Why are consumers only able to open milk cartons on one end? Why not both?

Answer: You are only able to open milk cartons on one end by design. The seal on the
bottom of the container must be very strong to withstand the handling and
transportation abuse which occurs. The other end of the top of the carton can be
opened, its seal is slightly stronger than the normal opening.

 "QUALITY BUILT INTO PRODUCTS – BY PEOPLE WHO CARE"

Mr. Paul C. Rosa
March 10, 1994
Page 2

4.   Are the best milking cows rewarded with additional hay, oats or beverages?

Answer: No, rather all milking cows are provided with a continuous and plentiful supply
              of complete, balanced and highly palatable food and plenty of water.

5.   When cereal companies use milk is their commercials, must they pay residuals to the
ADA?

Answer: According to Tom Jenkinson, general manager for the Western Dairyfarmers
              Promotion Association, our local affiliate of the American Dairy Association:

              "No, cereal companies do not pay the dairy industry to have milk appear in their
              commercials. In fact, it is a benefit in and of itself to the dairy industry to have
              milk appear in commercials simply because milk is an integral part of a cereal
              breakfast, cereal commercials sell more milk."

I hope these answers are what you had in mind. The T-shirt was supplied by the Western
Dairy Council. If I can be of any further assistance, please pen me a missive.

Sincerely,

Mark L. Johnson
Quality Assurance Manager

MLJ/sb

119 E. Espanola St.
Colo. Springs, CO 90907
February 21, 1994

Customer Service Department
First Alert Smoke Detectors
Pittway Corporation
780 McClure Rd.
Aurora, IL 60504-2495

Attention Fire Marshals,

Fire, wind, and rain. All of the earth's essential elements were created by these powerful forces! The bible states over and over again that fire is the sign of great evil (Satan, if you like) and should be duly avoided! Ever since 1974, when my Uncle Roberto expired, along with his farm house, in an immense fire ball, I've respected the good book's passionate warnings. Granted, Roberto's gas lines were as damaged as Joe Piscopo's current career, but the important message shone through, nevertheless: "Don't mess with 'the flame!'"

Given the pivotal issue of paragraph number one, I decided (in August of 1986) to purchase one of your handsome smoke detectors at a local hardware store. As a meticulously neat fellow-and knowing the incredible importance of blaze protection-I decided to treat your handsome product (model no. 83R) with unprecedented kid gloves. Wrapping the smoke detector in several layers of aluminum foil and plastic (to prevent contamination), I stashed it securely in the back of the top shelf of my refrigerator, a place my three-year-old (Bo) couldn't reach. A sense of wellness came over me as I realized I had "done my family right." And the years serenely passed.

Then one night, four months ago (October), having long forgotten the so-called "trusty detector," I was awoken by my barking dog (Jesse). The house was already beginning to fill with smoke, and I was soon thunderstruck to realize that the kitchen was frightfully ablaze. In the ensuing fire (apparently started by a "bad wire"), I lost an antique Finnish dining table (circa 1865), my collection of Larry McMurtry novels, and an exquisite set of Parker Fountain Pens. But this wasn't what made me angry, folks; allow me to explain in the next paragraph...

Although my kitchen quarters were now <u>completely</u> filled with smoke and heat, your (nearby!) product -completely *undisturbed* for over seven years- failed to issue a ring, chime, or buzz of warning! Thankfully no one was injured and my home is insured, but this does little to diffuse my blistering rage. Few things elevate my dander higher than a product that doesn't work as designed!!

In the enclosed (pre-addressed) envelope, I encourage you to address the complaints outlined in the preceding paragraphs and (consequently) sentences. I am always open to a fair discussion, so please rush a response! Finally, do you carry (XL) T-shirts? Always choose American, please.

Fortunate to be alive,

Paul Rosa

Paul C. Rosa

780 McClure Road, Aurora, Illinois 60504-2495   (708) 851-7330
FAX (708) 851-1331

March 18, 1994

Mr. Paul C. Rosa
119 East Espanola Street
Colorado Springs, CO 90907

Dear Mr. Rosa:

I am writing in regard to your recent letter concerning the operation of
your smoke detector. We can appreciate your concern.

Smoke detectors will not sense smoke that does not reach them. Your smoke
detector was wrapped "in several layers of aluminum foil and plastic"; smoke
would not have reached it. Further, detectors need to be installed on the
ceiling (or in some cases on the wall), in order to give early warning of
a developing fire.

Smoke detectors are designed to be as maintenance-free as possible, however,
to keep your detector in good working order, you must test the detector weekly
using the test button, replace the detector battery once a year and open
the cover and vacuum dust off the detector's sensing chamber at least once
a year.

From the description you provided in your letter, it appears that your detector
could not possibly have alarmed because it was shielded from the smoke. We
urge you to install it following the instructions given in the enclosed USER
MANUAL, test and maintain it.

Finally, we have no T-shirts of any size. Please feel free to contact me
if you have any questions concerning this matter.

Respectfully,

Beth Weber
Customer Service

119 E. Espanola St.
Colo. Springs, CO 80907
February 25, 1994

Customer Handlings
Trident Chewing Gum
201 Tabor Rd
Morris Plains, NJ 07950

Dear Jaw Strengtheners,

I am in a state of absolute euphoria as I sit proudly in front of my computer, transcribing my thoughts to a company (Trident) that means *almost* as much to me as my very family itself (wife, Samantha, and children, Rusty, Sheeba, Ned, Otis, Carmen, BiBi, and Selma)! However, I'd be truly foolish to rush into my fascinating tale without first meticulously providing the important "factoids" and details (if you will) which are, in fact, the very ingredients necessary for a credible offering. And, as everything I'm about to tell you is the God's truth, I'll proceed with efficiency, patience, and precision! You deserve it!

Chewing gum has always been an enormous part of my life. My parents (Ed and Sue) were avid gum-chewers, and they were thorough when explaining to me the many benefits of keeping the jaw moving in a consistent, determined, straightforward fashion. I was permitted my first stick of gum on Christmas day, 1965 (age 4), and have been a consistent "chewer" ever since! I can't begin to describe the sense of calmness and...purity I achieve when I have a healthful stick of Trident (especially Cinnamon flavored) in my mouth. Suffice it to say, my days always include ten to fourteen hours of aggressive chewing. And, as a fiercely (and proudly) frugal fellow, I had been known to use the same stick of Trident for long periods of time. The next paragraph will fully detail this understatement, friends! Let's meet below!

Welcome to paragraph three, and thanks for your undivided attention. On February 25, 1984, while studying for a Geological Sciences examination at Penn State University, I popped a refreshing piece of Trident Cinnamon Gum into my eager mouth. Little did I know how devoted I would be to this "stick of history!" As a fervent follower of the Guinness Book of World Records (I'm a "data fanatic"), I soon decided to attempt a record. I had heard of many folks who had used the same stick of gum for long periods of time, but they blithely removed it for regular intermissions. Unimpressed, I decided to keep the aforementioned product in my mouth *constantly,* for as long as possible! Now *that's* loyalty!

I would chew for approximately twelve hours daily, tucking the gum beneath my *upper* lip during meals and "rest periods." Believe it or not, this gum wasn't removed (ever!) until today, exactly ten years later! As an educated man, I have kept detailed records and documentation of my proud achievement, so I decided to contact you first with my potential record! Is it one? Do you maintain contact with the Guiness folks? Kindly respond swiftly in the enclosed "SASE," as I am extremely excited! Finally (and I don't wish to impose), could you send a souvenir in the form of an (XL) T-shirt? Thanks so much!

A goal-setter,

Paul Rosa

Paul C. Rosa

March 21, 1994

Mr. Paul C. Rosa
119 E. Espanola Street
Colorado Springs, CO 80907

Dear Paul,

Thank you for your enjoyable letter. I award you with the Trident
record as the most loyal customer. To show our appreciation for
you loyalty, enclosed is a lifetime supply (120 pieces) of Trident
Cinnamon for you to enjoy. Treat yourself to a fresh piece of gum
every now and then.

As far as the Guinness Book of World Records is concerned, Warner-
Lambert has no contact with them. You will need to contact them on
your own.

Again, thank you for your enthusiasm and good luck with the record
book.

                              Sincerely,

                              Tracy Pollastri
                              Marketing Assistant
                              Trident

TP1-9.94

201 TABOR ROAD, MORRIS PLAINS, NJ 07950   **When You Can't Brush....Chew Trident !**

119 E. Espanola St.
Colo. Springs, CO 80907
February 27, 1994

Potential Competitor Inquiries
Iditarod Trail Committee
P.O. Box 870800
Wasilla, AK 99687

Hello, event organizers, associates, and the like,

Ah, the mighty Iditarod! For years men (or women) and their proud, sturdy dogs have gathered annually to test their mettle by mushing a sled through hundreds and hundreds of miles of desolate, frigid wilderness. The winner (I'm a Susan Butcher fan!) could take pride in the fact that they *alone* were indeed the "most vigorous of the assemblage!" Their fine, noble accomplishment would (I imagine) forever hold a special place in their psyche, giving them strength and self-assurance. And you, my organizing-committee friends, are to be held in high esteem for your tireless efforts toward creating the "perfect product." Bless you!

Since my college days at Maximillian State University (B.S. in Textile Management), I have dreamed of one day taking part in the Iditarod as a resolute contestant. Several times a month over the past decade I have woken up in a cold, clammy sweat, attempting to recover from my latest, exalted Iditarod dream. This dream has remained unrealized, however, as my working life has been tirelessly devoted to the breeding and raising of beautiful Chinese Crested Dogs. With the largest stable of purebred Chinese Cresteds in the midwest, I am satisfied that my life's work has been a complete success. Well, not *entirely*. I'll explain.

Last night, instead of my customary, upsetting Iditarod mental images, I experienced what could only be described as a "thunderbolt of inspiration." As I leapt from my sleeping surface, I shouted to my wife (Shimino), "Why the hell not compete in the Iditarod with my sturdiest Chinese Cresteds?!" Shimino, forever supportive, instantly rallied to my side (not far, ha ha!) and encouraged me to passionately follow my dream.

Well, my friends, I am ready to begin arduous training sessions with a small group of my hardiest canine companions. At twenty to thirty pounds of sinewy muscle apiece, these compact beasts are ready to tackle the momentous task at hand...with your approval, of course! Enclosed is a picture of my lead dog, Galileo, who will hopefully navigate his companions (Sparky, Jesse, Agnes, Boomer, etc.) and myself through the wicked Alaskan wilderness. Is it permissible to enter the race without the customary huskies as sled dogs? And I'm about fifty pounds overweight, but I believe I can be in tip-top shape within a few months! Please send your ideas about my possibilities in the next big race, and, if feasible, send an (XL) T-shirt. I am breathlessly looking forward to the competition!

Soon buying a Stairmaster,

Paul Rosa

Paul C. Rosa

"GALILEO"

diarod Trail Committee, Inc.
P.O. Box 870800, Wasilla, Alaska 99687 USA • Phone (907) 376-5155 • Fax (907) 373-6998

April 30, 1994

Paul C. Rosa
119 E Espanola Street
Colorado Springs, CO 80907

Dear Mr. Rosa:

I have read and re-read your letter of February 27, trying to determine whether or not your were indeed serious. I must confess that I have not heard of a breed of dog called Chinese Crested. However, that means nothing. I'm sure there are many breeds of dogs I haven't heard of.

Iditarod race rules require that dogs racing in this event be northern breeds, further defined as double coated dogs. This requirement was put in the rules for the protection of the animals racing in harsh weather conditions.

The race rules for 1995 will be published in June of 1994, I hope. In the meantime, I am enclosing a copy of the 1994 race rules, as I doubt they will change too much.

Right now, a rookie, one who has never finished an Iditarod Trail Sled Dog Race, is required to qualify for running the Iditarod by completing a minimum of 500 miles in no more than two sanctioned qualifying races during the immediate two years preceding his/her running the Iditarod. (If you run the 1995 Iditarod, you must complete your qualifiers between January of 1993 and February of 1995. That qualifying requirement could change. It has been stiffened a little for 1994 from previous years and there is talk of making it even stiffer down the road.

As it stands right now, one doesn't have to be qualified to enter the next Iditarod. The entry fee, at least the present entry fee, is $1,249. In order to be listed as an official entry, that entry fee must be paid. That can be sent to the Iditarod in the form of a check or money order or may be charged.

Additionally, mushers must be members of the Iditarod Trail Committee. If you are not a member now, you may want to go ahead and take care of that so that you can begin getting Iditarod's mailings.

There are application forms and other forms that must be completed, but we usually send those out after one has sent in his/her entry fee. We will officially begin taking entry fees for 1995 on

Paul C. Rosa   April 30, 1994
                                                                                           page 2

June 25, 1994. As it stands right now, we will accept entry fees through midnight December 1, 1994.

You may call our toll free number, 1-800-545-6874, to order any of our T-shirts. We are just about to get a new catalog off the press and will be glad to send you one. Just call Carol or Patty at that number and ask for one.

Good luck!

Sincerely,

Joanne Potts
Race Director

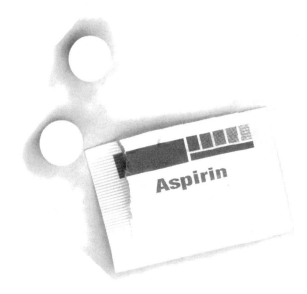

119 E. Espanola St.
Colo. Springs, CO 80907
March 1, 1994

Marriage License Bureau
El Paso County Government
200 S. Cascade
Colo. Springs, CO 80903

Dear Wedding Advisers,

As a young man who is *very* much in love, I felt it would be prudent to solicit some information and advice from your learned office. The topic (naturally) deals with the issue of marriage and all of the legal, social, and emotional ramifications that are the inevitable consequences of such a momentous passage. A commitment of this magnitude is arduous enough under normal circumstances, but *my* situation is truly one of a complicated nature. If you would afford me the luxury of a few more minutes of your undivided attention, I will fill in the gaps (if you will) of my passionate, true story!

You see, my patient friends, the "lady" of my dreams is, in fact...a cat. Now, by "cat" I don't mean someone who is suave (i.e. a "cool cat"). Actually, your initial prognosis was accurate; the love of my life is a *feline!* I rescued Jesse from the Humane Society three years ago, when she was a frightened, undisciplined two-year-old. Within months, however, she "grew" into a confident, proud, beautiful young lady. Our love blossomed over the following years, while we consistently reminded ourselves that we were (sadly and undeniably) members of separate species. Consequently, our relationship has remained <u>completely</u> Platonic, but we would still like to officially affirm our wonderful bond. That's where you come in!

Is it legal for a man to obtain a marriage license when the bride in question is not actually...human? I realize the minimum age for marriage without parental consent is eighteen, but Jesse is *technically* thirty-five, not five (cat years!). Does that make a difference? Much of our society doesn't embrace unconditional ("inter-specied") love as freely as I do, but I am willing to be somewhat of a pioneer in this area! I assure you that our relationship contains every bit as much devotion and respect as the best human marriages. We sleep together (remember, no sex!), travel together, bathe together, and dine together. Please write to me promptly, addressing all of the aforementioned issues. I anxiously await you pivotal reply. Thank you kindly.

Willing to be different,

Paul Rosa

Paul C. Rosa

Authors note: Apparently there is no law against marrying one's cat, given the feline is at least 18 years old (2.57 in cat years)!

⟵⟶

I hope the enclosed "statutes" will be helpful.

Joyce Manning
Recording Department

Ardis W. Schmitt
EL PASO COUNTY
CLERK AND RECORDER

TITLE 14

DOMESTIC MATTERS

ADOPTION - ADULTS

ARTICLE 1

Adoption of Adults

14-1-101. Adoption of adults.

The effect of an adult adoption and a child adoption are different. A person adopts an adult to make such person his or her intestate heir. Matter of Trust created by Belgard, 829 P.2d 457 (Colo. App. 1991).

Considering the circumstances at the time the trust was executed and the s___'s reasonable expectations, the phrase "persons legally adopted" was held to include adopted children only, not adults. The court held that the respondent was using the adult adoption statute to entitle his wife to a remainder of the trust estate, contrary to the setilor's intent as

set forth in the instrument. Matter of Trust created by Belgard, 829 P.2d 457 (Colo. App. 1991).

The general assembly's desire to place adopted and natural children on par with one another does not extend to permit adult adoptions for the purpose of giving them an interest in property already specifically designated. Such an adoption decree did not have the power to affect the disposition of such interests, it only granted the right to inherit through intestacy. Matter of Trust created by Belgard, 829 P.2d 457 (Colo. App. 1991).

ADOPTION - ADULTS

ARTICLE 2

Marriage and Rights of Married Women

Law reviews: For article, "Marital Agreements", see 18 Colo. Law. 31, (1989).

PART 1

UNIFORM MARRIAGE ACT

14-2-105.	Marriage license and marriage certificate.
14-2-106.	License to marry.
14-2-107.	When licenses to marry issued - validity.
14-2-109.	Solemnization and registration.
14-2-110.	Prohibited marriages.

PART 1

UNIFORM MARRIAGE ACT

14-2-105. Marriage license and marriage certificate. (1) (b) If either party has previously been married, such party's married name and the date,

1

14-2-106

Domestic Matters

place, and court in which the marriage was dissolved or declared invalid or the date and place of death of the former spouse;

(d) Whether the parties are related to each other and, if so, their relationship, or, if the parties are currently married to each other, a statement to that effect.

Source: (1)(b) and (1)(d) amended, L. 93, p. 437, § 1, effective July 1.

14-2-106. License to marry. (1) (a) When a marriage application has been completed and signed by both parties to a prospective marriage and at least one party has appeared before the county clerk and recorder and has paid the marriage license fee of seven dollars plus an additional fee of ten dollars, except as provided in paragraph (c) of this subsection (1), such additional fee to be credited to the Colorado children's trust fund pursuant to section 19-3.5-106, C.R.S., and an additional amount established pursuant to section 25-2-121, C.R.S., such amount to be credited to the vital statistics records cash fund pursuant to section 25-2-121, C.R.S., the county clerk shall issue a license to marry and a marriage certificate form upon being furnished:

(III) Repealed, L. 86, p. 711, § 1, effective July 1, 1989.

(c) The additional ten-dollar fee authorized in paragraph (a) of this subsection (1) to be credited to the Colorado children's trust fund shall not be assessed after the balance in such fund exceeds five million dollars.

(2) Repealed, L. 86, p. 711, § 1, effective July 1, 1989.

Source: IP(1)(a) amended and (1)(c) added, L. 89, p. 936, § 2, effective July 1; (1)(c) amended, L. 93, p. 927, § 4, effective May 28.

14-2-107. When licenses to marry issued - validity. Licenses to marry shall be issued by the county clerk and recorder only during the hours that the office of the county clerk and recorder is open as prescribed by law and at no other time, and such licenses shall show the exact date and hour of their issue. A license shall not be valid for use outside the state of Colorado. Within the state, such licenses shall not be valid for more than thirty days after the date of issue. If any license to marry is not used within thirty days, it shall be void and shall be returned to the county clerk and recorder for cancellation.

Source: Entire section amended, L. 93, p. 437, § 2, effective July 1.

14-2-109. Solemnization and registration. (1) A marriage may be solemnized by a judge of a court, by a court magistrate, by a retired judge of a court, by a public official whose powers include solemnization of marriages, by the parties to the marriage, or in accordance with any mode of solemnization recognized by any religious denomination or Indian nation or tribe. Either the person solemnizing the marriage or, if no individual acting alone solemnized the marriage, a party to the marriage shall complete the marriage certificate form and forward it to the county clerk and recorder within sixty days after the solemnization. Any person who fails to forward the marriage certificate to the county clerk and recorder as required by this section shall

be required to pay a late fee in an amount of not less than twenty dollars. An additional five-dollar late fee may be assessed for each additional day of failure to comply with the forwarding requirements of this subsection (1) up to a maximum of fifty dollars. For purposes of determining whether a late fee shall be assessed pursuant to this subsection (1), the date of forwarding shall be deemed to be the date of postmark.

(2) If a party to a marriage is unable to be present at the solemnization, such party may authorize in writing a third person to act as such party's proxy. If the person solemnizing the marriage is satisfied that the absent party is unable to be present and has consented to the marriage, such person may solemnize the marriage by proxy. If such person is not satisfied, the parties may petition the district court for an order permitting the marriage to be solemnized by proxy.

(3) Upon receipt of the marriage certificate, the county clerk and recorder shall register the marriage.

Source: (1) amended, L. 89, p. 781, § 1, effective April 4; (1) amended, L. 91, p. 359, § 19, effective April 9; entire section amended, L. 93, p. 438, § 3, effective July 1.

14-2-110. Prohibited marriages. (1) (a) A marriage entered into prior to the dissolution of an earlier marriage of one of the parties, except a currently valid marriage between the parties;

Source: (1)(a) amended, L. 93, p. 438, § 4, effective July 1.

A common law marriage cannot be **found** where decedent knew that plaintiff was **legally** married to someone not the decedent at the time the decedent died despite anything decedent may have said regarding an intention to marry plaintiff and plaintiff's acquisition of a retro-active divorce after decedent died. The court will not speculate as to what the decedent might have intended regarding marriage had he been aware of the removal of the legal disability during his lifetime. Crandell v. Resley, 804 P.2d 272 (Colo. App. 1990).

14-2-111. Putative spouse.

Knowledge that one is married to **another** person negates good faith belief **required of** putative spouse. People v. McGuire, 751 P.2d 1011 (Colo. App. 1987).

A common law marriage cannot be **found** where decedent knew that plaintiff was legally married to someone not the decedent at the time the decedent died despite anything decedent may have said regarding an intention to marry plaintiff and plaintiff's acquisition of a retro-active divorce after decedent died. The court will not speculate as to what the decedent might have intended regarding marriage had he been aware of the removal of the legal disability during his lifetime. Crandell v. Resley, 804 P.2d 272 (Colo. App. 1990).

PART 2

RIGHTS OF MARRIED WOMEN

14-2-201. Married woman's own property.

1. GENERAL CONSIDERATION.

Law reviews.

For article, "Ownership of Personal Property Accumulated During a Marriage," see 17 Colo. Law. 623 (1988).

Marriage and Rights of Married Women — 14-2-106

(2) The executive director of the department of health shall prescribe the forms for the marriage license, the marriage certificate, and the consent to marriage.

Source: R & RE. L. 73, p. 1016, § 1; C.R.S. 1963, § 90-1-5.

14-2-106. License to marry. (1) (a) When a marriage application has been completed and signed by both parties to a prospective marriage and at least one party has appeared before the county clerk and recorder and has paid the marriage license fee of seven dollars plus an additional amount established pursuant to section 25-2-121, C.R.S., such amount to be credited to the vital statistics records cash fund pursuant to section 25-2-121. C.R.S. the county clerk and recorder shall issue a license to marry and a marriage certificate form upon being furnished:

(I) Satisfactory proof that each party to the marriage will have attained the age of eighteen years at the time the marriage license becomes effective; or, if over the age of sixteen years but has not attained the age of eighteen years, has the consent of both parents or guardian or, if the parents are not living together, the parent who has legal custody or with whom the child is living or judicial approval, as provided in section 14-2-108; or, if under the age of sixteen years, has both the consent to the marriage of both parents or guardian or, if the parents are not living together, the parent who has legal custody or with whom the child is living and judicial approval, as provided in section 14-2-108; and

(II) Satisfactory proof that the marriage is not prohibited, as provided in section 14-2-110; and

(III) (A) Documentary evidence of rubella immunity as required by subsection (2) of this section.

(B) This subparagraph (III) is repealed, effective July 1, 1989.

(b) Violation of paragraph (a) (I) of this subsection (1) shall make the marriage voidable.

(2) (a) Before any marriage license is issued by an official authorized by law to do so, each female applicant under the age of forty-five shall file with said official documentary evidence of rubella immunity. Rubella immunity shall be shown by record of previous rubella vaccination or previous test for immunity. Applicants unable to provide a record of rubella immunity shall file with said official a certificate which states that the applicant has been given a standard serological test for rubella immunity. The certificate filed by the applicant shall be from a physician licensed to practice medicine, and the physician shall obtain blood samples from the female applicant and cause a standard serological test to be made for rubella immunity by serological methods specified by the department of health, and he shall provide her with his certificate stating that such test has been made and inform her of the results of such test and its medical significance; except that, whenever the physician finds that the female applicant is incapable of bearing a child because of prior surgery or other physical condition, the standard serological test for rubella immunity shall not be required, and his certificate shall so state.

(b) If a physician's certificate is required, it shall be accompanied by a statement from the person in charge of the laboratory making the test or

---

Domestic Matters — 4

14-2-102. Purposes - rules of construction. (1) This part 1 shall be liberally construed and applied to promote its underlying purposes.

(2) Its underlying purposes are:

(a) To strengthen and preserve the integrity of marriage and to safeguard meaningful family relationships;

(b) To provide adequate procedures for the solemnization and registration of marriage.

Source: R & RE. L. 73, p. 1016, § 1; C.R.S. 1963, § 90-1-2.

14-2-103. Uniformity of application and construction. This part 1 shall be so applied and construed as to effectuate its general purpose to make uniform the law with respect to the subject of this part 1 among those states which enact it.

Source: R & RE. L. 73, p. 1016, § 1; C.R.S. 1963, § 90-1-3.

14-2-104. Formalities. A marriage between a man and a woman licensed, solemnized, and registered as provided in this part 1 is valid in this state.

Source: R & RE. L. 73, p. 1016, § 1; C.R.S. 1963, § 90-1-4.

14-2-105. Marriage license and marriage certificate. (1) The executive director of the department of health shall prescribe the form for an application for a marriage license, which shall include the following information:

(a) Name, sex, address, social security number, date and place of birth of each party to the proposed marriage; and for such purpose proof of date of birth may be by a birth certificate, a driver's license, or other comparable evidence;

(b) If either party has previously been married, his married name and the date, place, and court in which the marriage was dissolved or declared invalid or the date and place of death of the former spouse;

(c) Name and address of the parents or guardian of each party;

(d) Whether the parties are related to each other and, if so, their relationship.

Law reviews. For comment, "Adoptive Sibling Marriage in Colorado; Israel v. Allen", see 51 U. Colo. L. Rev. 135 (1979).

There is no doubt that the public policy of Colorado favors marriage. Lewis v. Colorado Nat'l Bank. 652 P.2d 1106 (Colo. App. 1982).

But policy will not void a forfeiture-on-remarriage trust provision. A forfeiture-on-remarriage provision in a trust is not void on public policy grounds as a restraint on marriage. Lewis v. Colorado Nat'l Bank. 652 P.2d 1106 (Colo. App. 1982).

The policy of the law favoring marriage is without sufficient vigor to overcome the policy in support of maintaining a settlor's intention. Lewis v. Colorado Nat'l Bank. 652 P.2d 1106 (Colo. App. 1982).

Applied in Israel v. Allen. 195 Colo. 263. 577 P.2d 762 (1978).

14-2-106   6   Domestic Matters

from some other person authorized to make such report, setting forth the results of the standard serological test, the date this test was made, and the name and address of the person whose blood was tested.

(c) The above-mentioned certificate of physician and statement of person authorized to make reports for the laboratory shall be on a form to be provided and distributed by the department of health to all officers authorized to issue marriage licenses and to approved laboratories in the state.

(d) For purposes of this section, a "standard serological test" means a test for rubella immunity, approved by the department of health and made at a laboratory approved by the department to make such tests.

(e) Such laboratory tests as are required by this section may be made on request without charge at the department of health laboratory.

(f) Before the licensing officer issues any marriage license, he shall attach thereto either the previous record establishing rubella immunity or the certificate form of the female applicant specified in paragraph (a) of this subsection (2). No minister or other person authorized to perform marriage ceremonies in Colorado shall perform any such ceremony unless either the previous record establishing rubella immunity or the certificate form of the female applicant is attached to the marriage license, and they shall remain so attached until the marriage certificate is filed.

(g) Any judge of a county or district court within the county in which the license is to be issued is authorized and empowered, on joint application by both applicants for a marriage license, to waive the requirements as to a laboratory test and certificate and to authorize the county clerk and recorder to issue the license, if all other requirements of the marriage laws have been complied with and the judge is satisfied, by affidavit or other proof, that the test is contrary to the tenets or practices of the religious creed of which the applicant is an adherent and that the public health and welfare will not be injuriously affected thereby.

(h) This subsection (2) is repealed, effective July 1, 1989.

Source: R & RE, L. 73, p. 1017, § 1; C.R.S. 1963, § 90-1-6; L. 75, p. 583, § 1; L. 79, p. 635, § 1; L. 84, pp. 742, 1118, §§ 1, 9; L. 86, p. 711, § 1.

A failure to obtain the blood test (now rubella immunity documentation) does not invalidate a marriage, since § 14-2-113 provides for penalties only, in the event of violation. Young v. Colorado Nat'l Bank, 148 Colo. 104, 365 P.2d 701 (1961) (decided under repealed § 90-1-6, CRS 53).

Am.Jur.2d. See 52 Am. Jur.2d. Marriage, §§ 14-16, 33-35, 37, 38, 41.
C.J.S. See 55 C.J.S. Marriage, §§ 11, 24, 25.

Law reviews. For article, "Common Law Marriage in Colorado", see 16 Colo. Law. 252 (1987).

14-2-107. When licenses to marry issued - validity. Licenses to marry shall be issued by the county clerk and recorder only during the hours that his office is open as prescribed by law and at no other time, and such licenses shall show the exact date and hour of their issue. A license shall not be valid for use more than thirty days after its date of issue. If any license to marry is not used within thirty days, it shall be returned to the county clerk and recorder.

Source: R & RE, L. 73, p. 1018, § 1; C.R.S. 1963, § 90-1-7; L. 75, p. 583, § 2.

---

7   Marriage and Rights of Married Women   14-2-109

C.J.S. See 55 C.J.S. Marriage, § 23.

14-2-108. Judicial approval. (1) The juvenile court, as defined in section 19-1-103 (17), C.R.S., after a reasonable effort has been made to notify the parents or guardian of each underaged party, may order the county clerk and recorder to issue a marriage license and a marriage certificate form:

Editor's note: This introductory portion to subsection (1) is effective October 1, 1987.

(a) To a party aged sixteen or seventeen years who has no parent or guardian, or who has no parent capable of consenting to his marriage, or whose parent or guardian has not consented to his marriage; or

(b) To a party under the age of sixteen years who has the consent to his marriage of both parents, if capable of giving consent, or his guardian or, if the parents are not living together, the parent who has legal custody or with whom the child is living.

(2) A license shall be ordered to be issued under subsection (1) of this section only if the court finds that the underaged party is capable of assuming the responsibilities of marriage and the marriage would serve his best interests. Pregnancy alone does not establish that the best interests of the party would be served.

(3) The district court or the juvenile court, as the case may be, shall authorize performance of a marriage by proxy upon the showing required by the provisions on solemnization, being section 14-2-109.

Source: R & RE, L. 73, p. 1018, § 1; C.R.S. 1963, § 90-1-8; L. 87, p. 315, § 15.

Law reviews. For comment, "Adoptive Sibling Marriage in Colorado: Israel v. Allen", see 51 U. Colo. L. Rev. 135 (1979).

14-2-109. Solemnization and registration. (1) A marriage may be solemnized by a judge of a court of record, by a retired judge of a court of record, by a public official whose powers include solemnization of marriages, or in accordance with any mode of solemnization recognized by any religious denomination or Indian nation or tribe. Either the person solemnizing the marriage or, if no individual acting alone solemnized the marriage, a party to the marriage shall complete the marriage certificate form and forward it to the county clerk and recorder. Any person who fails to forward the marriage certificate to the county clerk and recorder as required by this section is guilty of a misdemeanor and, upon conviction thereof, shall be punished by a fine of not less than twenty dollars nor more than fifty dollars.

(2) If a party to a marriage is unable to be present at the solemnization, he may authorize in writing a third person to act as his proxy. If the person solemnizing the marriage is satisfied that the absent party is unable to be present and has consented to the marriage, he may solemnize the marriage by proxy. If he is not satisfied, the parties may petition the district court for an order permitting the marriage to be solemnized by proxy.

119 E. Espanola St.
Colo. Springs, CO 80907
March 2, 1994

Consumer Suggestions (*New Features*)
Gazette Telegraph Newspaper
30 S. Prospect St.
Colo. Springs, CO 80901

Dear (fellow) News Hounds,

If I've said it once, I've said it 15,000 times: Data and information are (succinctly stated) my life! I've devoted my very existence to the acquisition and mental collating of facts, figures, and "nuggets" of knowledge. My curiosity was set in motion during high school in Pittsburgh, Pennsylvania (class of 1980) by a devoted, thoughtful English teacher named Helen Agnes Shoolmaine. Her passionate lessons have forever occupied a special portion of my psyche, as I make my way through life on this fascinating planet we fondly call, "earth!" I soon matriculated at Coleson Tech Institute (class of 1985), and my dual careers (Geologist and aquarium shop co-owner) subsequently thrived. I have also had the fortune of marrying a magnificent woman (Yewela) and siring two sets of twins (Ken, Tip, Felicia, and Minny)!

For the past six years I have also diligently pursued my fascinating hobby of <u>squirrel scrutinization</u>. With my powerful binoculars, handy (Panasonic) camcorder and assorted camouflage outfits, I can often be seen in the numerous area parks, meticulously collecting statistics (and such) on this exciting, bushy creature. With my powerful lenses I enjoy recording their various, intriguing activities (i.e. nest building, mating, nut gathering, and, of course, good-natured tomfoolery!). Most of these area rodents (Rodentia: Any of a very large order of gnawing mammals, including rats, mice, squirrels, beavers, etc., characterized by constantly growing incisors adapted for gnawing or nibbling) have even been named by me. Down in Monument park live Wayne, Susan, Sammy, Ed, Renee, Pika, and Big Kurt. Over in Memorial Park, Gypsy, Nicki, Jesse, Russell, Megan and Boris can be found. No one in southern Colorado has a better understanding of this (often misunderstood) creature! No one.

But you may now be asking yourselves why I chose to write! Well, although I have absolutely no journalism experience or official zoology credentials, I feel I can "bring the squirrel" to Colorado Springs residents better than anyone. What I lack in accreditation, I easily make up for with savvy and passion. I would like to suggest a daily column about squirrels (and their ways) for the Gazette Telegraph. With all of the outdoor lovers in the area, I feel my column would be embraced with unprecedented enthusiasm. I have already completed two reports on my favorite rodents (squirrels!), dealing with tree-climbing and scolding. I look forward to your quick, concise reaction to my suggestion, and humbly request an (XL) T-shirt. That's that!

The trees are the source,

Paul Rosa

Paul C. Rosa

COLORADO SPRINGS
GAZETTE TELEGRAPH

30 S. Prospect St., P.O. Box 1779, Colorado Springs, CO 80901
(719) 632-5511

119 E. Espanola Street
Colorado Springs, CO 80907
May 18, 1994

Dear Paul C. Rosa,
    Your suggestion for writing a column for the <u>Gazette Telegraph</u>
on the subject of squirrels living in local parks has made its way
to me. As supervisor over the Features and Metro sections, I am the
logical person to make the call on this one.
    Your hobby, I am sure, is fascinating. However, when we
either contract outside or assign inside a column for our news columns,
we must give our readership and their interests the first priority.
As you must be aware, news columns are precious and valuable. So, our
decisions on what to put there must be guided on what will appeal to
the broadest audience. While squirrels are all around us, I do not feel
there is sufficient broad-based appeal on that subject to warrant
a regular column in the <u>GT</u>.
    However, that is not to say that you and your avocation are not
interesting to us. Do not be surprised if you hear from a GT reporter
some time in the future. While I cannot guarantee that this will happen
-- news of the day always dictates what we do and when we do things --
your unusual hobby has caught our attention.
    Thank you again for your kind offer.

Regards,

Terri Fleming
Deputy Managing Editor

119 E. Espanola St.
Colo. Springs, CO 80907
March 6, 1994

Earl Scheib Automobile Painters
World Headquarters
P.O. Box 92184
Worldway Postal Center
Los Angeles CA 90009

Dear Pigment Replenishers,

Byrdstown, Tennessee. Population 884. Simple town, simple folks. A place where honesty and integrity once came guaranteed with each (and every) handshake. Written contracts and such were practically unheard of when I was a boy, because a man's word was as good as anything that appeared on parchment. Sadly enough, attitudes in Byrdstown have changed with the times, and this enchanting little town now contains its share of lawyers and the like. But this does little to sully my memory of a tranquil, healthy childhood spent in a town that epitomized many of the proud American traditions of the 1960's and early 1970's. If you have trouble understanding how this story applies to you, my friends, I merely request that you read on; the relevant point is swiftly approaching, I assure you.

On February 9 of this year, my car (1982 Nissan Sentra) was the recipient of a deluxe paint job (black) at the Colorado Springs Earl Scheib location on North Nevada Avenue. For roughly $250, my reliable Japanese vehicle received the "facelift" required to take years off its appearance. After completing the transformation with four shiny, new hubcaps, I was amazed when, as a result, my social life actually picked up! An admiring young woman (Ri Ann) soon approached me in a local K-Mart parking lot, remarking how impressive she thought my automobile looked. Well, I am pleased to announce that I have been courting said woman ever since, and the word, "love" is actually dancing merrily through my subconscious. Life is good. And now, I will deliver the aforementioned (promised) relevant point!!

On the sales slip I received from your affiliate, I noticed your motto, **"The World's Largest Auto Painter."** I immediately remembered my summers in Byrdstown, when I helped my Uncle Ned in his small, successful automobile painting shop. Through sheer hard work and determination, Ned built a thriving business which many naysayers claimed would "fold like a card table." Well, Ned proved (and still proves) them all wrong by working tirelessly, despite carrying a colossal 575 pounds on his 5'8" frame! And now comes my point: Are you absolutely sure that Earl Scheib is indeed the "world's largest" auto painter, given the (factual) monstrous dimensions of my proud uncle?! He's far too timid to cry, "false advertising," but I would like to challenge your lofty claim! Just how big is Mr. Scheib, and how can you be 100% certain that he is truly the largest auto painter in the world?! Presumably there may also be larger painters (aside from Ned) in Europe, Australia, and parts of Africa! I look forward to your respectful reply and wish to remind you again how grateful I am for the terrific work! God bless!

A stickler for honesty,

Paul Rosa

Paul C. Rosa

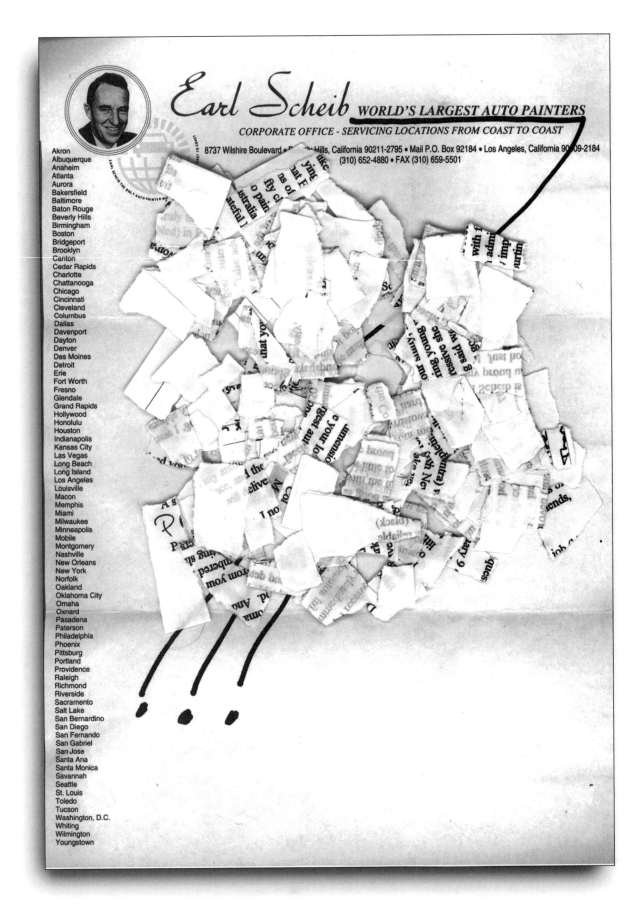

119 E. Espanola St.
Colo. Springs, CO 80907
March 9, 1994

Patron Questions
International House of Pancakes
525 North Brand Blvd., 3rd Floor
Glendale, CA 91203

Dear Morning Mavericks,

I love sausage. I love eggs. I love pancakes. I love toast. I love hash browns. I love bacon. But (damn it) I _really_ love the International House of Pancakes. As a *very* regular patron of your superb restaurants in Colorado Springs (66 Southgate Rd. and 512 North Chelton Rd.), I want to congratulate you on the fine job of establishing two proud, sanitary affiliates. Although I recognize you primarily serve breakfast items, I occasionally enjoy a lunch or supper excursion, featuring delectable chicken, savory hamburgers or juicy steaks. I would estimate that I dine at your restaurants approximately nine times per week. Yep, that's living!

It is no surprise to me that the <u>International</u> House of Pancakes can be found in all corners of the earth (what *corners*?). When a restaurant offers such an unprecedented array of delicious entrees, it's certainly no surprise when success quickly follows in the form of global (i.e. "international!") success. I've long dreamed of sampling your chow on other continents, but have never had adequate funds for such an ambitious trip. In fact, given the meager wages I've earned as a dog groomer, my farthest excursion has been to Byrdstown, Tennessee to attend my uncle Ned's funeral yesterday. Uncle Ned, weighing an unfathomable 575 pounds, collapsed while painting a 1982 Nissan Sentra in his small auto shop. His heart simply couldn't handle the strain, but he died doing what he loved!

Anyway, I was thrilled to discover that Ned left me $35,400 in his will! I have decided to visit Paraguay, Saudi Arabia, Zambia, Tunisia, Thailand, Finland, and New Zealand (my cousin Jesse's home). As an impassioned supporter of International House of Pancakes, I have written to request the "IHOP" restaurant locations in the aforementioned countries. It gives me great comfort to realize that I can continue to enjoy the exact same foods I consume in America! Your international scope will surely serve to help make my trip a rip-roaring success! I look forward to your fleet, thorough report. God bless and keep cooking!

No cereal for me,

Paul Rosa

Paul C. Rosa

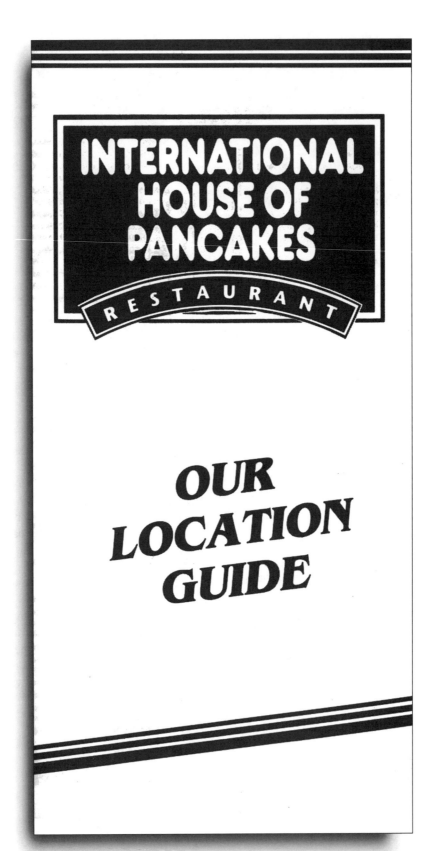

119 E. Espanola St.
Colo. Springs, CO 80907
March 9, 1994

Consumer Anger
Kinko's Service Corporation
P.O. Box 8000
Ventura, CA 93002-8000

Attention you people out there in California!

I'm a hard-working man who spends ten to fourteen hours each day working on his ranch, tending to over 75 head of cattle, hundreds of chickens, 200 acres of crops (turnip, beets, etc.) and a medium lumber yard. Since 1971 I've worked my fingers to the bone, doing the Lord's bidding and providing for my proud, Baptist family of seven. Having given up the evils of urban America soon after graduating from Porter High School (1968), I've found a lot of happiness in the outdoors...close to God.

Anyways, I recently began to have trouble with <u>really</u> chapped lips until I decided I had to do something about them. I refuse to see those high priced, quack city doctors, so I decided to travel into town (Colorado Springs) and see if I could find a remedy of some sort or another. My wife (Myrtle) asked to come along, but I wouldn't hear of it. I won't have those sinners looking at her legs and getting them filthy, dirty ideas that men get all the time. I think she should be happy staying home with the kids (Burt, Sue, Agnes, Bo, and Joe) until I get back. Maybe that's old fashioned but the old ways are the best ways. She soon agreed.

So feeling a little nervous I drove my pick up truck (Ford) into town and stopped at the first store that looked clean to me. I wash up at least five times a day, so I like to be near things that are really clean too. I could see them city eyes on me as I walked through the door, so I decided to try and make a quick choice. I'd seen those adds on the television for that chap stick stuff that's supposed to be good for sore lips, so I looked around the store like a hawk over my ranch eyeing a chicken. I was happy to see some of the stuff (called Kinko's Glue Stick), and I quickly paid the gal in cash. On the drive back to my spread, I put some "Kinkos" on my lips and it felt good at first. But soon it felt real sticky and got to tasting nasty as all get out! My lips didn't feel any better, in fact I started feeling kind of sick! It was awful, I tell you!

So, I decided to type you out a letter and let you know that your lip product doesn't help at all! In fact it made me furious to drive into town and come back with such a horrible item. Please write to me and explain and let me know if others have complained. Finally, my son, Joe, asked that you send an (XL) T-shirt. Please read the bible.

Hoping to forgive,

Paul Rosa

Paul C. Rosa

kinko's
the copy center

Kinko's Service Corporation • 255 West Stanley Ave. • Ventura, CA 93002-8000 • 805-652-4000

June 14, 1994

Paul C. Rosa
119 E. Espanola Street
Colorado Springs, CO 80907

Dear Mr. Rosa:

Thank you for taking the time to tell us about your experience at Kinko's.

We apologize for any discomfort you encountered when you applied Kinko's glue stick to your lips. Our product is not designed for any use other than as an adhesive, and other than your letter, we have not had any prior complaints about this specific use of our product. Additionally, we regret that we will be unable to send your son a Kinko's tee-shirt. You may inquire about purchasing "Kinko-Wear" at your local Kinko's Copy Center.

Sincerely,

Paul J. Orfalea
Chairperson of the Board

PJO/tpr

cc: Tim Stancliffe, Partner
        Karen Lauersdorf, Regional Manager
        K-Graphics, Inc.
        7112 W. Jefferson Ave., #312
        Lakewood, CO 80235

        Ted Young, Manager
        Kinko's - Colorado Springs I

Over 600 locations nationwide • Call 1-800-743-COPY for the location nearest you.
This recycled paper contains 100% post-consumer waste.

119 E. Espanola St.
Colo. Springs, CO 80907
March 19, 1994

Consumer Affairs
Safeway, Inc.
2800 Ygnacio Rd.
Walnut Creek, CA 94598

Dear Meal Makers,

As you know, I've written twice before concerning "serving suggestions" on TV dinners and toilet tissue information. In both cases I was cordially and swiftly answered by Safeway, and came away from the experiences with a general sense of well-being. Be advised, I have consistently shopped at the Safeway outlet on North Wahsatch Avenue for over eight years. As a boy I would visit the store with my father (Lincoln Charles Rosa, God rest his noble, hard-working soul), and thereafter ventured into the facility alone. You see, my mother (Ramona) has an inoperable, billiard-ball-sized cyst on her nose and simply refuses to leave the sanctuary of our modest home. Admittedly, she is at times tedious, but I promised my father (on his deathbed) that I would care for this fragile woman. So be it.

I pride myself on my honest, Christian demeanor -I recently embraced the Baptist faith-but several incidents happened at Safeway this year that make it difficult for me to sleep more than three hours nightly. My friend, a minister I will refer to as "Pete," urged me to seek forgiveness by confessing my sins to you. After several days of introspection, facilitated by long walks through several local parks and museums, I have decided to do as "Pete" suggests. So, without further ado, I shall unburden myself.

On February 22 (a Tuesday) I visited Safeway to buy a few breakfast items (cereal, jam, etc.) and a medical item. The item-and this is rather sensitive-dealt with...incontinence. As I checked several labels of promising packages, I lost my footing and began to crash earthward. Attempting to right my 350 pound frame on a shelf, I pulled roughly "six feet" of products onto the floor. But instead of confessing to security officials, I simply sneaked to the next aisle, mortified. My shame is still all-consuming.

Several weeks later, on March 4 (a Friday), I was at the incomparable Safeway produce section, retrieving bananas, and beets. I placed the aforementioned items in separate plastic bags and secured them with the convenient plastic "fasteners" provided *free of charge* by the good people of Safeway. Suddenly I decided that a fastener would prove effective as a clip for my mother's medical tubing (she has *various* maladies). Assuming the small item would never be "missed," I blithely slipped it into the pocket of my tweed blazer. I now realize I am a shoplifter. Again, the remorse is too great to ignore.

I have enclosed the (stolen) fastener but urge you to let me know the consequences of my above crimes. I'd certainly appreciate it if the police weren't notified, but I am willing to accept this eventuality. Be assured that I will diligently peruse the New Testament for strength! Your mercy is appreciated.

Seeking compassion,

Paul Rosa

Paul C. Rosa

SAFEWAY INC.
6900 S. YOSEMITE
ENGLEWOOD, CO 80112-1412
(303) 843-7600

P.O. BOX 5927 T.A.
DENVER, CO 80217

April 14, 1994

Mr. Paul C. Rosa
119 E. Espanola St.
Colorado Springs, CO 80907

Dear Mr. Rosa:

Thank you for your letter of March 19th, 1994. I have forwarded
your remarks to our Management people for their review.

We always appreciate hearing from our customers, and hope you
find on your next visit to our store that you are given the same
service as all of our customers.

The fastener you enclosed is put in the produce departments to be
used by our customers for their purchases. If they choose to use
them for other things around the house, that is great. Just
another way of recycling or re-using a product.

Thank you again, for taking the time to write. We value your
patronage and hope that we may continue to serve you with money
saving values at Safeway.

Sincerely,

Loret

Loret Babcox
Customer Service
Coordinator

cc: Marketing Operations Manager

 Recycled Paper

119 E. Espanola St.
Colo. Springs, CO 80907
April 3, 1994

Customer Letters
Russell Stover Candies, Inc.
1000 Walnut St.
Kansas City, MO 64106

Hi you guys!

My name is Paul and I am seven and in the second grade in Mrs. Willisnerson's class. Today is Easter (we learned that Jesus came back from behind a rock) and I have eaten a really good chocolate rabbit that I got yesterday. I was at a Easter egg hunt at the park with my friends Kurt, Willie, Sanchez, Tim and Gwyneth who is okay even though she is a girl. I found the egg with the big gold star on it in a tree root so I won the best chocolate prize out of all of them. It was a Russell Stover chocolate rabbit with pecans and I ate all of it in one day even though my friends but not Gwyneth shared it with me. My Uncle Sammy who was in Vietnam keeps on saying that it is really important to share so I did it even though Tim and Willie never do that for me ever. But I don't care cause I couldn't eat it all without getting sick anyway.

I usually don't write this good but my mom is helping me learn the computer and is standing right here next to me now helping me spell! She's a German lady who has been in Europe lots of times and works at a bank!! And my dad is Hungarian with a moustache! So I had some questions about the Easter bunny and others and Easter eggs so mom said I should write to you and ask you some stuff since I want to be an expert zoologist on rabbits some day and teach other people. I love the computer so I decided to send you a letter now. I just hope that you are not so busy that you don't feel like writing to me because that would make me feel bad. But you probably will, right?

Where does the Easter bunny live? I know Santa Claus lives on the north Pole, but I never learned where the Easter bunny lives! Not even my teacher knew the answer, so I figured since you make chocolate Easter bunnies you would know. I would like to write to him like I write to Santa and say that I love him!! Also, do Easter eggs come from the easter bunny or from an Easter chicken or robin or something. It's really weird that a rabbit would lay eggs isn't it? Is he married to a bird maybe or something? My last question is about that crazy Energizer battery bunny rabbit who keeps on going and going and going. Is he the same type of rabbit as the easter bunny or not? Sanchez says it is the same bunny but I think that would be too much work don't you think so? Please write quick because this was hard! Thanks! And my dad likes the Playboy bunny isn't that funny?

I love chocolate so much!!

Paul Rosa

Paul Rosa

P.S. Do you think I'm gross if I said I kind of like Gwyneth because she is nice?

1000 WALNUT STREET KANSAS CITY, MISSOURI 64106-2198
TELEPHONE (816) 842-9240

May 25, 1994

Mr. Paul Rosa
119 East Espanola Street
Colorado Springs, Colorado 80907

Dear Paul:

Thank you for your recent letter requesting information on the Easter Bunny. The Easter Bunny lives in Countryside, Illinois.

Easter eggs come from a chicken. The Easter Bunny is just the one who delivers the eggs.

The Energizer bunny is not related to the Easter Bunny, however, the Easter Bunny does have to have a lot of energy to deliver all of his eggs each Easter.

Again, thank you for writing and we hope you have many opportunities to enjoy our candies.

Sincerely,

RUSSELL STOVER CANDIES, INC.

Cheryl A. Woolley

caw

119 E. Espanola St.
Colo. Springs, CO 80907
April 5, 1994

Employment Office
Delta Airlines, Inc.
Hartsfield Atlanta International Airport
Atlanta, GA 30320

Salutations, Transporters!

The moment is at hand, friends! Since I was barely eleven I have dreamed of one day serving an established airline in the capacity of male stewardess (I believe they are known as "stewards"). Dutifully, I maintained a near-perfect (3.961) grade point average (GPA) in high school and soon matriculated at Chatoom Industrial College (C.I.C.) In seven weeks I shall graduate at the top of my class with a dual degree in Hotel/Motel Management and Consumer Affairs. Be assured, these disciplines were mastered in order to guarantee I would be viewed with reverence when applying for the aforementioned airline position. Yes, all of the hard work and dreams have paid off and I now stand on the threshold (if you will) of a lifelong commitment to airborne patrons! And that is why I am dispatching this very missive!

While my college transcripts *are* available upon request-they feature a sparkling 3.886 GPA-I felt it would be prudent to contact you with this introductory "get-to-know-me" note first. It is no secret that I have narrowed my choices to three noble airlines: Delta, United, and TWA. These folks are the front-runners in the "Rosa Sweepstakes" because of their passion and devotion to meticulous service. You see, I wouldn't *dream* of a lesser commitment, given my pride. I shall now proceed to describe myself further, thereby heightening your interest (or concerns, whichever the case may be). I appreciate the time it takes to review the credentials of a young lad such as myself. Onward (downward)!

Due to a troublesome (hereditary) glandular problem, I carry roughly 470 pounds on my five foot, six inch frame. This same genetic misfortune has saddled me with a horrific case of acne which has left my face looking not unlike (i.e. like) the surface of Mars. Finally, a severe combination of asthma and episodal vertigo (chronic dizziness) has made prolonged, strenuous exertion *extremely* inadvisable, even foolhardy. However, with the new, relaxed hiring policies concerning stewardesses and stewards, I assume my physical shortcomings will be smartly swept under the proverbial (politically-correct) rug. Aside from the effects of unpredictable bouts of stuttering and <u>mild</u> epilepsy, I have been described (by professors and relatives alike) as "cordial and efficient," the very traits needed by prospective stewards!

In summation, I am clearly interested in arranging an interview and addressing the intense competition that surely exists in this exciting field. Based on the above "factoids," can I interest the Delta folks in such a meeting? May I forward further credentials and references? Your swift reply is appreciated ("SASE" enclosed, friends!), as I hope to be joyfully employed by July. Do you have (XXL) T-shirts?

With an unfettered passion for living well,

Paul Rosa

Paul C. Rosa

Dear Applicant:

Thank you for your recent inquiry regarding employment with Delta Air Lines.

We would appreciate your completing and returning the enclosed application form. We have many qualified applicants who have expressed an interest in employment and, unfortunately, there are relatively few vacancies. However, we shall be pleased to notify you if we can offer you encouragement for employment.

Your interest in our company is warmly appreciated.

W. L. Gregory
Manager - Employment
Delta Air Lines

119 E. Espanola St.
Colo. Springs, CO 80907
June 2, 1994

W. L. Gregory, Manager of Employment
Delta Airlines, Inc.
P.O. Box 20530
Hartsfield Atlanta International Airport
Atlanta, GA 30320-2530

Dear Top Employment Executive (i.e. "Mr. or Ms. Gregory"),

First of all, what does the "W. L." in "W. L. Gregory" stand for, my friend? I've discussed the myriad of possibilities with my older sister (Kate) and we feel "Wilson Lee" is a strong possibility (if you are a man!). Since you've obviously advanced impressively in the vast Delta empire, we assumed that you would have a strong, proud name (how close were we?). I once had a chum (in Tennessee) named Wilson Gessler, but his promising young life dissolved into a series of nightmarish, drug-induced stupors. But alas, that's another story altogether and really wouldn't interest you!

I was pleased when I received the crisp packet from you a few *short* weeks after applying for a steward position in April. However, I was a bit saddened to come across the thick, tedious "Application For Employment." Not only has this particular form of "weeding out" applicants been proven primitive, but my schedule is such that a one hour (or longer) commitment to petty, inconsequential details is simply...unacceptable! In my first letter (copy enclosed), I smartly included all relevant data; enough information (I felt) to justify an interview! With a 3.886 GPA from Chatoom Industrial College (summa cum laude!), I assumed I could be "hurried" through the tedious interviewing process (including applications) and be invited to Atlanta-at once-for an interview. Last week I *graduated*, and I have been inundated with so many offers that my office looks like the far recesses of Hades itself! I understand that the "typical" applicant must be thoroughly measured (if you will) in order to separate him/her from the teeming pack but my credentials are such that this eventuality becomes (plainly) mute.

W. L., please consider me for employment without demanding that the voluminous forms you sent me be addressed! I believe the first letter I sent (along with this one) offers plenty of data to prove I should proceed to the next steps (transcripts, references, etc.). I certainly hope my various medical maladies are not daunting obstacles, but I welcome your response on this issue as well as the aforementioned one. Although Delta is my __first__ choice, I *have* received several offers from other (competing) airlines, so I encourage you to accelerate my "file" and relate the options available within the week. Positive or negative, I welcome your forthcoming decision. Lastly, how about that (XXL) T-shirt? Bless you!

Cutting through the red tape,

Paul Rosa

Paul C. Rosa

P.S. On the bottom of the application (not enclosed), it reads, "This application is not to be sold." First of all, why would anyone *buy* it when they are available at no cost? Secondly, if someone *did* wish to purchase it from me, what's the harm? Thirdly, what *does* "W.L." stand for?!!

▲ DELTA AIR LINES, INC.

EMPLOYMENT OFFICE
P.O. BOX 20530
HARTSFIELD ATLANTA INTERNATIONAL AIRPORT
ATLANTA, GEORGIA 30320-2530 U.S.A.

July 7, 1994

Mr. Paul C. Rosa
119 E. Espanola Street
Colorado Springs, Colorado 80907

Dear Mr. Rosa:

With regard to your letter of June 2, 1994, you have been advised of our
requirements to become an applicant of Delta Air Lines. It is your
decision whether you wish to comply with those requirements.

Our employment opportunities are currently limited to temporary positions
in the Customer Services Agent and Associate Reservations Sales Agent
categories in various locations across the Delta system.

Again, should you be interested in being considered for one of these
positions, please complete and return the application which was previously
mailed to you.

Thank you for contacting Delta.

Sincerely,

W. L. Gregory
Manager - Employment

WLG:lam

119 E. Espanola St.
Colo. Springs, CO 80907
April 8, 1994

Colorado Department of Transportation
4201 E. Arkansas Ave.
Denver, CO 80222

Ahoy, Mileage Moguls!

Tens of thousands of miles of free limited-access highways, toll limited-access highways, other four-lane divided highways, principal highways, other through highways, unpaved roads, and scenic routes (I'm quoting Mr. Rand McNally himself!) criss-cross this stupendous land we enjoy calling, "America!" Having traveled a great many of this nation's highways and by-ways (what *is* that?) myself, I have been consistently impressed with the matchless performance of our wonderful departments of transportation. My seven "preferences" include: Vermont, Idaho, Utah, Ohio, Colorado, Tennessee, and Michigan. As I haven't declared my *overall* "favorite," I now take great pride in naming my home state (Colorado) victorious! I've decided to have my mother (Jesse) bake the fine folks of the Colorado Department of Transportation a delicious "triumph" Sachertorte (German pastry) if the acceptance of unsolicited food is indeed allowed at your department. Is it? And now, compliments and kudos appropriately registered, I shall graduate to the "query" sections of this letter. Your patience is appreciated, good people.

Many times while traveling along in my 1982 Chevy Van (blue), I've noticed the road signs reading, "END CONSTRUCTION." This bizarre suggestion has consistently confused me! I believe "END APARTHEID" is a good sentiment, as is "END COMMUNISM," but "END CONSTRUCTION?!" Construction is a (proven!) necessary component of our diverse society and the hooligans who are espousing such fanatical views must be apprehended and incarcerated! The Department of Transportation doesn't support this radical opinion, does it? It would seem so...self-defeating as construction is clearly pivotal to the very success of your organization!!

Next, when approaching a highway "work area," I am impressed with the fact that a *worker* is inevitably displaying a "SLOW" sign. If this sign were held erect by some kind of simple "mechanical holding mechanism," (or hole!) wouldn't this save the American taxpayers considerable money? Imagine if we paid people to hold up street signs and traffic lights; that would be madness!! Also, why is the "SLOW" sign holder always (always!) a woman? In this age of equal rights, why don't men ever receive this plum of a job (i.e. clutch sign, smile at motorists, and occasionally utilize the decelerate, palms-down signal)? Does this job pay as much as the ones that require exertion? If so, I would be truly angered, friends!

Well, as I always like to keep my correspondences to one page, I will "wind down" this fact-finding missive. Please educate me on the above topics concerning pastry acceptance rules, the heinous "END CONSTRUCTION" signs and the *sexist* "SLOW" sign-grasping policy (women only?!). I look forward to your rejoinder and request an (XL) T-shirt. Bless you and keep on truckin'!

Avoiding potholes,

Paul Rosa

Paul C. Rosa

STATE OF COLORADO

DEPARTMENT OF TRANSPORTATION

4201 East Arkansas Avenue
Denver, Colorado 80222
(303) 757-9011

May 5, 1994

Mr. Paul C. Rosa
119 E. Espanola St.
Colorado Springs, CO 80907

Dear Mr. Rosa:

Thank you for your letter, regarding the issues of "End Construction" signs, a mechanism for holding and turning the stop/slow signs and the gender of the individuals turning these devices.

The "End Construction" sign is a mandatory sign required at the end of construction projects. This device is used to indicate the termination of a work zone. This traffic control device is required by the national standard for all traffic control devices otherwise known as the Manual on Traffic Control Devices. This manual has recently been changed to provide for a more descriptive message. The new message will read "END/ROAD WORK". This new design is optional depending upon the complexity of the project, as well as the length of time the project will be active and is used at the discretion of the engineer.

The role of the flag person is often misunderstood. The flagger's job is critical - the safety of the motorist and the construction/ maintenance crew depend on the conscientiousness and quick thinking of the flagger. Flag people get the heavy equipment in and out of the construction zone safely and are often responsible for the flow of the traffic through the work zone. For these reasons we require that all flaggers in Colorado be trained and certified.

Related to the last item, you asked why the gender of the flag people is always female. Well, believe it or not, there are male flaggers as well. I can't tell you why all of the flag people you have seen are women but you can rest assured that there are male flaggers and we don't have any requirements that limit this job to women.

Thank you for your letter and positive comments. As for your offer of Sachertorte, it sounds wonderful, but being the weight conscious person that I am, I must decline the offer. Thanks again!

Sincerely,

Dan Hopkins, Director
Office of Public and
Intergovernmental Relations

119 E. Espanola St.
Colo. Springs, CO 80907
April 10, 1994

Consumer Affairs
The U.S. Playing Card Co.
P.O. Box 12126
Cincinnati, OH 45212

Dear "Card Sharks,"

I began playing cards when my older brother, Jesse, was sent to Vietnam in the summer of 1968. My family, never ones to openly discuss stressful situations, chose instead to immerse themselves fully in (as Mother used to say) "busy-bee activities." Our unofficial motto seemed to be: "Keep your mind occupied and things will *seem* somewhat better." Well, I adhered to this questionable philosophy-I was only a small lad-and spent countless hours playing Hearts, Bridge, Poker, and the like, as we anxiously awaited news from "the front." Thankfully, Jesse returned with only a few bumps and bruises and proceeded to carve out a lucrative career as a fine-luggage salesman in southern Louisiana.

Perhaps card-playing *isn't* always the best way to handle such trying situations, but it's certainly preferred to chronic nail-biting or even anti-social behavior (graffiti, loitering, littering, etc.)! So, my helpful confidants, your product has consistently (then and now) served to ease my occasionally-troubled mind. As The U.S. Playing Card Co. has played (get it, ha, ha?) such a *huge* part in the passion play (there it is again!) which was/is my life, it amazes me that I've never written to you. Well, I'm remedying that transgression now, so please be patient if my queries prove somewhat numerous!

Here we go! What does the "U.S." in your company name stand for? My sister (Jenny) insists that it stands for "undoing stress," but she has been tested at a paltry 85 I.Q. (Intelligence Quotient), so her findings must be treated with kid gloves! Next, what is a "Jack?" It seems that a "King" and "Queen" should be followed by a "Prince," not a "Jack!" The fellow often *looks* like a prince but he's always referred to as a "Jack!" What gives, folks?! Was there a "Prince Jack" somewhere, perhaps Sweden? Thirdly, when a "wise-acre" is labeled a "card," I often wonder what the origin of this expression is! Perhaps you can shed some light on this anomaly! Finally (and fourthly), as a Geometry teacher (tenth grade), I wish to encourage you to start printing playing cards on shapes other than the rectangular variety. I believe that some towel manufacturers will soon begin producing triangular and pentagonal-shaped offerings to encourage math excellence in teenagers. Do you think you can "chip in" as well? Alas, I fully recognize how busy you must be, so I'll stop the inquest here and now!

I am enclosing a convenient self-addressed, stamped envelope ("S-aSE"), and encourage you to respond at your earliest convenience (soon, I hope!). As I have been using your cards for twenty-six years, I believe your rejoinder will feel like...a letter from a friend! Thank you, God bless, and eat well, friends!

With a trip to Las Vegas planned,

Paul Rosa

Paul C. Rosa

119 E. Espanola St.
Colo. Springs, CO 80907
April 10, 1994

Consumer Affairs
The U.S. Playing Card Co.
P.O. Box 12126
Cincinnati, OH 45212

Dear "Card Sharks,"

I began playing cards when my older brother, Jesse, was sent to Vietnam in the summer of 1968. My family, never ones to openly discuss stressful situations, chose instead to immerse themselves fully in (as Mother used to say) "busy-bee activities." Our unofficial motto seemed to be: "Keep your mind occupied and things will *seem* somewhat better." Well, I adhered to this questionable philosophy-I was only a small lad-and spent countless hours playing Hearts, Bridge, Poker, and the like, as we anxiously awaited news from "the front." Thankfully, Jesse returned with only a few bumps and bruises and proceeded to carve out a lucrative career as a fine-luggage salesman in southern Louisiana.

Perhaps card-playing *isn't* always the best way to handle such trying situations, but it's certainly preferred to chronic nail-biting or even anti-social behavior (graffiti, loitering, littering, etc.)! So, my helpful confidants, your product has consistently (then and now) served to ease my occasionally-troubled mind. As The U.S. Playing Card Co. has played (get it, ha, ha?) such a *huge* part in the passion play (there it is again!) which was/is my life, it amazes me that I've never written to you. Well, I'm remedying that transgression now, so please be patient if my queries prove somewhat numerous!

United States

Here we go! What does the "U.S." in your company name stand for? My sister (Jenny) insists that it stands for "undoing stress," but she has been tested at a paltry 85 I.Q. (Intelligence Quotient), so her findings must be treated with kid gloves! Next, what is a "Jack?" It seems that a "King" and "Queen" should be followed by a "Prince," not a "Jack!" The fellow often *looks* like a prince but he's always referred to as a "Jack!" What gives, folks?! Was there a "Prince Jack" somewhere, perhaps Sweden? Thirdly, when a "wise-acre" is labeled a "card," I often wonder what the origin of this expression is! Perhaps you can shed some light on this anomaly! Finally (and fourthly), as a Geometry teacher (tenth grade), I wish to encourage you to start printing playing cards on shapes other than the rectangular variety. I believe that some towel manufacturers will soon begin producing triangular and pentagonal-shaped offerings to encourage math excellence in teenagers. Do you think you can "chip in" as well? Alas, I fully recognize how busy you must be, so I'll stop the inquest here and now!

I am enclosing a convenient self-addressed, stamped envelope ("S-aSE"), and encourage you to respond at your earliest convenience (soon, I hope!). As I have been using your cards for twenty-six years, I believe your rejoinder will feel like...a letter from a friend! Thank you, God bless, and eat well, friends!

With a trip to Las Vegas planned,

Paul Rosa

Paul C. Rosa

A BRIEF HISTORY OF PLAYING CARDS

Playing cards as we know them today have a documented history of over 600 years! One of the earliest mentions of them is noted in the treasury records of Charles VI of France, authorizing the payment of 56 sols to the painter Gringonneur, for the illumination of three decks for the amusement of the king. The date of this record was 1392, before the invention of printing.

We can only guess that cards were invented in China, where paper was invented. European cards appear to have been invented in Italy in the form we know as a tarot deck, containing 78 cards: 22 trump cards with symbolic designs and 56 number cards which included four court cards, king, queen, mounted knight and page.

Being hand-painted of course meant that these early cards were limited only to those who could afford this luxury. With the invention of printing in the 1400's, Germans began to produce cards for the masses. The Germans were the first to change the suits from the Italian swords, batons, cups and coins, using leaves, acorns, (falcon) bells and hearts instead.

Also in the 1400's the French designed their own deck, and it is from these early French cards that our own cards today are derived. The French discarded the 22 trump cards of the tarot deck, combined the knight and page into a single card, our jack, making 52 cards. At the same time, they designed the suits we use today: hearts, clubs, diamonds and spades. They also simplified the suit symbols into a flat, simple design using only two colors, red and black, thus speeding up the printing process.

It is important to remember that these were the Middle Ages, days of knights in shining armor. The court cards represent the heroes of the time and the very use of court cards, kings, queens and knights, reflects society as it was then recognized. The four suits, regardless of which set of symbols is used, reflect the structure of medieval society: hearts (cups or chalices) represent the church; spades (swords), the military; diamonds (coins) the merchant class, and clubs (batons), agriculture, which was the basis of medieval life.

The French identified their court cards, printing the names on the cards.

The king of spades is David. On French cards he holds a harp referring to the Psalms which he wrote. On English cards he carries a large sword belonging to Goliath whom he slew.

The king of hearts is Charlemagne and he swings a sword over his head.

The king of diamonds is Julius Caesar who carries a battle-axe. He is shown in profile because his appearance was known only from coins which were struck during his lifetime.

The king of clubs is Alexander the Great. He holds an orb, symbol of the world that he conquered.

The four kings represent the four civilizations which made up the Western culture: the Hebrews, the Holy Roman Empire, the Romans and the Greeks.

Page 2

The queen of spades is Pallas Athena, Greek goddess of wisdom and war. She is the only armed queen.

The queen of hearts is Judith of Bavaria, daughter-in-law of Charlemagne, married to his eldest son, Pippen.

The queen of diamonds is Rachel, wife of Jacob and mother of the twelve sons who founded the Twelve Tribes of Israel.

The queen of clubs is Argine, considered to be an anagram for the word "regina" or "queen".

The jack of spades is Hogier, a Dane and knight of Charlemagne. In early single-ended cards, he had a dog at his heels for he was patron of the chase. He carried a halberd or large sword on French cards, a marriott or beribboned pike on English cares. He is shown in profile.

The jack of hearts is "La Hire" whose name was Stephan de Vignoles, a knight in the court of Charles VII. He carried a battle axe surrounded by "faces", a symbol of authority.

The identity of the jack of diamonds is less definite. Some early decks identified him as Roland, while later ones identified him as Hector. He carries a "Welsh hook" or weapon.

The jack of clubs is Lancelot, chief knight of King Arthur's Round Table.

Although the identity of the court cards and the general design was the same, each area of France had its own design variations which helped the government levy taxes on the cards.

English royalty and her soldiers alike spent much time in France, where they learned about cards. At first, not manufacturing paper themselves, the English imported cards from France, Rouen being the closest source. When they began to manufacture cards themselves, the designs were based on French models, though the English imposed their own personality on these cards. The English kings are dressed in the costume of Henry VIII, while the queens are in the dress of his mother, Elizabeth of York. The Yorks were fighting the Lancasters in the War of Roses: a white rose was the symbol of the Yorks and a red rose for the Lancasters. Elizabeth of York married Henry of Lancaster, bringing an end to the War of Roses.. Henry then became King Henry VII of England, father of Henry VIII. The bi-colored roses held by the queens symbolize the end of this war.

The jacks are dressed as the Squire who is described in Chaucer's Canterbury Tales. English decks kept the French names though not printing them on the cards...everyone knew who they were!

Early printing techniques limited the design of cards. Those wood block designs from the 15th century are therfore strong, dynamic, proud to proclaim popular heroes. The designs have changed very little through the ages, refined only by technical improvements. Card players are a superstitious lot and are reluctant to change anything which might interfere with their luck! Although there are isolated examples of double-ended cards earlier, they did not become acceptable until the middle of the 19th century. At about the same time, experiments were made with ways to index cards: miniature cards in the corners, numbers and suit signs running around the borders, and

Page 3

finally, the index system found on today's cards was accepted.

From time to time, different cards have been tried, suit signs changed, new color systems introduced, but none ever were successful. Attempts were made several times to eliminate the royal reference, after both the French and American revolutions, for instance. In war time, patriotic themes have been introduced with limited appeal. In the year 1502, a German scholar, Thomas Murner, was able to introduce the only successful deviation from the normal deck. He designed a deck of cards to help his university students understand and thus learn, a difficult lesson in logic. Although he was nearly burned at the stake for being a heretic, Murner's students were successful and so were his cards. Especially popular during repressive regimes or religeous restirctions, educational playing cards have never ceased being popular.

It is hoped that this brief history will pique your curiosity and encourage you to look farther into the fascinating history of playing cards. The Playing Card Museum, a public service of The United States Playing Card Co., has the world's largest collection of antique playing cards, going back to the late 15th century. Please check for museum hours. (513-396-5700 or 513-396-5731).

119 E. Espanola St.
Colo. Springs, CO 80907
April 25, 1994

Kleenex Tissues
Kimberly-Clark Corporation
Dept. MFT, P.O. Box 2020
Neenah, WI 54957

Dear Nose Pals,

A handful of product brands are so special, so lofty (if you will) that their very <u>names</u> are synonymous with the products themselves! Band-Aids (adhesive bandages), Xerox (duplicating machines), and Chap Stick (lip balm) are a few obvious examples of which I speak, but any sane discussion of this sociological phenomenon must begin with the "Grand-Daddy" of them all...**KLEENEX** (tissues)!!!!! When an unfortunate "patient" requires something with which to wipe/blow his/her oozing proboscis, they invariably utter the line that has been heard for (literally) decades: "Hand me a *Kleenex*, won't you?" You see, when you desire the best, you must ask for it by <u>name</u>. This explains the unprecedented success of the above products (Band-Aids, Xerox, Chap Stick, and, of course, Kleenex)! God bless you folks for making the life of an allergy-sufferer a bit more bearable. That's right, "***GOD*** <u>BLESS YOU</u>!!!" Perhaps it's not "fashionable" to be religious in these permissive times, but to that I say, "pish posh!" The Lord governs me and I'm proud of that!

And now it's time to graduate to the gist of this memorandum, as I realize how arduous your schedules must be! I would guess that a fifty or sixty-hour work week is commonplace for the employees of the number one "nose comfort" suppliers in the nation (perhaps the world), and I have often dreamed of toiling tirelessly as a chemist in a Kimberly-Clark laboratory. Sadly though, my high school grades were unimpressive (2.67 GPA), and I was expelled from college (in Ohio) for (stupidly) burglarizing a mineral sciences exhibit, so the dream shall remain just that. However, I've become a truly productive citizen-I've embraced yoga-and continue to "idolize" your firm! But alas, the aforementioned "gist" of this note remains undelivered, so paragraph three shall serve to right this wrong! Again, God bless you!

Ten to twenty times weekly, I blithely toss a used Kleenex into the various metal canisters (i.e. "trash receptacles") in one of the corners of <u>each</u> of the seven rooms of my rental property. Recently I began wondering if this "nose broth" had any *practical* uses or should simply be considered "waste," along with saliva, sweat, urine...I think you get my point, friends. As a fervent recycler, I have fantasized of using the aforementioned fluid as an ingredient in a hair conditioner or even as a skin cream (creme?) additive. I have an impressive chemistry set in my basement, but felt it would be prudent to consult the experts before wasting any precious time! I look forward to your (fleet!!) reply, and, perhaps, a souvenir (XL) T-shirt. Thank you, keep up the fine work, and (of course) God bless you!

Interested in science,

Paul Rosa

Paul C. Rosa

✝ (He died for our sins!!) ✝

⊕ Kimberly-Clark   **Consumer Services**

May 13, 1994

Mr. Paul C. Rosa
119 E. Espanola Street
Colorado Springs, CO 80907

Dear Mr. Rosa:

Thank you for contacting us about KLEENEX® facial tissue. It is always
nice to hear from a loyal customer, and we appreciate the opportunity
to respond.

Over the years, we have conducted research on many issues involving
facial tissue. However, we are unaware of any practical use for "nose
broth" and have not researched this particular subject. I am sorry we
cannot be more helpful.

We value you as a customer and hope you will continue to use our
KLEENEX tissue. Please accept the enclosed coupons as our way of
thanking you for your interest in our product.

Sincerely,

Joyce M. Drace

Joyce M. Drace
Consumer Representative

JMD/cl

1477817A

119 E. Espanola St.
Colo. Springs, CO 80907
May 9, 1994

Customer Affairs People
Scrabble Board Game
Milton Bradley Co.
443 Shaker Rd.
East Longmeadow, MA 01028

Dear Word Experts,

I will try to get straight to the point because I probably know how busy you executives there can be! I am now 32 years of age (I'm a Scorpio), and me and my family have been playing Scrabble regular since I was a small fella here in Colorado. No one in my family has ever made it to college, but we still try to practice our words by reading a lot (I like them romance novels) and playing Scrabble each and every Sunday night at my Aunt Irene's on the west side. It's always real fun because the game is usually very close and sometimes we even order a pizza and hope the Domino's delivery person takes a long time so's we can get a $3.00 discount. The people who usually play are me, my sister (Jesse), my mom (Agnes), my aunt (Irene) and my uncle (Phil). My daddy left home when I was seven, so he doesn't play of course. But now I need to tell you why I'm writing cause I don't want to waste your time anymore!

The problem to us is Phil. He doesn't play every week (maybe two out of three), but when he does, he does something I think is illegal in the game but I'm not sure. Phil has a real bad stuttering problem so he talks different than the rest of us players do and thinks he should get special priviliges! Yesterday he used three straight P's in one word (on a triple word score!) cause he sometimes says P-P-Park instead of Park like the rest of us do. He says if that's the way he says it, that's the way he spells it! I think once he used Q-Quiz on a double letter score and got about a million points!! My family about killed him when he did that, but we really weren't sure of the rules ourselves! That's the main reason I am writing to you nice folks. Who is right, Phil or the rest of us who are angry? Whatever you say, we agreed to let you be the tiebreakers of the fight, so who wins?!

Lastly, I don't know if you are the ones who make Trivial Pursuit too, but I had a really funny dream last week. First of all, my family is really bad at that game and can hardly get any of the answers, but we try hard and have fun just the same! Anyways, my dream was that I was playing Trivial Pursuit with God and that Alfred Einstein fella. It was really frustrating and funny cause they were getting all the answers really quick and I just stood there looking foolish and all. When I woke up to go to work at the lumber yard, I was real releived and started laughing. My sister thought I'd about gone nuts.

So if you do make Trivial Pursuit tell me what you think of my dream! Maybe you can use it on TV! But whatever you do, please answer the rule about Phil's stuttering. We're getting real tired of his ways! Also, my buddy (Ned) is here clammoring for an (XL) T-shirt if you got an extra. God bless all of you!

I try to read a book each month!

Paul Rosa

Paul C. Rosa

MILTON BRADLEY COMPANY
A DIVISION OF HASBRO, INC.

SINCE 1860

May 13, 1994

Paul C. Rosa
119 East Espanola Street
Colorado Springs, CO 80907

Dear Mr. Rosa:

Thank you for your letter of May 9th regarding Scrabble. I will be glad to answer your question about the game rules.

All words used in Scrabble play must be real words and must be spelled correctly. For spelling verification any standard dictionary will do. If a player stutters, the words he plays would still be spelled the same as those used by a non-stutter. Referring to your example, the word "pppark" is not a real word and if challenged by another player, would be removed from the board and the player would lose their turn. Remember, phonetic spelling and correct spelling are two different issues and in Scrabble correct spelling is what wins games.

I hope this information will help resolve any controversy among your co-players and that you will all continue to enjoy playing Scrabble.

Sincerely yours,

D. K. Wood
Consumer Services Coordinator

ps: Trivial Pursuit is manufactured by Parker Brothers of Beverly, Massachusetts (508-927-7600).

119 E. Espanola St.
Colo. Springs, CO 80907
May 15, 1994

Consumer Department and Question Section
Lite Beer from Miller
3939 West Highland Blvd.
Milwaukee, WI 53201-8322

Dear Brew Masters,

Another weekend has just gone by and I have drunk another delicious case (almost!) of your great, great beer! This was a really good weekend cause there was lots of basketball on the boob box! I watched the Houston Rockets and the Atlanta Hawks and the Chicago Bulls and the Utah Jazz and the Denver Nuggets and a bunch of other exiting teams run all over the place dunking the ball. I can't hardly believe how quick and strong some of those guys are and I like to drink a lot of beer when I watch the sports on television. My family (wife, Shelby and kids, Danny, Rupert, Casey, Sarah, Priscilla, Felix, and our adopted daughter from Korea, Kwan Li) and I barbeqed on Saturday night and I must've had about eight beers in the back yard there alone!! It's delicious stuff, damn it!!!! I didn't mean to cuss.

I've been drinking Lite Beer since the 1980s when you had those hystericall funny commercials where those old timer athletes would holler at each other over and over and over again, "Tastes great!! Less Filling!! Tastes great!! Less Filling!!" It would go on and on and me and my friends would be on the floor laughing and rolling at those great old athletes like Dick Butkus and those guys. That was some funny stuff alright!! And nowadays you have those great commercials where folks are watching sports on TV and can't agree on which one to watch so someone will wack the TV with a beer bottle and suddenly the two sports are together as one (like sumo diving or luge bowling)! Now that is some funny stuff my good friends. I can't understand why people laugh at that Woody Allen or David Letterman when you guys have the funnyest stuff on the air today. Or ANY day. Your commercial making team must be a hoot to hang around with, always cracking up and stuff.

Although your beer is the best on earth including Germany, I do have a small complaint about the beer itself in your cans. Whenever I open a can of Lite the beer on top is really cold and good the way I like it!! But in the middle of the can the beer is always not as cold but still tastes good. When I get to the bottom of a can the liquid down there is always kinda warm and not as good!!!! Why can't you make the beer <u>all over</u> the can really cold or at least mix it better so's the temprature is the same all the way through?!! It makes me sad when the bottom tastes not cold enough after I really enjoyed the beginning of the can! Now I'm gonna give you all one of those prestamped envelopes and would like an answer if you have the time! And finally please send a huge tshirt for my oldest boy, Danny. Thanks!

It is Miller time!!!

Paul Rosa

Paul C. Rosa

MILLER BREWING COMPANY

July 18, 1994

Mr. Paul C. Rosa
119 E. Espanola St.
Colorado Springs, CO 80907

Dear Mr. Rosa:

Thank you for your letter praising our Miller Lite beer.

We enjoy receiving complimentary comments about our products, and hope
you remain a satisfied customer for many years to come. Consumers, like
yourself, have helped to make us one of America's leading breweries.

Regarding your beer getting cold by the time you get to the middle of the can,
there is nothing that we could do in the manufacturing of our products to
remedy this situation.   However, I am enclosing a promotional items catalog
which features many different can wraps which are specially designed for the
purpose of keeping a beverage cold. Possibly you may want to try purchasing
one of those. They are on pages 55, 57, 105, 108 and 120.

If your travels should ever bring you to Milwaukee, please make plans to take
a tour which includes our world famous caves and enjoy some beverages in
our Miller Inn.

As a token of our appreciation for taking the time to write, please accept the
enclosed gift.

Yours truly,

Ruth A. Harmon
Consumer Affairs Representative

Enclosures

119 E. Espanola St.
Colo. Springs, CO 80907
May 22, 1994

Consumer Outrage
Crouch Fire & Safety Products, Inc. (Formerly the Fyr-Fyter Co.)
415 Warren St.
Dayton, OH 45402

Dear Flame Failures,

Fire. It's not always a pleasant word. It's not always a (quote, unquote) *good* word. But each and every one of us-from the smallest child to the most jaded adult-should agree it is a *powerful* word! Undeniably, fire can do much good-witness the benefits of heat, light, and cooking possibilities. And a romantic evening by the fireplace (with one's "sweety") is truly a way to fan the flames (excuse my wordplay) of a stalled relationship! But alas, this same wonderful "force of God" can also be the harbinger of unfathomable despair, evil, and distress; the devil's work, if you will. And I was the victim of a dose of this anguish one night last October. But perhaps it's best to first construct the foundation, the infrastructure, of my epistle before I proceed. As a senior citizen, I *am* patient. And thorough.

Thirty-seven years ago I was living serenely with my wife (Kapa) and my small son (he was two). As a Hungarian immigrant (having escaped Communist rule), I worked proudly in the factory of a local jelly canner by day, baking fresh pasta by night. No, it wasn't a lot of money, but along with Kapa's income from her award-winning knitting projects, we managed to eke out a comfortable existence. Inspired by love for my young family, I decided-in August of 1957-to invest some hard-earned wages in "fire protection." I purchased one of your massive fire extinguishers at a local hardware store (it shall remain nameless for litigation purposes). Having this device in my home allowed me to sleep soundly at night (seldom during the day), as I assumed any and all fires would be...manageable. All was well for many years (my son graduated from Yale in 1976), but one day, almost four decades later, "it" happened.

Last October I was woken by my barking, six-year-old Schnauzer (Jess), who "urged" me to follow him! After irritably donning my slippers and stumbling downstairs, I learned that my smoke detector had failed to warn me in any manner whatsoever, as my kitchen was frightfully ablaze (it pains me to tell this story over and over again)! Naturally, I remembered the fire extinguisher, retrieving it from a lower shelf in my attic study, where it had stood, <u>untouched</u> for all these many years. Dashing back downstairs, I was shocked to realize the flames were *now* licking the kitchen ceiling! Without further hesitation, I hurled your "Fyr-Fyter Instant Loaded Stream Anti-Freeze Fire Extinguisher (U.S. Patent No. 1,976,056)" <u>directly</u> into the very core of the flames. "Sweet Jesus!" I then bellowed, realizing the product was doing nothing to control the blaze!! The fire department soon arrived, but not before I lost several valuable Peruvian artifacts and a priceless collection of Hungarian mementos. Why your extinguisher did not perform as designed has confused and enraged me for many months now!!! This is why I write.

I simply refuse to run off to a lawyer every time I feel slighted, so I offer you the chance to defend your product and return a missive in the enclosed, fully-prepared "SASE." Please respond promptly!

Hot under the collar,

Paul Rosa

Paul C. Rosa

JOHN T. CROUCH CO.

Fire + Safety Products, Inc.

June 27, 1994

Mr. Paul C. Rosa
119 East Espanola Street
Colorado Springs, Colorado 80907

Dear Mr. Rosa:

Your letter requesting information on old, obsolete,
Fyr-Fyter Co. products has reached our company as we are
perceived locally as being the only remaining connection with
the defunct Fyr-Fyter Manufacturing organization originally
headquartered here in Dayton until the mid-1960's.

A brief explination of that connection is that our non-
manufacturing wholesale/retail distributorship was first
established as the Fyr-Fyter Products Co. following WW II by
John T. Crouch Jr. operating as a primary local distribution
outlet for Fyr-Fyter Mfg. At that time, Mr. Crouch's function
was to assist in developing a distributor marketing program
for Fyr-Fyter manufactured products. As Fyr-Fyter Mfg. became
more diversified, Mr. Crouch, for whatever reason, became
dissatisfied with existing arrangements. Although still
representing Fyr-Fyter, he broke away from being a captive
distribution outlet adding many other lines of fire protection
equipment, fire fighter's gear, paramedic, rescue, emergency
lights & sirens and workplace safety supplies.

In the mid-1960's, Fyr-Fyter Mfg. was purchased by Norris
Industries. The plant in Dayton was closed and all operations
were moved to Newark, N.J.. From that point on until 1977-78,
various of it's divisions were sold-off until nothing was left.
Manufacture of Fyr-Fyter Brand products, finally ceased in mid-
1978.

We extend our regrets and sympathy for the unfortunate
house-fire experience your well-written letter described.Beyond
this sincere expression, and in view of the information provided,
we can offer no surmise as to the exact nature of your difficulty
with the near antique Fyr-Fyter "Instant".

Kindest regards,

Rich Oxley, Co-Owner &
Chief Operating Officer

415 Warren Street • Dayton, Ohio 45402-2894
Phone (513) 223-8801 • 1-800-837-8801 • FAX: (513) 223-4282

119 E. Espanola St.
Colo. Springs, CO 80907
May 22, 1994

Consumer Section
AutoZone
3030 Poplar Ave.
Memphis, TN 38111

Dear Car Buffs,

As the proud owner of southern Colorado's largest dealer of used ("Pre-Owned" we like to say!) medium-sized, American automobiles, I make it my <u>business</u> to be acquainted with all of the local "car parts" dealers! Oh yes, there's Checker, NAPA, Champion, Western, and *then* there's AutoZone! As there is little discernable difference in quality among the Big 5 (as I mischievously like to call them), I've decided to let television commercials be the tie-breaker! But perhaps some history is in order, friends!

I was born in the south-western part of Finland, emigrating to the states (United) with my loving parents, Gunner and Eva Rojsavajuk, and my retarded sister, Nijka, in the autumn of 1957. For convenience reasons, my father shortened the family name to "Rosa," and he soon began laboring in and around the shipping docks of Pittsburgh, PA. Dad built a comfortable life for his family in the suburbs and I was soon surrounded with many fun-loving, diverse friends (Tip, Wing-Lee, Kurt, Jesse, Naomi, Raftsakan, and Cap). Many a summer were spent playing wiffle-ball and collecting toy cars (hot wheels, etc.) and here my love for automobiles was born. I soon owned a classic Ford Mustang which I returned to its original, mint condition. Graduating from Sansterman Technical College with a degree in Mechanical Engineering, I moved to Colorado and began building the biggest (aforementioned) dealer of its kind in the area! However, why don't we pick it up where we left it at the end of the first paragraph?

Your splendid, warm-hearted commercials are "head and shoulders" above the paltry offerings of your competitors, so I've declared you the winners of my patriotic little contest! In particular, I enjoy your advertisement featuring "the campers." The heavy man regales his companions (around the campfire) by <u>thoroughly</u> explaining how an AutoZone employee (admirably) talked him out of buying a battery by revealing the true, less-expensive problem area. As an avid outdoorsman, I appreciate a warm-hearted, story told in the wilds!! Those men (needless to say) are hanging on his every word!! I also love your offering featuring the thin, balding chap who concludes the sales pitch (to the lovely strains of a hidden acoustic guitar) with something like this: "When folks come to AutoZone, well...that's how we make *friends*." Then he smiles warmly, ear to ear. So few corporations seem interested in making friends, and I am delighted that you choose to "buck the trend!" A third "spot," featuring a slim gal, cleverly explains, "Some customers just want to come in, pick up what they want, and <u>get out</u>." How very true!!!

Anyway, a great deal of business is (justifiably) coming your way, my creative friends! Please send the complete story behind your <u>brilliant</u> commercial campaign and an (XL) T-shirt. Bless you (and such)!

Appreciating genuine warmth,

Paul Rosa

Paul C. Rosa

P.O. Box 2198, Memphis, TN 38101-9842 / (901) 325-4600

Paul C. Rosa   June 29, 1994
119 E. Espanola Street
Colorado Springs, CO 80907

Dear Paul,

Thank you for the wonderful letter about our company. It was an absolute joy to read, and I apologize for not getting back to you sooner. I am happy to hear that our advertising has made such a favorable impression on you, and I hope AutoZone continues to deliver the kind of service that will exceed your expectations. Please accept the enclosed T-shirt as a token of our appreciation.

As far as the story behind our TV campaign goes, I'm sorry to say that it is probably not as interesting as you might think. But here goes. . . . AutoZone has a history of developing projects and systems "in-house"; just as we locate potential sites, design and merchandise the stores, develop our own electronic parts catalog, and so on, we also create our own television advertising.

We typically spend three to six months kicking around story ideas that we hope will communicate an honest and warm feeling about AutoZone. Once we are comfortable with the story, we then try to create a setting that will allow the story to be told in a relaxed, sincere manner—i.e. "Hey, maybe we just have a bunch of guys sitting around a campfire telling stories. . . ." We then just have to find actors who are good story tellers, and who seem to be friendly, likeable personalities who are representative of AutoZone and of our customers. We give them the script and a bit of license to tell it in their own words. Most of the people who have speaking parts are hired actors, and most of the background people are actual AutoZoners, family members and friends.

For various reasons, we have had to film the commercials in several different locations—Arizona, Tennessee, Florida, Utah, Colorado, Illinois, Indiana—to name a few. And obviously, we can't close the stores down to film the interior scenes, so we film the store shots during the night. Once we've got all the scenes on film, we spend a week or two editing, add a little original music and sound effects and *presto!* we've got another TV spot.

It may not be as dramatic or glamorous as you hoped, but all in all it's a fun, rewarding process. And when letters come in like yours, the feeling is all the more meaningful. Again, Paul, thank you very much for your kind words.

Sincerely yours,

Dean Rose
Vice President, Advertising
Customer Satisfaction
AutoZone

THE BEST PARTS IN AUTO PARTS

119 E. Espanola St.
Colo. Springs, CO 80907
June 1, 1994

Buyer Complaint Department
Johnson Wax -Shout Power Stick Product
S.C. Johnson & Son, Inc.
1525 Howe
Racine, WI 53403

Hello Complaint Department there,

Sometimes I work sixteen hours in the day, tending my cattle and making sure my fields are mantained proper. I'm still a young man (33 this November, a Scorpio) so's I can work almost nonstop without taking a break, just like my daddy before me and his daddy before that. I've got me some polled herefords (cattle) and some prize winning vegetables so I know that hard work is the best way to getting good results. My wife (Sarah Anne) and my four kids (Jason, Trent, Becky Lee, and Kimba) are treated right and there's always a hot meal on the table for them. I think I'm a pretty good daddy cause I always treat em' fairly and hardly hit em' at all unless they do something really bad (Trent set fire to the shed last year!). And when I'm working so hard, I don't worry about sweating and feeling clean and stuff like that. No, hard work and being clean smellin just doesn't go together in this neck of the woods, my friends. In many ways this is still cowboy country and we keep our work and socalizing seprate! But now I'll get to the point I been trying to make to you. You see, I don't do to much writing but I do my best anyways!!

When I take a break from workin (nights usually and a few holidays) I like to put on my clean trousers and a fresh shirt. But first I like to take a long, hot bath and shampoo my hair with that good head and shoulders soap. I then shave with my electric razor, brush my teeth (Crest) and put on the underarm cream. I like to shop around for good deals on this and also try new products to see what's working the best and I've already tried Arrid and Sure and Rightguard and Mennen. The other day I saw your Shout product on the grocer's shelves (Shout it out! it said) and thought what the hell why not give it a chance too! This past Saturday after my usual hot bath with shaving and tooth brushing, I rolled some of your product under my armpits there. It went on smooth but didn't feel right and smelled too lemony like some sort of detergent or something!! After awhile my underarms got to hurting and feeling like it was burning me!! I didn't have no cuts or nothin so it didn't make no sense to me so I thought it would be best to write and complain to you folks in Wisconsin who make this product!!

Please let me know if there have been some other bad Shout rollons reported by other folks and answer me what could have happened to me. If I hadn'tve washed that stuff off quickly it would have felt even more awful and stinging!! I'll put in an envelope to make it easy to answer and my son (Jason) is now asking for a super large tshirt if you got any in your werehouse. Thanks for writing quick!

My uncle served in Korea,

Paul Rosa

Paul C. Rosa

S.C. Johnson & Son, Inc.
1525 Howe Street
Racine, WI 53403-5011
Phone: (414) 631-2000

June 28, 1994

Mr. Paul Rosa
119 E. Espanola Street
Colorado Springs, CO 80907

Dear Mr. Rosa:

Thank you for contacting us about SHOUT Stick Laundry Stain Remover.

We'd like you to know that SHOUT Stick Laundry Stain Remover has been formulated, designed and tested only for those uses described on the label. We hope you'll understand that we are unable to recommend using it the way you described.

The guiding philosophy of SC Johnson Wax has always been to market products that are superior to those of our competitors. When our products are used according to label directions, we hope our high standards will be quickly recognized by consumers.

To show our appreciation, some coupons are enclosed. If we can be of help in the future, feel free to contact us again.

Sincerely,

Janice Brown
Consumer Specialist

File reference: 1193574

119 E. Espanola St.
Colo. Springs, CO 80907
June 13, 1994

New Patient Questions and Issues
American Society of Plastic and Reconstructive Surgeons, Inc.
444 E. Algonquin Rd.
Arlington Heights, IL 60005

Dear Face Molders,

"Vulcan Boy," "Dumbo," "Cobra Kid," even "Bat Child"...I've been called everything! You name the indignity, I've suffered it. Ever since I was a homely lad in Pueblo, CO (pop. 99,822), a disfigured head has made my existence a living hell. One can argue that it is society's tragic prejudices that make life unbearable for me, but that doesn't seem to "lighten my load." After hiding inside my home for the past five years, I've decided enough is enough. Working as a semi-successful Romance novelist -you may have heard of "Sweet Submission"- and having all of my necessities delivered has allowed me to remain completely secluded. But it's time to end this self-imposed hibernation. That's where you come in, miracle workers!

I have attached (below) a weathered, xeroxed copy of the last photograph taken of me (in 1986, when I was sixteen). As you can see, there is considerable room for improvement, my friends. My ears are a colossal seven inches in diameter, my mouth (agape in its natural position) is occupied by numerous sharp "fangs," my eyes are frighteningly "owl-like," and my scalp is completely hairless. My parents aren't exactly fetching, but there's simply no explanation for *my* lot in life. And I want it changed!

Based on the aforementioned picture, I would like information provided on the help available to me. **Please don't merely send me a "list of local physicians," as I would *first* like to know if your industry has (or has not) successfully tackled cases as daunting as mine!!** Cursed with a shrill, whiny, almost indecipherable voice, I have chosen never to use my phone (except for emergencies), so I would appreciate a prompt return <u>letter</u>. A convenient, self-addressed, stamped envelope (CSASE) is enclosed. Please "inject my life with hope" by responding quickly, my friends. Finally, please send an (XL) T-shirt.

I've got nice skin though!

Paul Rosa

Paul C. Rosa

AMERICAN SOCIETY OF
PLASTIC AND RECONSTRUCTIVE
SURGEONS

PSIS — Plastic Surgery Information Service

FOR INFORMATION
CONTACT:
DEPARTMENT OF
COMMUNICATIONS
EXECUTIVE OFFICE
444 EAST ALGONQUIN ROAD
ARLINGTON HEIGHTS, IL 60005
(708) 228-9900

Thank you for contacting the American Society of Plastic and
Reconstructive Surgeons Information Service.

Unfortunately, we do not maintain the information you are
requesting. Our service can supply you with a list of five plastic
surgeons who are certified by the American Board of Plastic Surgery
along with an educational brochure. If you already have the name
of a plastic surgeon, we can varify if they are certified by the
American Board of Plastic Surgery.

If you would like this information, please call (1-800-635-0635)
and a PSIS representative will be happy to assist you.

Sincerely,

Plastic Surgery Information Service

119 E. Espanola St.
Colo. Springs, CO 80907
June 15, 1994

Consumer Concerns
Columbia House Record Club
1400 N. Fruitridge Ave.
Terra Haute, IN 47811

Dear Music Dispatchers,

Whether it's Beethoven, Billie Holiday, or Bon Jovi, there's something for each and every one of us in the wonderful world of "music reproduction!" I was raised to the soothing sounds of classical music (mostly Mozart) in southwestern Kentucky in the 1960's and 70's. My father (Rupert) would place the speakers in the window facing the garden and tackle his chores with the zeal of a man breaking a fast with sweet nectar! As a teenager (eager to fit in) I began to embrace the aggressive sounds of rock and roll music. My friends and I would sneak onto the Alcooma golf course (since closed) at night, crack open some chilled lagers and enjoy various offerings from Led Zeppelin, Queen, Kansas, Rush, Styx, REO Speedwagon, and Journey. In the summer of 1978 I met my future (now "ex") wife, Silia, who also shared a passion for Journey's exemplary album, "Infinity." Anyway, my friends, to make a long paragraph approximately 9% longer, music continues to play a vital role in my life to this day!

Recently I fell on hard times, and I would like to reveal the details to you since it is relevant to this letter. In the 1980's I owned and operated the largest novelty shop in southern Colorado. "Paul's Pranks" featured whoopee cushions, artificial feces, noise-makers, magic kits, gag gum, and a huge assortment of items for the practical joker in all (most) of us. Business was good until a tragic fire struck in November of 1989. Due to defective smoke detectors and fire extinguishers, the blaze consumed the business in its entirety. A clerical error on my part meant that insurance settlements would not materialize and, within months, I was penniless. The word "penniless" will soon prove pivotal to this letter. Stay tuned.

Due to a chronic eating disorder, and a fierce, unexpected case of agoraphobia (fear of open spaces), I have been a virtual recluse for several years now. Unable to earn a living but too proud to accept handouts, I survive on the yield from my humble vegetable garden and a modest dose of old-fashioned chutzpah. My love for music endures, and I am very eager to join your record club, but as the above paragraph reveals, I am truly (and utterly) destitute! It is somewhat ironic that I still have two stamps left (to mail this missive and include a "SASE"), because otherwise I am (again) *penniless*! And herein lies my dilemma as well as the very backbone of this letter. Would it be possible for me to bypass the requirement of sending one cent (a penny) in order to join your club? Your generosity and understanding would be truly appreciated!

Please send me a hasty reply, folks! In the meantime, I will devote every ounce of strength to my pursuit of respectability. As a final aside, please send an (XL) T-shirt. And remember the Bible (John 3:15)!

Asking for compassion,

Paul Rosa

Paul C. Rosa

1400 NORTH FRUITRIDGE AVENUE • TERRE HAUTE, INDIANA 47811

2L02631
1282304
072195

JULY 28, 1994

PAUL C ROSA
119 E ESPAÑOLA ST
COLORADO SPGS   CO   80907-7428

Dear Customer:

We have received your recent correspondence regarding enrolling in
the Club.

It is not required that you send 1¢ with your application.
However, depending on the application submitted, you will be
charged for shipping and handling for the Enrollment Package. You
will also be required to purchase a certain number of regular Club
priced selections for receiving your Enrollment Package at such a
low cost.

The purchase of each cassette or compact disc will count as
follows toward your Enrollment agreement:

$ 7.98--$19.97 one unit ($12.98--$19.97 for CDs) $19.98--$29.97
two units $29.98--above three units (Some higher priced selections
may count as more than 3 units and will be noted in the Club
magazine as such.)

Once you have completed the agreement, the purchase of any of the
above allows you to take an equivalent number of compact discs for
as low as $3.99 plus mailing and handling; or cassettes free plus
mailing and handling.

If you decline your Bonus selection at the time you make your
regular price purchase, we will send you a certificate which may
be used to order your bonus recording at a later date.

We are unable to send you any merchandise until you are a member
of the Club.

We hope we have clarified the matter, and if we may be of further
service, please let us know.

                                         DAVID TSANGARIS
                                         CUSTOMER SERVICE

03/092

Encl: ENPRE

Entertaining America...One Person at a Time.℠

119 E. Espanola St.
Colo. Springs, CO 80907
June 15, 1994

Dial Soap - Customer Milestones
1850 N. Central Ave.
Phoenix, AZ 85077

Dear Shower Friends,

"Cleanliness is next to godliness," my mother (Lisbeth) would repeatedly counsel me as she carefully scrubbed the far recesses of my young, developing body with Dial Soap in the early (to mid) sixties. My tiny body would ecstatically writhe in the kitchen sink as she playfully returned me (time and time again) to my preferred, sparkling condition. However, soap is not embraced with only fond memories, as roughly once a week the bar was used for washing out my mouth after an incident of profanity or unnecessary complaint. Yes, my parents raised me with the proverbial "iron fist" - my father, Gunter handled the periodic beatings - but, consequently, I've become a model citizen. For this, I say, "Bless you, good people!" And you (the folks of Dial) are to be congratulated for keeping me "squeaky clean" for the past thirty years. Oh sure, I've been tempted to sample some of the pretenders (Coast, Ivory, etc.) but my devotion to your product has proved thorough enough to thwart these dangerous feelings!!

One fine morning, on October 18, 1987 (when I worked as a Junior Systems Analyst in Northern Virginia), I completed my daily, invigorating shower only to discover what could best be described as "an oddity" appearing on my bar of soap. The capital letter "L" had been clearly (and unintentionally) formed by a hair that had been washed from my person. As a collector of things...unusual, I decided to have the aforementioned L-containing soap piece sealed, for all posterity, in clear Lucite. For several months it served as a playful conversation piece at my office until -on December 21, 1987- I discovered the letter "M" in a practically-new bar of Dial. Again, I preserved this collector's item in Lucite and realized a hobby, nay, an obsession, had been born! I was soon cheering in the shower, hoping for that new as-yet-unrealized capital letter to appear (strictly by chance) in my soap!

Well, the months flew by and the collection grew, as did my excitement. Some of the letters ("C," "D," "S," etc.) appeared quickly, as they are uncomplicated (architecturally speaking), but eventually the tricky ones blessed my showers as well. By January of this year I had twenty-four "hair-letters-in-soap" sealed in Lucite, and I decided to shower twice daily to increase my chances of securing the letters "X" and "Q." X is tricky as it presumably requires two hairs, and Q is geometrically intricate. Well, my friends, I "landed" the letter X on March 28 (a Monday) as I prepared for an important speech at my office. I was almost too excited to speak later, but it went off without a hitch (as they say). Anyway (drum roll please) I was almost moved to tears when I discovered an almost-flawless "Q" in my bar of dial this morning, and decided to let you know at once. Perhaps you can use my twenty-six Lucite specimens in an advertising campaign this fall! My family can personally guarantee that I haven't tampered with the hairs - they all formed randomly! Please contact me at once and let me know your ideas (I'm so excited!). Finally, please forward an (XL) T-shirt and other free samples!

Pondering a *new* hobby,

Paul Rosa

Paul C. Rosa

The Dial Corp

Consumer Products Group

Dial Tower
Phoenix, AZ 85077
Phone (602) 207-2800

September 9, 1994

Mr. Paul Rosa
119 E. Espanola St.
Colorado Springs, CO 80907

Dear Mr. Rosa:

Thank you for your letter and suggestion regarding the bar soaps in Lucite. I have passed your idea to the proper management team but they have so many projects in the works that they are not interested in pursuing the matter further.

We do thank you for thinking of Dial and for your longterm use of the soap. It certainly is the most effective deodorant bar and we are pleased that you enjoy it.

As a token of our esteem, I am sending you a set of coupons for some of our Dial products. Thank you again for your interest in Dial and for sharing your novel hobby idea.

Sincerely,

Nancy Dedera
Nancy Dedera
Director Consumer Affairs

The Dial Corp

Consumer Products Group

**Consumer
Information Center**

15101 North Scottsdale Road
Mail Station 5028
Scottsdale, Arizona 85254
Tel: 800-258-DIAL

October 10, 1994

Mr Paul C Rosa
119 E Espanola St
Colorado Springs CO 80907

Dear Mr Rosa:

Thank you for taking the time to contact The Dial Corp concerning Dial
Soap. I'm pleased to have this opportunity to respond to your
comments.

The Dial Corporation has a policy of accepting ideas submitted only by
our employees or through our advertising agencies. Because of the
obligations of confidentiality, and other legal issues, we cannot
review or consider your idea. Experience has taught us this policy
avoids any possible confusion or misunderstanding.

Your letter is quite extraordinary and we are very pleased you shared
it with us. Your devotion to Dial products is greatly appreciated
also. Unfortunately we do not have any promotional t-shirts or free
samples to send.

We have, however, enclosed product coupons for you to use on your next
shopping trip. Again, thank you for sharing your comments with us.

                         Michal Bradshaw
                         Consumer Information Specialist

0676382A

ACKNOWLEDGMENTS

This book is dedicated to the small spider that's been living in the southeast corner of my basement for the past three years.

I'd also like to thank Cloris Leachman and the Mandrell sisters.

Thanks also to Rusty Staub, Jesse Rosa, Geddy Lee, Agnes, Homer Simpson, Joan Jett, David Letterman, Bob Whitley, Jeff Spicoli, Lisa Galvin, George Costanza, Mrs. McAleese, Brenda Vaccaro, Uncle Siegfried, Stanley Mrose, Cher, and my future wife. And Yanni.

Finally, thanks to the brave men and women who buy this book.

ABOUT THE AUTHOR

Paul Rosa's company (Idiot, Ink.) is the leading seller of bumper stickers in the world. He is the creator of "My Kid Beat Up Your Honor Student," "<u>DARE</u> To Keep Cops Off Donuts," "Discourage Inbreeding—Ban Country Music," "I Think You Left the Stove On," and many others. Most of the stickers can be found at *Spencer Gifts*, while *all* of them can be found at the web site, *www.idiot-ink.com*. To date, Idiot, Ink. has sold over 3/4 million stickers.

Paul Rosa has moved!...
Since the completion of this book Paul Rosa has moved and can now be reached at:

Paul Rosa
Idiot, Ink.
P.O. Box 9368
Colorado Springs, CO 80932

If a reply is requested, please enclose a S.A.S.E.!